It's Not About Perfect

COMPETING FOR MY COUNTRY
AND FIGHTING FOR MY LIFE

SHANNON MILLER

WITH DANNY PEARY

THOMAS DUNNE BOOKS
ST. MARTIN'S PRESS ✺ NEW YORK

THOMAS DUNNE BOOKS.
An imprint of St. Martin's Press.

www.thomasdunnebooks.com
www.stmartins.com

Designed by Anna Gorovoy

Library of Congress Cataloging-in-Publication Data

Miller, Shannon, 1977–
    It's not about perfect : competing for my country and fighting for my life / Shannon
Miller with Danny Peary.
        pages cm
    ISBN 978-1-250-04986-5 (hardcover)
    ISBN 978-1-4668-5084-2 (e-book)
    1. Miller, Shannon, 1977–   2. Gymnasts—United States—Biography.   I. Peary,
Danny, 1949–   II. Title.
    GV460.2.M55A3 2015
    796.44092—dc23
    [B]
                                                                    2015002589

First Edition: April 2015

10 9 8 7 6 5 4 3 2 1

For Rocco and Sterling, my two miracles

ACKNOWLEDGMENTS

I am so thankful for all of those who have supported me, strengthened me, and inspired me.

I thank God; "With Him all things are possible" (Matthew 19:26).

To my parents, Ron and Claudia, who taught me to dream big and work hard, who continue to encourage me in all of my endeavors, with honesty and love, thank you.

To my sister, Tessa, and brother, Troy, I will forever be grateful to you for keeping me grounded, keeping me going, and helping me soar, all at the same time.

To my husband, John, my rock, you inspire me every day to be the best person I can be. Thank you for your love; thank you for the laughter.

To my phenomenal coaches Steve Nunno and Peggy Liddick, thank you. You will always hold a special place in my heart for all that you have done for me, from life lessons to helping me travel the world competing in a sport I love.

To Nick Furris, an admirable mentor, a tremendous business partner, and, above all, my friend, thank you for taking a leap of faith with me on this incredible journey.

To Lauren Fox, for your limitless enthusiasm, creativity, dedication, and passion for the mission, thank you. You are an absolute gem.

To Jackie Culver, thank you for your expertise and your energy. You wear many different hats each day and you wear them all with style.

To Jerry Clavier, my very first coach, thank you for fostering my love of gymnastics, the endless hours waiting for me to *finally* leave the gym for the night, and your selflessness in encouraging me to spread my wings.

To USA Gymnastics for the many tremendous opportunities and outstanding memories—above all, the chance to represent my country on the world stage.

To the United States Olympic Committee, it has been an honor to work with such extraordinary people throughout the years. Thank you for allowing me to play a small part in such an incredible movement.

To Dr. Stephen Buckley, Dr. William Long, Dr. Thomas Virtue, and all of my extraordinary doctors and nurses. Thank you for your positive attitude even during the darkest moments; thank you for all that you do for me and each one of your patients.

And to all caregivers who give endlessly, selflessly, and heroically to make the way just a little bit easier for those in need. (Please don't forget to take care of yourself along the way.)

To Danny Peary, thank you for helping me share my story; the gymnastics years in particular were filled with both thrilling moments and those that I might rather forget. However, it was often these trying times that became critical in my success and in forming who I am today. I'm thankful for your ability to pull so many moments of my life together in a way that sheds light into my own trials and triumphs that are reflected in the lives of so many. And thank you to your wife, Suzanne, daughter Zoë, and the gymnast in your family, granddaughter Julianna, for sharing you over the past many months.

To Al Zuckerman at Writers House for believing in this book and that it might help many out there who are facing obstacles and battling the many issues that life throws at each of us on a daily basis.

To Rob Kirkpatrick, for your guidance, excitement, and support for this project. You are an amazing editor and I thank you for your thoughts and ideas. Congratulations to you and your wife on the beautiful addition to your family!

To Jennifer Letwack, it has been a pleasure to work with you. Thank you for all of your help along the way. Particularly in narrowing down thirty-seven years of photos!

To my copy editor, Justine Gardener; dust jacket designer, Danielle Fiorella; book publicist, Jessica Lawrence; marketing manager, Karlyn Hixson; and the many others who worked tirelessly behind the scenes at Thomas Dunne/St. Martin's to create a work that is, I hope, beautiful both inside and out. And thank you to Elina Mishuris, a splendid transcriber.

To the very kind and gifted photographers Dave Black, Liliane Hakim, Renee Parenteau, Mike Proebsting, Sable Tidd, and Matthew White, who graciously shared their art, their work, throughout this book.

To my amazing fans, you have stuck by me through the ups and downs of my career and my life. You give and give and give and I cannot thank you enough for your support.

Finally, for all of those affected by cancer, you are not alone . . . let's keep fighting!

Don't judge me by my successes but rather how many times I fell and got back up again.

—NELSON MANDELA

It's Not About Perfect

PROLOGUE

Dr. Virtue didn't sugarcoat it. He looked me in the eye and said bluntly, "Shannon, I've discovered a cyst on your left ovary that is about seven centimeters in diameter."

Pow.

For me, this confirmed that life can change in the blink of an eye.

In my gymnastics career I'd taken many hard falls and suffered numerous painful injuries, from a fractured elbow to severe hamstring pulls to a ripped stomach muscle, but never had I felt such seismic shock to my body as when I heard my doctor's words.

I just thank God I heard them. I'm ashamed to confess that I had almost postponed my appointment, a routine examination with my gynecologist, that memorable morning in mid-December 2010. My days were no longer filled with chalk dust and sweat. Having traveled a long and arduous road, I had found my passion as an advocate for women's health. My mission was (as it still is) to help women make their health a priority. But was I listening to my own words and those of the endless experts, doctors, nurses, and survivors I'd interviewed or spoken to over the years? I knew the importance of keeping my scheduled appointments, but because of my own demanding schedule, I'd called my doctor to postpone.

I was put on hold, and in those few seconds, I felt a tinge of guilt for not practicing what I preached. I could swear I heard from above a whispering in my ear, "Don't delay!" I didn't wait. In fact, I took the first available appointment, that very morning. Within an hour of my hanging up the phone, my life had changed forever.

The second blow came just weeks later when an ultrasound showed a large mass on my left ovary. Surgery followed and then there was confirmation that the mass was a malignant tumor.

I had cancer.

To be precise, I had ovarian cancer.

I felt that my body had betrayed me. I wondered how it was possible that I was so out of touch with my own body that I didn't realize I had something the size of a baseball growing inside me. In gymnastics, my body was my instrument, so I had no choice but to understand it, take care of it, and focus on it. When I was tumbling backward on a four-inch piece of wood or performing a difficult dismount off the uneven bars I had to focus 100 percent on every aspect of my body. And if I experienced an injury, I would have to know my body well enough to decide whether I could push through or needed to back off while it healed. But after I retired from competition, and busied myself with law school, marriage, and work, I quickly lost that focus.

With my first pregnancy came a renewed focus on my body but in a different way than before. During pregnancy, I thought of my body as a home, one that I needed to take care of for my son. But after he was born in late 2009, my body went through all kinds of changes that were completely foreign to me, which every new mother can relate to. That was part of my rickety explanation after the tumor was found for why my relationship with my body wasn't as close as it had always been. I had simply stopped paying attention. When I did have an issue it was quickly swept aside as insignificant. There were more important things to do than worry about a little tummy ache, or even multiple tummy aches.

As a gymnast I would have immediately tried to figure out the problem and get it taken care of. Not so anymore. When I didn't feel well or had stomachaches as an adult and as a new mom, I thought about the e-mails I "needed" to return, errands I "needed" to run, and travel arrangements I "needed" to make for my business, as well as taking care of all my baby's needs. So I'd take some Pepto-Bismol and keep racing around rather than questioning whether those stomachaches and some weight loss were symptoms of something more serious. Like many new mothers, I felt I should tough it out. My concern was my child, my marriage, my work; everything but me. We all *need* to be focused on our bodies, and if we experience something out of the ordinary, we *need* to get it checked out. Too many of us think we have to wait for permission to take care of ourselves.

Now, after my diagnosis, I no longer felt the need for permission to make my own health a priority.

I had to calm down, assess the situation, and begin my battle. I am a planner and a perfectionist by nature, but I found early on that while it's admirable to shoot for perfection, it's not about perfect. It's about going out and giving it your best every single day. It's about getting back up after you've been knocked down.

I admit it took a while, but when I was told I needed to undergo chemotherapy, I finally faced the fact that I really had cancer and couldn't just wish it away. I had cancer and it didn't matter that I was fairly young. It didn't matter that I was a wife and new mother of a child who needed me. It didn't matter that I didn't have time for this.

However, it did matter that I was an advocate and spokeswoman for women's health because I had learned a great deal about battling life-threatening illnesses from those who had experienced it, including my mother. And though it was irrelevant that I was Shannon Miller, Olympic gold medalist, it was vital that I had learned tremendous lessons to become a successful gymnast. Cancer was by far the biggest obstacle I had ever faced. I was forced to put it into perspective and see it as one more challenge in my life, not a death sentence. I firmly believed that being diagnosed early increased my chances dramatically of not being counted among the thousands of women who succumb each year to this dreaded disease.

I knew how to take on challenges because I had done it, under extreme pressure, since I was a child. Other women who battle cancer and other life-threatening diseases mine their own unique sources of strength. I relied on the many lessons I learned from my parents and then my coaches when I first put on a leotard:

- Set goals.
- Put in the work if you want results.

- Utilize mistakes as a way to learn and grow.
- Eliminate negative thoughts (and, when possible, negative people).
- Search for the positive in the negative.
- Don't place limits on yourself.
- Accept help from others.
- Never give up.
- Most of all, believe in yourself.

These life lessons served me well throughout my twenties as I searched for my identity outside of gymnastics and also well into motherhood. I would lean on them during the most difficult challenge of my life, my battle with cancer. They would be my weapons against this disease. The question was whether what I learned as a child could save me as an adult.

1

I have traveled constantly since I began my gymnastics career in the mid-1980s, and in America and abroad, in big cities and remote places, I run into people from Oklahoma. "Hey, Okie!" they'll call. We'll talk like old friends, although we've never met before. That's just the way it is when you're from the heartland. That wonderful sense of community between everyone from the Sooner State makes me feel at home wherever I go. I am so proud to hail from Oklahoma and am so grateful for the love of its people and, of course, the unavoidable reminder of my Olympic medal count that I experience every time I drive into my hometown of Edmond. I think of that large sign that honors my accomplishments as a tribute to the community where I grew up, a community that supported me every step of the way, win or lose. Having grown up in Edmond, trained mostly in Oklahoma City, and attended college in Norman, I am grateful to be forever identified as an Oklahoman. Indeed, it surprises people to learn that I was born in Missouri.

Both my parents are actually from Texas. My father, Ron, had family in Indiana and lived there when he was nine, and my mother, Claudia, had a grandmother in Tampico, Mexico, but they both grew up in San Antonio and met there while attending Trinity University. Ron Miller, cerebral and analytical, received a bachelor of science in physics, and was accepted into graduate school at the University of Missouri at Rolla. Claudia Murff, with a body that was always in action and a mind as sharp as a razor and always going a mile a minute, got a BA in political science and received a full scholarship to law school at Washington University in St. Louis. She was third in her class in her only year there, but withdrew so she could follow her heart to Rolla and marry my father on June 19, 1971. There were no law schools in the area and the newlyweds needed money while my father attended school, so my mother took a job as an assistant manager at the university bookstore.

While my father worked on his PhD in atmospheric physics, my parents rented a house in Rolla. That's where they were living when my sister, Tessa, was born in 1975 and I was born on March 10, 1977. My parents claim they named me Shannon simply because they really liked that name, but I suspect they might have been expecting a boy, because it was a boy's name back then. Its Irish roots can be traced to my grandmother, whose maiden name was Shockey. My middle name, Lee, came from my father's mother, Mabel Lee Miller. His side of the family was primarily Swiss-German.

I weighed only five pounds, six ounces, but my pediatrician assured my parents that I was perfectly healthy and that "great things come in small packages." She did point out that my legs turned in a little and that this might lead to problems. At first she advised my parents to try therapy each day at home, but after a month she determined that something else needed to be done. It was a concern for my parents as they prepared to move out of the state.

My father completed his doctorate in the spring of 1977, building a cloud chamber as his thesis project, and accepted a position as a professor in the physics department at Central State University, about 375 miles away in Edmond, Oklahoma. (The college would be renamed the University of Central Oklahoma and my father's department became engineering physics.) So the family packed up and moved to Oklahoma when I was about five months old.

My parents purchased a five-year-old, two-story house with a big backyard about two miles from town. It is where they raised three kids and where they now entertain their grandkids. At the time, before scores of

new houses were built and it transformed into a nice but heavily popu-
lated suburban neighborhood, we lived in "ranchin' country," with wheat
fields and pastures, stables and horse trails. We often heard cows mooing
in the morning. We literally lived on Easy Street, in a setting as relaxing
as that name. There were wide open spaces, clean air, blue skies, all kinds
of animals, and snow in the winter. While we had to weather the occasional tornado, it was a wonderful place to call home. There were nearby
churches, schools, and even a well-stocked candy store by the filling station that kids would walk to when they had quarters burning holes in their
pockets. My father was set to teach in the autumn and my mother was
hired to work in a bank, so life was grand for the Millers. Except for one
thing: My legs showed no signs of straightening out.

The pediatrician in Missouri got in touch with one in Oklahoma
and asked him to examine my legs. He agreed they were growing too
inward and fit me with special booties with the toes cut out so that my
feet could grow. He said, "She'll probably have to wear them for a year to
eighteen months so that her legs will straighten out." My parents were
mortified that those little white shoes were attached to a big steel bar that
went from one shoe to the other. It would keep my legs in a fixed position,
but, as the doctor said, "She's not going to like it."

That first night I cried and moaned. The second night I was still uncomfortable but didn't do much fussing. My mother recalls that by the third
night I had a determined look on my face that told her I could handle it.
For the first time in my life, I was faced with a physical obstacle that I
would not give in to. Even at that age I refused to be limited and made
the best of a bad situation. My mother remembers that when I was about
eight months old, I began crawling and pulling myself up in my crib, as if
I had no impediment. Before my first birthday, the doctor took off the bar
and examined my legs. He said, "Wow, they look straight!" I never had to
put on those shoes again, but I still keep them as a souvenir, a reminder
of challenges overcome.

The doctor broke it to my parents that because I wore the special shoes
I would begin walking later than most kids. As it turned out, I crawled at
eight months and walked before my first birthday, just as Tessa had. Maybe
I didn't realize that not every child had a bar to drag around. I was ready
to move and if I had to take that bar with me that was fine by me. I had

proved the doctor wrong. For years to come I would make it my mission to defy the expectations of people who said I was too young, too small, too shy, too injured, and, toward the end of my gymnastics career, too old. It would be a recurring theme in my life that I tried to match or better people's expectations. Even today, I feel the need to prove my worth by disproving someone else's contention that I can't do something. Maybe it stems from my competitive spirit or simply a lifelong desire to please everyone.

That first time I proved someone wrong about me it wasn't by design. I was too young for that. But I feel certain I was motivated. I couldn't afford to be slowed down; I had to keep up with my older sister in everything she did. When I was eighteen months old and Tessa was three and a half, my parents bought an old jungle gym at a garage sale. Tessa quickly learned to climb to the top and stand on the platform, and, sure enough, soon after I doggedly climbed to that platform myself. Perhaps this foreshadowed my aspiration to stand on podiums during my gymnastics career.

When I was four, my mother enrolled six-year-old Tessa in a jazz and ballet class with a few of her friends. Naturally, since Tessa was taking dance I was desperate to take it as well. My mother wanted both of her daughters to enjoy dance, but money was tight and she was hesitant to pay for lessons for me until I was old enough to reap the benefits. Oh, I wasn't happy. I had a special relationship with my grandma Rosemary Murff, so when I next spoke to her on the phone I tactically shed a few tears until she promised to pay for my dance lessons. She told my mother that "if she doesn't get anything out of the lessons, it will be my money wasted, not yours." Maybe my mother thought dance was a smart alternative to my racing my new baby brother, Troy, around in my doll cart, because she gave in and signed me up for dance twice a week.

I learned what was considered jazz dance and a little ballet, but at that age, I was simply gaining a foundation. Still I fell in love with dance and couldn't wait to perform at the December recital. I was so shy that I let Tessa talk for both of us when we interacted with strangers, yet I was thrilled to have the opportunity to perform in front of an audience and show what I'd learned. The timid girl just vanished when I put on my leopard recital costume. I wore it around the house and for several years it was my Halloween costume. I don't know how well I actually danced, but my mother was surprised that I was just as studious and serious about the lessons as Tessa. Had I proved her wrong?

Both my parents were physically active, playing tennis on the neighborhood courts and racquetball at the YMCA. But my mother took it to a different level. She participated in a number of activities over the years to keep active including swimming, softball, horse jumping, and even just climbing the stairs at work on her lunch break. She was constantly in motion. Mom wanted her kids to follow her lead. When she was a young girl, her father, my grandpa Chester Murff, urged her to do as many push-ups and sit-ups and run as fast and far as her brother, Lloyd. No limits. No excuses. Now she encouraged her own daughters to be as physically active as any boys our age. We had unbridled energy and were eager to try any daily activity to fill the time between our dance lessons. She didn't care what we chose as long as we stopped spending our free time tearing up her furniture. So when we begged for a trampoline for Christmas, she didn't object.

My parents were able to purchase a trampoline at a yard sale for a hundred dollars, a huge gift for us. When they brought it home, it was snowing and the temperature was in the single digits, but we couldn't wait to try it out. So we ganged up on my poor father, who was one of four boys in a military family and could build or fix anything. He had set it up for us, finishing a good ten seconds before we were bouncing on it. He would be the only one in our family not to use it over the three decades it remained in the backyard. Even my mother did a front flip or two.

Tessa and I loved jumping and doing flips on our "awesome" Christmas present. What made it even more of an adventure was that we had a big, crazy dog that we could get past only by doing a mad dash from the back door to the trampoline. In truth, Ebony wasn't dangerous, just a little rambunctious, but to us, my goodness, we were trying to escape from a terrifying monster. While my parents were glad to see us having fun doing an activity, they had no idea we could be such caution-to-the-wind daredevils and began to worry. They became concerned that their fearless young girls would kill themselves on that old-style trampoline. It had no netting or pads, and when we'd bounce off the springs we'd fly off onto the grass.

Around this time Tessa decided to move on from dance, and I begrudgingly gave up my first love, too, so that I could follow my big sister to whatever she did next. For a while, all we did to pass the time were stunts on the trampoline. Determined to find something safer to occupy us and channel our energy, my mother opened the yellow pages and looked for "Gymnastics."

2

My mother randomly called three local gyms and enrolled Tessa and me at the first one that got back to her. It was called Adventures in Gymnastics and was located a five-minute drive from our house in a large concrete building. Walking through the door for the first time was not as magical as entering a gorgeously manicured ballpark or stately arena. It was just a sweaty, nondescript facility with a lot of floor space and really high ceilings. Having never watched gymnastics on television, I looked around for trampolines. There were none. I didn't recognize any of the apparatuses that were spread about into four areas that were not entirely separate from each other. My eyes widened as I watched some girls tumbling and flipping around on mats and other equipment. I thought, "Oh, I want to learn to do that! I know I can do it!" I was excited and couldn't wait to do somersaults!

Although I had no clue what gymnastics was, it never occurred to me that I couldn't do anything those girls could do, even the older ones. My down-to-earth, rational, hardworking parents had instilled in Tessa and me the idea that if we dedicated ourselves, there were no limits to what we could accomplish. *Dream big and go for it*. I combined that lesson with my innocent childhood belief that nothing was too scary to try and my stubborn determination to not give up until I reached my goal. That was the surefire recipe I'd follow as I entered this new, challenging world of gymnastics.

Adventures in Gymnastics was run by Jerry Clavier, who was the perfect first coach for me, although I thought he was too tall to have been a gymnast himself. Away from his gym, he worked as a nurse. When Tessa and I first arrived, Jerry told us to put one leg forward. She put her right leg forward; I put my left. I am right-handed when I write and when I throw a ball or swing a bat, but it turned out that I was a lefty in gymnastics. That meant I would twist left, split better with my left leg, and lunge with my left leg forward.

Of course when you begin gymnastics you can do very little that looks like actual gymnastics. Early on, tumbling was what I loved most. What I learned to do first were forward and backward rolls, cartwheels, and handstands. My mother remembers that I quickly learned from Jerry how to do a back handspring (a backward flip with support from your hands), a backflip, and even a full twist. I also apparently experimented on my own and did a whip back, which is kind of a back handspring but without your hands touching the floor. It was a fun skill because you literally whip yourself through the air backward.

Meanwhile, I learned that the vault, uneven bars, balance beam, and floor exercise were the four apparatuses, or events, in gymnastics. On television the terms "apparatus" and "event" are pretty much interchangeable, with "apparatus" being more formal. On each apparatus, you learn skills and the skills make up a routine that you might do in a competition or exhibition. Adventures was a recreational gym that taught skills and fundamentals but didn't enter its young gymnasts in competitions. At the time, I didn't know there were even such things as gymnastics competitions and was more than satisfied to learn and practice new skills. I wasn't one of those kids who grew up dreaming of being an Olympian. I grew up wanting to be my sister.

At five years old, I went to the gym for an hour in the afternoon five times a week. I wanted more. Jerry believed both Tessa and I had the potential to merit more hours. Tessa, who was in a different class, decided she had too many other interests, including swimming, to make such a commitment and decided to leave the gym. For the first time, I didn't follow her. She was probably a bit relieved that her kid sister wouldn't be tagging along anymore, just as she was when my parents built an addition to our house and she no longer had to share a bedroom. But we had an unbreakable sisterly bond and would find time to do things together on weekends and in the summer.

My decision to stay at Adventures in Gymnastics meant Tessa and I would spend less time together, but I refused to give up this sport that had captured my heart and imagination. It wasn't only that I had so much to learn, which excited me, but that I was a bashful, timid, scrawny, and awkward little girl who had found her self-confidence and self-esteem in this gym.

Fortunately, my shyness wasn't a hindrance in gymnastics but helped me block out distractions and focus on learning skills quicker than most. At the gym I was so focused that I truly didn't notice all the hoopla around me. I was good friends with the four scrappy girls I trained with every day—we were a tight-knit group—but when I was learning a skill, it was just me and the equipment and the rest of the world didn't exist.

From the very start, Jerry believed that this tiny, knobbed-kneed, wild-haired girl had potential. He liked that I listened and quickly picked up some of the foundational skills. I was eager to learn anything and everything. Every day I worked on a variety of skills. There are a few that can be learned in a day or two, such as a roundoff, which is simply a cartwheel landing on both feet, and a split leap on balance beam. However, most take months, even years, to learn properly. So I never ran out of skills to learn and then attempt to perfect. Jerry was an ideal coach for me because he realized I didn't want to be consoled when I fell or couldn't learn a skill quickly, but rather wanted to be told what I was doing wrong and be given the corrections I needed to do it better the next time. I craved constructive criticism, even at an early age. *If I don't know what I'm doing wrong, how am I going to fix it?*

As his student, I learned there are multiple progressions in every event, which means each skill needs to be learned before you can move on to the next, more difficult skill. It became my goal to learn skills in all four events, one after another.

I began learning beam skills on the floor, doing my moves on a tape outline. Then I worked on a low beam and finally a high beam. Of the four apparatuses, I felt the most comfortable on the beam. A lot of coaches told their gymnasts to turn their feet out on beam, but I thought that odd because I wasn't as stable that way. My feet still naturally turned in a little bit, and in the end I think that helped me. My little toe was on one edge of the beam, and my big toe was on the other edge. With this technique I had a good grip on the beam and better balance.

I wasn't particularly strong, flexible, or powerful, but I thought, "Everyone else seems scared of beam and if I don't get scared maybe I can be really good." I have no memory of being competitive in the gym, but my mother remembers that I was proud I could do beam better than the other girls. My small size and the fact that I didn't have any fear seemed to help me. The more I learned about the event, the more I loved it. So Jerry just kept teaching me more difficult skills and I ate it up. On the high balance beam, I didn't start out learning major skills; I started by walking on it forward and backward and then I did some dip walks and sideways walking. Then I learned such skills as a forward roll, cartwheel, and leap. I wasn't too young to learn how to do a backbend and a handstand, then a backbend kickover, and finally a back walkover.

At the time I was working on the back walkover I was just six, an age when my favorite TV show was *Scooby-Doo* and I made sure not to miss Bozo the Clown every morning before leaving for school. Over the summer break, we took a trip to Aurora, Colorado, to visit my uncle Roger, my father's oldest brother. He and his wife had just come back from Turkey and there were quite a few pricey mementos on display in his living room, so he was uneasy that I was practicing back walkovers and cartwheels and jumping off his couch. Before I broke something, my mother took me to a nearby gymnastics facility. She told them I had just turned six and she would like to sign me up for just three days. They said, "Sorry, we only let gymnasts on the national team train a few days at a time." She assured them I could do a lot of skills and I just needed to burn off some energy. A coach standing nearby said I was too young to try doing skills and might hurt myself.

Then bashful little me, who never spoke up, stated proudly, "I've got skills!"

"What skills, honey?"

"I can do a back walkover and a back handspring."

"Really?"

"Really. I can do a back walkover on the high beam."

My mother thought the coach would come unglued. He was trying so hard not to laugh as he said, "Show me."

And show him I did. I climbed up on the high beam and stuck a back walkover. He ran out and came back with four other coaches and I did a back walkover and even a back handspring on the high beam for them, too. They went crazy. They couldn't believe this little girl. They wanted to sign me up for an accelerated program. My mother said, "Well, we live in Oklahoma." They said, "Well, have you thought about moving here?" That must have been my mother's first glimpse that this gymnastics bug that bit me wasn't going away.

Mastering the back walkover allowed me to move on to a back hand-spring and, finally, a back handspring–back handspring. In Mrs. Taber's first-grade class at Haskell Elementary School, I was usually reluctant to raise my hand. Yet on Show-and-Tell Day I had enough confidence to vol-unteer to demonstrate the back handspring for my teacher and the other kids. They cleared the room and moved some desks out of the way so I could do it. Since my first day of school, I was not known as "Shannon, the gymnast," but "Shannon, Tessa's little sister." The teachers expected me to be as brilliant as Tessa, but nobody could be. So I was under the long shadow she cast. But that day I felt special. In the third grade I'd happily give an encore performance.

Dismounts off the beam also followed a progression. I learned to do a cartwheel, then a roundoff—the cartwheel-like move that ends with both feet together—then a roundoff off the end of the beam, then a tuck-back and a layout, then a roundoff layoff with a full twist, and then, when I was eight, a roundoff layout double full. The double-twisting dismount was considered a very difficult skill for someone so young. So was a consecu-tive back handspring series. I loved beam from the start because it was a constant challenge. There was nothing better than sticking my dismount. It's a pretty tough thing to do because of your horizontal momentum and the small room for error. To glue your feet to the floor on a landing and not move was an incredible feeling.

Uneven bars took me a little bit longer because I didn't have much upper-body strength. Gymnastics is a full-body sport, but since we don't walk on our hands all day our upper-body strength doesn't typically match our lower-body strength. I needed to condition my arms, shoulders, and core in order to do swings, back-hip circles, and other uneven bar skills.

The big move to learn on uneven bars is the kip. You learn a substantial number of other skills before you first try it, but the kip is that key skill you need in order to progress on this event. You can do the kip on either bar, but you learn it on the low bar. You jump off the floor, stretch your body, and grab the low bar with both hands. Next you swing your body underneath the bar into a stretch position. Then you pull your toes up to where your hands are on the bar. That's followed by a move we called "pulling on your pants." You pull the bar up to your shins, knees, and quads, and wind up with your hips on the bar and your arms in a support position. That is the kip, and in those days you needed to do it in order to do any significant skill on bars. After nearly two years of trial and error, I learned to do the kip when I was seven.

My mother reminds me that I didn't love bars right off the bat because I was a little frightened, a rarity for me. I picked up most skills pretty fast, but the giant swing, which is a fundamental skill on bars, was difficult for me. Back then girls had to use what were basically boys' parallel bars, which were much larger and more oval-shaped than what women compete on today. I had small hands, so my fear was that when I swung around I was going to slip off and fall hard to the mat. I tried it as many times as I could despite my trepidation. I couldn't keep count of how many times I stayed late, after gym, working on it. I just couldn't swing around the bar in a straight-body position. I would get 345 degrees around, but never the full 360 degrees. Late one night, I was working tirelessly on a boys' parallel bars with one bar taken out. Jerry was ready to shut off the lights and my mom was eager to drive me home, but I kept trying and trying. Finally she said, "You can try one more time, but then we really have to go." So at nine thirty at night, I tried one last time, and I got over the bar!

My mother had enrolled me in gymnastics at an early age because she wanted me to have an activity safer than jumping on the trampoline in our backyard. Though I learned to do high-risk skills in gymnastics, like the giant swing, they came about so gradually, and under supervision, that she never really worried about my getting hurt. At my age, I would try anything and if I felt any fear cropping up, I had the ability to just shut off my worried mind and go for it anyway. Still, as my mother understood, I wasn't a kamikaze-type, one of those kids who did things without thinking twice about it. In the gym, I would process the situation before going for it. Whereas on roller skates I did a lot of crazy stunts I felt my mother and my coaches didn't need to know about—for instance, on the big concrete slab in our backyard, I'd jump, do a full turn down the stairs, and somehow land without cracking my head. However, when it came to gymnastics, I was safety-conscious. I always took time to analyze the situation. I was like my mother in that I was physically active but like my dad in that I took the time to step back and say, "Let me get my bearings, let me observe a little bit, let me understand the situation, and let me then create a plan."

The first time I heard the word "vault," I thought someone was speaking a foreign language. I didn't have any immediate feelings about that apparatus, good or bad. Everything in gymnastics can be dangerous if you're not properly spotted and trained, but what we beginners did on vault was very simple. We just ran as fast as we could down the runway and sprang over the vaulting horse. You ran, jumped on the springboard, and vaulted yourself up and over the horse, landing either on a big fluffy mat or safely into a big foam pit. It wasn't artistic; it was pure fun.

Floor was a lot of fun, too, because I got to tumble. It wasn't until I was about eight and we did a few exhibitions that a choreographer incorporated a little dance and music. That's when I began to learn that floor exercise was a mix of artistry and power. Of course, the routines created for the five of us to perform together were by no means true routines; they were just a way to show what we'd been working on. We would dance for about twenty seconds and then tumble, then dance for about ten seconds and tumble again.

Because we didn't yet compete, I really looked forward to those exhibitions so that our team at Adventures could show what we could do. So I could show what I could do! It was an exciting opportunity to put on a pretty uniform with rainbow colors and carry my nifty rainbow gym bag.

All dressed up, I felt like a real gymnast as I tumbled in front of an appreciative audience. It was so much fun.

One July 4, Jerry was invited to bring his athletes out on a football field in Edmond. We ran and tumbled and I did some back handsprings. It built my confidence when the crowd cheered loudly. I also loved parades, which usually took place on holidays in downtown Edmond. I was still only seven the first time Jerry's group marched. I would have been absolutely terrified to speak in public or deliver a line in a play, but I was dying to show the world my back walkover. I could do it easily enough on a mat, but this was hard asphalt and as much as I wanted to do it, I was a little nervous. My angel of a mother ran along the edge of the crowd and when she got the signal—my arms stretched up high—she ran out to me and placed her hand near the small of my back in case I lost my balance. At some parades our group marched after the horses, which is why it was extremely important to learn very quickly how to do an aerial: a cartwheel with no hands. You learned to do anything so you didn't have to put your hands down. I loved all the opportunities I had to perform outside of the gym. No doubt I would have been thrilled to go to gymnastics competitions if I knew they existed.

Adventures was a recreational gym and I had no experience otherwise in the sport, but I already had a tremendous competitive spirit. That had been evident since around the age of six, when I ran my first mile at an event my mother put together called Jog for Genesis, which raised funds for Genesis House in Edmond. As I approached the finish line there was a man in front of me who was likely completing a 5k. I wasn't a fast runner, but my competitive juices kicked into high gear and I started to sprint. My legs were on fire; the crowd was cheering wildly for this little girl who was trying to beat a grown man to the finish line. He didn't let up, but I finished a hair in front! It must have been a sight!

At around age seven, during the summer, I increased my time in the gym to two hours a day during the week and three hours on Saturday. When school started I went only three weekdays but for two and a half hours each time. I still trained with the other four girls, but Jerry also put me in a class with older girls and invited me to participate in "open gym" on Saturdays to work on more difficult skills. My parents worried my new schedule was too intensive for someone so young, but they saw I was enjoying myself and fully supported me despite time and financial commitments on their part. (Finances would become a much larger concern as I began to compete and travel.)

We all came to think of Jerry as family and got to know his wife, Teresa, and their young son, Kurt. A couple of years later my mother began coaching the preschool kids in his gym, and my dad helped him out by building a foam pit at the end of the vault runway and also the huge covers that could be raised and lowered over the pit. I have great memories of those times my mother would pick me up in the evening from Adventures, and Jerry would go with us to The Kettle, a diner where you could get breakfast all day. I'd pour syrup over my scrambled eggs and the three of us would talk. Our conversation would be about making sure I was having fun and enjoying the sport, as well as my learning new things so I'd feel challenged and not bored.

I certainly didn't consider myself the most talented girl in the gym or even in my age group. I don't think I ever did in my entire career. I just assumed every girl was doing what I was doing and more. But Jerry believed I had special talent and entered me in the USAIGC program that would allow me, if I passed a very difficult two-part performance test, to work with other coaches at a training camp.

I didn't have much time to train for the first test being held in Waco, Texas, but Jerry felt it would be good for me to get a better understanding of what to expect so I'd be more prepared the next time around. My mom drove and we went with Jerry and his wife and stayed overnight with his relatives. I tried my best and went pretty far but didn't pass the strength and flexibility test that would have qualified me to take the skills test. Nevertheless, Gary Goodson, the tester, was impressed and told Jerry, "You've got to take our material on the tests home, spend a few months working with her on it, and then bring her back for the next test. I think she can pass it."

Jerry had accepted three or four other skilled girls to his gym who were maybe a year older than me. He trained us hard for three months and brought us to the next test. We all passed the strength and flexibility part of the test and moved on to the skills part. And the skills were very hard. They had us do a giant swing with a pike between the narrow bars, which is more difficult than on a single rail because you have to learn the proper timing. We also had to do two back handsprings in a row without a break on the high beam and complete a roundoff layout dismount. The eight-year-olds didn't make it through.

To pass the test, I had two chances to do the required roundoff lay-out dismount. I thought I did the skill well on my first attempt, but Gary Goodson gave me a zero! We were all stunned. He explained, "If you're ever going to learn a doubleback, you can't go straight backward; you have to go upward. You have to create time in the air to complete two somersaults. But you couldn't do that because you had no block." "Block" is where you move the horizontal energy to the vertical energy, and if you don't have that you have no vertical rise. Fine. Okay. That made perfect sense, so I did my second attempt with that correction in mind and got a high score. I was Jerry's only gymnast invited to the USAIGC camp.

I also got to spend a weekend that summer at the gymnastics camp run by legendary coaches Béla and Márta Károlyi at their gym in Hous-ton, Texas. A few of Jerry's girls, including my training partner and best friend, Lisa Heckel, got to go. I knew next to nothing about the Károlyis or Olympic history, but would soon learn that the Hungarian-born Béla had coached the Romanian women's gymnastics team in 1976 and 1980 that included Nadia Comăneci, whose perfect tens during the Montreal Olympics did much to popularize gymnastics internationally. The Károlyis had defected to the United States in March 1981 and set up their gym-nastics facility and camp.

Among Béla's pupils was Mary Lou Retton, who became America's first all-around gold medalist at the 1984 Summer Olympics. Word was that "Mary Lou is in the building" and a few of us found her practicing on beam in the back gym. I got to watch her in action for five or ten minutes be-fore we were ushered along and told that she needed privacy. Later, I spot-ted my future friend running through the parking lot to her red Corvette with a paper bag over her head so that she wouldn't be recognized. "Too late, Mary Lou, we love you!"

At camp, they held different contests on different days and I revealed my latent competitive nature by winning one that entitled me to toss a whipped-cream pie into Béla Károlyi's face. That was my introduction to this legendary coach! At the end of our time there, Béla asked his coaches to select girls to do uneven bar and tumbling exhibitions. I was ecstatic to be singled out for both bars and floor. Moreover, Béla spent about forty-five minutes personally coaching six of us on each event. My mother snapped a picture of Béla and me . . . and then had one of herself taken with the famous coach.

3

In 1986, soon after I turned nine, I took another trip that proved to be one of the most incredible experiences of my life. Gary Goodson arranged, as an International Gymnastics Training Camp program, for a delegation of Canadian coaches and female gymnasts to travel to Russia and train with Soviet coaches and their female gymnasts. Mr. Goodson invited several coaches, including Jerry, and representatives from other gymnastics clubs in the U.S., to accompany the Canadians. Of the thirty gymnasts who flew to Russia, four of us came from Adventures in Gymnastics. This invitation was a huge deal. The Soviet Union had boycotted the 1984 Summer Olympics in Los Angeles and relations between the two countries were strained in sports as well as politics. Significantly, this was the first time the Soviet Union allowed outsiders to witness their training methods. The Soviet women had won team gold medals in the last four Olympics in which they had taken part, so this was a once-in-a-lifetime opportunity.

The first time I stepped foot on an airplane, my destination was Russia! And it was certainly the first time I had ever flown on a double-decker plane. Gymnastics was already opening up the world to me in a way that went far beyond backflips and cartwheels.

Jerry came along and each athlete had a parent with her. My mother and her aunt Connie chaperoned me. Preparations had to be made in a hurry, and the girls' mothers sewed costumes and organized a bake sale, a car wash, and a gymnastics exhibition at my father's college to raise money for the expensive trip. On top of the money raised, my parents borrowed money from my well-traveled great-aunt. She was so excited about the trip that she came along.

Once we gymnasts arrived in the Soviet Union, we were given a strict schedule. We understood very quickly that we were there for one reason— to learn. Each day for two weeks, we took a bus from our hotel to an incredibly large gymnastics facility in the heart of Moscow and trained from 8:00 A.M. to 5:00 P.M., with just a short break for lunch. The Canadian coaches and American coaches—including one from Oklahoma named Steve Nunno, whom Mom met only briefly—took clinics with Soviet coaches on technique and methodology. All of the visiting gymnasts trained with Soviet girls under the supervision of the Soviet coaches.

The first thing they did was divide us into groups based on skill levels. So they had us do a few basic skills on each event to see where we fit. The next thing I knew, I was the youngest one in the highest-level group. They put me, a nine-year-old, into a group with experienced fourteen-year-olds. The rest of Jerry's kids were in younger groups. Rather than feeling daunted, I was thrilled to train with the older Soviet girls because I'd get the chance to do the more advanced skills they were working on. I really enjoyed being with them despite the language barrier, and I loved that they all wore pretty bows in their hair!

Trying to keep up with them was challenging every single day and required a great deal of work. When I had trouble learning a skill they excelled at, I'd often become impatient and emotional. My tears were those of frustration, not because I felt I was being worked too hard or I felt sorry for myself. In fact, I was delighted to be allowed to train with these amazingly gifted and elegant gymnasts who could do skills no one was doing in our gym in Oklahoma. I was so appreciative that the coaches, seeing I was willing to work hard, were excited to teach me the same things their girls were learning, like how to execute a double backflip on floor. They even tried to get me to do triple twists, which no nine-year-old was doing. Being a daredevil, I was happy for the chance to push my limits. "Can't" was not in my vocabulary.

The coaches wanted to get the most out of us and they had a great enthusiasm for how they went about it. Instead of telling us, "Go do twenty reps of that skill," they made it a game by asking, "Who can do that skill twenty times in the least amount of time?" I expected it to be tough, and it was. I hoped they'd push me to my limits, and they did. What I wasn't prepared for was how much pure fun I had and how much laughter was involved with high-level training. The coaches were strict but also understood that they got the best results when training was both tough and fun.

I was thrilled that dance was part of the training regimen. We had ballet every day and it proved to be a very comfortable style of dance for me. For the very first time, I had a glimpse of how classical music and dance can be incorporated into gymnastics. Three feet from where we trained on the floor exercise, there was an actual *grand piano*. It was thrilling to find myself working with a Russian choreographer on some true dance positions. I'd never had anyone work with me in such a detailed manner. Every finger placement, every shoulder placement, every toe placement, and every eye movement had to be done exactly the right way. She was strict and precise and had me do them over and over and over. Jerry was a fabulous coach, but I had never had someone who paid such close attention to every element of every move. Yes, I loved it! I'm not sure that I realized it then, but it changed me as a gymnast, and likely as a person. It wasn't okay to muddle through; I was expected to strive for perfection with every turn. *Every move counts.*

During our two weeks in Moscow, my mother, Aunt Connie, and I did a bit of sightseeing, but I was so tired after a full day in the gym that I usually preferred napping. I still haven't forgotten the gigantic meals that were always placed in front of us. I was such a picky eater that I would just grab handfuls of cherries and put them in my pockets to eat later in the hotel room. Mom and I shared a room and she had wisely brought from home a small, mint-green cassette recorder. She had the foresight to know that I would have trouble sleeping when it was still light outside. So she would close the drapes and play the Dolly Parton cassettes she'd brought with her. Night after night, I would doze off to the sounds of Dolly's version of "Downtown."

At the conclusion of the two weeks, the Soviet coaches held a big conference with all the American and Canadian coaches. Parents were not invited to attend, but Mom was allowed in with Jerry because she was, by this time, a bona fide gymnastics judge. Not content to just watch me, she had learned everything she could about her daughter's sport by earning a coaching certificate and becoming a judge, which she'd be from October to June for over ten years. (Eventually she would even take adult gymnastics lessons!) So she was privy to how the Soviet coaches evaluated all the girls.

They told our coaches, "Most of your girls will be only recreational gymnasts or do well competitively but not at an Elite level." I would learn that "Elite" is the highest level in gymnastics one can achieve, and only Elite gymnasts are allowed to compete for a spot on the national team and compete in a World Championship or Olympic Games. Continuing their critique, the Russian coaches said, "However, there are three girls who have Olympic potential." They identified two older girls and then began talking about "a young girl who got frustrated quite often, but who showed how determined she is to do well. Plus, she demonstrated a high skill level for her age." When they said her name was "Shannon Miller," Jerry and my mother almost fell out of their chairs.

Going to Russia was pivotal to my career as a gymnast. It not only opened my eyes to the exciting skills I could learn and how dance—particularly ballet—can be incorporated into the floor exercise, but also taught me to be more detail-oriented in every event. Most of all it showed me that gymnastics was larger and had so much more breadth than I had imagined. I'd had a cookie-cutter impression of gymnasts. Previously when I had looked in the mirror, I saw a quiet mouse with twiggy legs and a small frame and I didn't think I looked at all like a true gymnast. I didn't look like Mary Lou Retton, who had powerful legs and a big smile that reflected her peppy personality. She was the only champion gymnast that I knew of at the time and I assumed all the other *real* gymnasts were like her.

That trip allowed me to redefine in my mind who a gymnast can be. Having trained with some marvelous classically trained female gymnasts in Russia who had a body type similar to mine, I realized that I actually had a wonderful body type to be a successful gymnast. What a revelation! My mother started me in gymnastics to have fun and stay out of trouble, not because she was looking for a sport specific to my size. Somehow we had stumbled into a sport for which I was the right size and that I absolutely adored. Eventually, I would become a champion by forging my own path and fostering my own talents, rather than forcing myself to try to achieve a level of explosive power—or attempt a gregarious nature that was the norm during my era but did not come naturally to me. As I learned in Russia, grace and elegance can be just as effective as power. I now saw there were many styles that I could explore to find the one that best fit my personality.

Of equal significance was that my experience in the Soviet Union threw fuel on the fire in my belly to finally compete. I was very competitive by nature, whether I played board games with Tessa and Troy, gin with my grandma, or had contests with the other girls at Adventures. I hated to lose and when I did I wanted to quickly play again so I had a chance to win the next time. However, in my years at Adventures I had so focused on learning skills that I had not truly thought of gymnastics in terms of a larger competition. I didn't know any better. My competition was to complete a twist or stick a landing. But now I wanted to show the world what I could do.

I assumed I could learn what I needed to be a competitive gymnast at Adventures in Gymnastics and Jerry could put together a team of girls to enter in competitions. Jerry thought differently and said to my mother, "Look, I've decided we're not going to have a competitive team here, and frankly, I don't know that I can train a kid with that kind of potential to be a competitor. What if I mess her up? She needs a coach who can take her a lot further than I can. She needs to go to another gym where she can really develop into something special." By being so honest with my mother (as he was with the mothers of other talented girls in the gym) and suggesting I go elsewhere, he was looking after me, as he had always done.

I was so fortunate that I began taking gymnastics with Jerry and spent more than three years at Adventures in Gymnastics. It was the best thing that could have happened for my competitive career to come. I was able to work on the pure foundational skills that I would need to learn the bigger skills. Unlike girls in gyms where competition was emphasized, I had the time to focus on perfecting skills without worrying about the next meet. I didn't have to worry about what the judges would be looking at, or obsess over putting together complicated routines, or fret about being gone every weekend for a competition. I didn't have to train the same routine over and over, so each day I had the luxury of simply learning new skills.

But when I had learned all those skills, I needed to do something with them other than show them off at the next parade. I didn't think about medals or victories quite yet, but my desire to start competing in order to reach my potential intensified.

4

Of the two gyms that Jerry Clavier highly recommended to my mother, one was owned by Ralph King and the other by Steve Nunno. My mother had chatted with Steve in Moscow but not about me or the possibility that I might be changing gyms. First I worked out for an evening at Ralph King's gym in Oklahoma City, which was only a twenty-five-minute drive from Edmond. I felt comfortable and really liked the other girls there. But Jerry stressed, "Before you make a final decision, see how you feel about Steve Nunno."

So Mom drove me the forty-five minutes to Norman and I worked out at Dynamo Gymnastics, in a space at Bart Conner's Gymnastics Academy that Steve Nunno rented from the two-time gold medalist at the 1984 Olympics. I may not have watched gymnastics on television, but even I knew who Bart Conner was. Oklahoma, which was not a hotbed for gymnastics at the time, claimed Bart as one of its own, even if he was from Illinois. (I related because while I born in Missouri, I felt Oklahoma was my home.) Likewise, Steve had migrated to Oklahoma, having been born in New York and raised in Massachusetts. He'd been a gymnast in college and his degree from the University of Massachusetts was in sports administration. For a time, he ran his own gym, and then he spent a year in

Houston as an assistant coach to Béla Károlyi before working for three years as an assistant coach for the women's gymnastics team at the University of Oklahoma in Norman. Now, about thirty, he had high hopes of growing his new venture, Dynamo Gymnastics.

After I trained at both gyms, my mother fully expected me to choose the one run by Ralph King because she correctly surmised that Steve and I weren't sure we liked each other. My first impression was a long way from "Oh, I love it here and I really like him," as I had felt at the gym owned by Mr. King. So my mother was startled when I chose Dynamo. Something had clicked and I knew, "This is where I need to be."

Why did I choose Steve? At the time I had no dream of being an Olympic champion, but I did have a single-minded desire to be the best I could be as a gymnast. No doubt I could have had fun at the other gym club, but, while having fun was important, I wanted to make real progress in my sport. I needed the opportunity to learn the next new skill and the one after that. I had my mind set on competition and moving up levels one after the next until I reached the pinnacle of the sport: Elite! I expected a lot from myself and I wanted to be taken seriously. I didn't want someone to coddle me.

I wanted another coach like Jerry who could be honest with me and tell me what I was doing wrong, so I could fix it. I wasn't the type who needed to be told everything was peachy when it wasn't. I just had that instinct the first time in his gym that Steve was going to deal straight with me. I knew he wasn't going to let me get away with not giving 100 percent. He wasn't going to say, "Oh, sweetie, it's okay that you fell five times," or, "If you can't do twenty push-ups that's okay; just do fifteen. Do you need to sit down and rest?" That would have wasted his time and mine. Also, my parents were paying hard-earned money so I could take gymnastics lessons and I wasn't going to waste it. This was not a babysitting service; I was there to learn.

I thrived on structure and Steve had plenty of that. He had rules. Number 1: Look me in the eye when I'm speaking to you. Number 2: No sitting in the gym . . . period. Number 3: Gymnastics is about having fun, so train hard and enjoy it. How Steve expected me to behave at Dynamo was similar to how my parents had taught me to act in general: I was to pay attention, be respectful, and do my best.

Jerry thought I'd made a good, mature choice and called Steve with the news. Steve agreed to take me on a one-month trial basis to "see if it works." He seemed cautious, but my mother still tells me, "He was very impressed by you in Russia and the minute he got his hands on you, he had big plans." And I believed it was part of God's big plan for me to be at Dynamo.

I could not have stayed at Dynamo very long if Steve and I didn't get along. At the outset he wasn't all hugs and kisses, but we connected once I understood his rules and that his aspirations for me were the same as mine. His primary goal was that I become a successful competitor. He expected me to work to achieve that. My parents had instilled in me a very strong work ethic, so I was comfortable with his demands.

Within weeks, Steve decided that I was no longer on "probation." I think he was delighted that several of us from Adventures joined his gym. He had hoped to expand his business, become a full-time coach, and eventually own his own building. At the time, he was also selling real estate and it was amusing watching him arrive each day carrying a briefcase and wearing a suit and tie before changing into his gym garb.

People assume that the minute I joined Dynamo, Steve started signing me up for local competitions and that I was a phenom who blew away more experienced gymnasts and brought home medals every time. In actuality, I went from being a recreational gymnast to a competitive athlete through endless hours of training, pulled muscles, and frustration. I was quick to learn some skills, but it would take me longer than other girls to learn some of the skills that are critical to that level of competitor. For example, I would work on a doubleback (two flips) on floor exercise and also off the uneven bars for many months before I could land them successfully even 50 percent of the time. I was not even allowed to go to the first competition my gym went to because my new coach didn't think I was as ready as some of his other girls. I was not pleased.

My mother remembers that when Steve took me to Dallas for my first competition, I fell on both beam and bars. He was right; I wasn't ready. I had sporadic success in my early competitions over the next few months, but for the most part, I was shaky and had a rough time. Steve promised me that consistency would come, but his immediate solution was for me to get back to the gym to make the necessary corrections. I didn't have to be told that I needed to work even harder.

At the time I had arrived at Dynamo, Steve was training about ten girls, all older and at a much higher level of skills. So until some younger Class 2 girls joined—including Lisa Heckel and others from Adventures— he had no choice but to throw me in with some higher-level teenage girls, the "big dogs." In future years, I'd be asked by reporters to name my gymnastics inspirations. I felt I was expected to recall Olympic champions from the past, big names that everyone would recognize. But having never watched the Olympics, I hadn't even seen Mary Lou Retton or Bart Conner win their medals. I did know of University of Oklahoma star Kelly Garrison (who would compete in the upcoming 1988 Olympics), but only because she was born and bred in Oklahoma and had dropped in on a clinic Jerry Clavier took his Adventures girls to in her hometown of Altus. I remember that clinic, and I'm pretty sure Kelly remembers, too. I spent most of the break time riding piggyback on this future star! But in my bubble, my only real inspirations were Tracy Cole and Shelly Pendley, two of the older Class 1 gymnasts at Dynamo. Tracy in particular was always very focused, so I wanted to be like her and work just as hard. Becoming a Class 1 gymnast was a goal because it was just one level below Elite, the level I needed to reach in order to contend for the national team.

My problem was that I expected to be as good as Tracy and Shelly from the very start. When I fell on my fanny, I'd use up all my energy crying. At competitions I didn't cry as much when I failed to pull off a new skill, because I had to move on to the next rotation, but when I tried to learn a difficult new skill in the gym and didn't ace it immediately, my emotions would get the better of me. Steve began calling me Chicken Little because if things weren't going exactly as planned it was as if the sky had fallen and my life was over. He didn't do this in a derogatory way. It was more to bring on a smile and remind me that I could get back on track.

Steve saw that I wasn't being a bad sport or a spoiled brat who wanted everything to come easy; I was certainly willing to put in the work. I just couldn't fathom why I wasn't immediately doing every skill as well as his more experienced sixteen-year-olds. I didn't see why age made a difference. I wanted to be perfect.

Although Steve often got fed up with my roller coaster of emotions, he appreciated that I was driven and had exceptional perseverance. He thought, "Here's a kid I can help if I can get her to channel that frustration into positive energy." He recognized that I had the inner drive needed to advance from neophyte to Elite, and with the patience of a saint tried to get me to listen to him and help me refocus. Steve would stress that getting upset is tiring and you need that energy to get back up and work on the correction. He would say, "Forget the fall; concentrate on doing the next skill well."

I would try so hard to do what Steve said, and most of the time I was successful at handling my emotions. Of course there were other times when there was nothing anyone could say because I just needed to vent, to get the disappointment out. He realized there were times that this was the only way I could move forward. He stressed that I needed to maintain a positive attitude, but it would take me years of trial and error, of finding what worked and what didn't. And it took years before I understood that having a positive attitude didn't mean I wasn't allowed to feel a little disappointed when things didn't go my way. It was about regrouping the best I could and finding a way over, around, or through whatever obstacle stood before me. Having a positive attitude also meant finding the silver lining even under the direst of circumstances. The belief that there is always a silver lining would get me through numerous difficult times in my life, and it was instilled in me as a young gymnast.

Steve was a great motivator and kept gymnastics stimulating and fun for me, which was the reason we were a great combination from the start. He introduced the concept of goal-setting, the importance of which became colossal in my life. At the beginning of each year, he sat his girls down on the floor exercise mat and passed out index cards. On one side we had to write down our long-term goals. At first I wrote down something fairly conservative, as far as dreams go. Something like, "I want to compete at the state competition!" or "I want to be an Elite gymnast!" I'm sure other girls wrote down that they wanted to go to the Olympics, but that wasn't my heart's desire yet. Steve did not let us stop there. We had to turn the card over and on the back side we would painstakingly write down our short-term goals. Steve explained that these were those small things we had to work on daily in order to reach our long-term goals. Learning a new dismount off uneven bars and consistently sticking a landing were important short-term goals for me.

Steve talked a lot about always giving 100 percent. That meant on every skill we tried. If you were up on the balance beam to do a skill but weren't prepared to give it everything you had, you needed to get off the beam immediately and practice it on the floor or low beam until you were ready. It did no good to stand there and fret. You also didn't want to go halfway. I learned that lesson early on. As I was waiting my turn, I was watching my teammate do a series of skills on beam. Suddenly she stopped in the middle of her back handspring layout step out and landed on her head. It was scary to watch and though she was fine physically, she was pretty shaken up. Steve called the entire team over and said, "Look, you go zero percent or you go a hundred percent, you don't go anywhere in between, because that's when you get injured." I would never forget that.

I also worked on improving my strength and flexibility, as I had done during my time at Jerry's gym. In most sports you need primarily either upper-body or lower-body strength and flexibility, but since gymnastics is a full-body sport you need both. So Steve had me work on conditioning for my entire body, using my own body weight to gain strength in my legs, arms, and core. We would run for about fifteen minutes at the start of practice to loosen up, then do close to an hour of conditioning and stretching before even starting work on the individual events. It was a rigorous way to begin a workout, but it didn't take long for me to see the direct correlation between the strength and flexibility I gained and the more difficult moves I now was able to perform.

We also worked on my "game face," or competition mode. *Train like you would compete and compete like you've trained.* As a spectator, it's natural to think that some mistakes are made in competitions because of the distractions: people taking pictures; fans cheering for other gymnasts; loud music accompanying other gymnasts performing floor exercises; the noise and chaos around the arena; and the TV cameras. But that's just how it is in gymnastics, and as young athletes in the gym, we quickly learned to block out everything going on around us and focus. If you wanted to compete well, you needed to have that ability. We were at peace with the chaos around us, much like being in the calm eye of a storm. We trained while there was music blaring, toddlers running across the vault runway, other gymnasts walking across the mats, and coaches yelling out corrections, yet we were able to concentrate on our routines. In fact, many times when I was on beam during competitions, I'd hijack the music playing or the audience's cheers during another gymnast's performance and pretend it was for me. Gymnastics is an incredibly mental sport. Yes, you have to have a certain amount of talent, strength, flexibility, and artistry, but if you can't hold it together mentally you may never have the opportunity to show off all of those error-free routines you practiced.

Ironically, the hardest time for me to execute my skills at the gym was when there was nothing going on. When preparing for an important competition, Steve had us do what we called "pressure sets." He'd turn off the music and have everyone in the gym sit and watch each other perform full routines as if we were in a competition. There was complete silence and everybody in the gym was staring at you. That was the worst!

I'd go to school a full day and then train from 4:00 P.M. to 8:00 P.M. My father drove me to and from Norman, which took about forty-five minutes each way. In my family, education was a higher priority than gymnastics, so in the car I would diligently do what homework I hadn't finished at school, with the light on during the return trip after dark. My dad helped me with math and science, so I kind of had a personal tutor with me. He also gave me a primer course in physics to help me understand how my body could perform at optimum levels while doing moves in gymnastics. I'm sure some kids would have fallen asleep, but I wanted to know more. I just loved learning and my dad could put even the most complex ideas into examples that I could easily grasp. For instance, a piece of paper sliding off the dashboard as we made a turn became a fascinating lesson in centrifugal force. He truly was an amazing teacher!

I'd eat dinner at 9:00 P.M. with the rest of my family. That was one of the few times I got to spend with my equally busy siblings, who'd often just gotten home from doing their own activities. As much as possible, Mom cooked well-rounded meals like pork chops with broccoli and mashed potatoes, although pizza and cheeseburgers were not uncommon with our crazy schedules. I drank a full glass of milk every night. There was never a special menu because I was an athlete; there were no diets. We were active kids and my parents made sure we all got enough calories to give us the energy we needed each day. They wanted us to understand a balanced diet, which meant along with the carbs and protein we loved, we also had to eat our vegetables. That didn't come easy for me. As many children do, I balked at eating my greens. One night I was told I couldn't get up from the table until I finished my spinach. I tried to feed it to Tessa's cat, Yo-Yo, but he wouldn't touch it, either. After an hour Dad took pity on me and let me go, which was probably not a wise thing because it just hardened my resolve. I thought, "Okay, I won that one!" But over time each of us kids came to eat at least a couple of bites of everything put in front of us, including vegetables. During dinner, we all talked about what we did that day and what we were going to do the next day. Afterward, I finished my homework or went directly to bed.

On Saturdays, if there was no competition, I'd train during the day. There was no waking up at the break of dawn, no matter what day of the week. That's a bit of a myth about gymnasts. Rest is part of training. You have to give your body time to recover. During the summers, I'd be in the gym from 9:00 A.M. to 1:00 or 2:00 P.M. As the competitions became more serious, practices were sometimes split into two sessions for a total of six or seven hours, six days a week. I remember those Saturday mornings when my sister and brother would be in their pajamas watching Saturday morning cartoons and I'd be dragging my heavy gym bag downstairs to go off to a six-hour workout. Those were the times I'd need to pull out my index card and look at my goals for motivation. Seeing them in black and white, ink on paper, somehow made it more real. There were so many small goals I had to check off the list before I could achieve that ultimate dream.

It was a difficult schedule, no doubt, but I thrived on routine. Juggling gymnastics practice, competition schedules, and school could be tough, but it was all I knew, and I was comfortable with it. If for some reason the gym was closed for a day or I didn't have to go to school, I was much less productive than when I had a very structured schedule. I liked being busy and having every minute accounted for. When I didn't have something specific to do, I would simply create things like death-defying roller-skating jumps—*Helmet? What helmet?*—or ride bikes with my sister. Often, I would watch reruns of *The Brady Bunch* while twirling a laundry basket with my feet, whiling away the hours. I'd make up games for myself and my sister and brother. Of course, my games typically had so many rules and structure that we hardly ever got to the part where we actually played them.

Only on rare occasions did I do serious gymnastics at home. Gymnastics teaches you safety, and I knew better than to get from my bedroom to the kitchen by doing back handsprings. My dad did build me a small balance beam for the living room, covering it with carpet. I loved that beam so much. Having a balance beam at my disposal gave me an opportunity to try my hand at choreographing routines or working on less dangerous skills that I was still trying to perfect. For some crazy reason, I had Dad put up a bar in the backyard. It was a single rail with chalk to go with it. I was excited to try it out, but after that I didn't make much use of it. It's one thing to have a low beam for working alone on simple skills, but for bars you really need mats, a pit, and someone to spot you.

At home I mostly did stretching. Lots and lots of stretching. Flexibility was a weak area for me that I needed to improve. So I did quite a bit of homework in the splits. I even tried sleeping in the splits—left, right, and middle—but it didn't really take. I was always full of crazy ideas. For a while I was worried about my toe point. So I started sneaking Ace bandages into my room and binding my feet into a toe point each night. It was not the best idea I ever had, but at the time I thought it was worth a shot.

5

Steve began taking us to competitions most weekends. As long as there was a competition ahead, I felt all was right with the world, although I would be a bit on edge right before competing, as I would be my entire career. My schoolwork didn't suffer, but I fear my family did. I became a little hard to live with. This sweet little girl would suddenly become cranky and irritated over minor things, and I could be short with Tessa and Troy. As the middle child, I was always the peacemaker, always trying to please everyone, but not before a meet. At the time, I couldn't voice my emotions. I'm not sure I even understood them. "Please, everyone, I have a meet coming up and I'm scared." I'm sure everyone was relieved once the competition ended and the relaxed and happy Shannon would again emerge.

My father often drove to competitions and would borrow a video camera so that he could tape them for my mother. My mom's job at the bank didn't provide her with the same flexibility he had as a professor, so she had to stay behind. But before competitions, she would give me index cards with short faith-based sayings. She would consistently remind me, "Your thinking it's all on you. It's not. Give God His due because He is with you, always."

Tessa wished me luck when I left for a competition, but she seemed indifferent. Years later, my mother revealed that Tessa would sit with her and watch tape-delayed broadcasts of my meets on television. Mom says she would get so excited watching me. When Dad called home from competitions that weren't on television, Tessa would start yelling, "Did she win? Or did she fall? Ask Dad if she won!" If everything went okay, she would sigh with relief. Tessa never told me about this, and I was so touched to learn about it from Mom. Unfortunately, Tessa had a few years of disappointment while waiting for me to start winning.

Steve would have loved if the gymnasts he took to the various competitions made it to the podiums, but he cared more about our hitting the skills and routines we had practiced. He was keeping the bigger picture in mind. He entered me in competitions for which I was a little young so I could see how I'd do against older girls—he knew that being bested by them would make me hungrier to improve. He always wanted me to strive for more and this was part of his strategy to move me to the next level. He wanted me to have a taste of success so that I would want to keep going, but not so much success that I would become complacent. It was a bit like golf. You can have seventeen really bad holes and be ready to throw in the towel. Then all of a sudden you drain that twenty-five-footer for a birdie and that one good hole makes you want to keep coming back.

Steve also wanted me to use these opportunities to audition new skills in my routines, and see if I could do them without error in competitions. The first series I competed in beam competition was a gainer back handspring, back handspring, back handspring. This move required three back handsprings, one after the next, with no stops in between. The first, called a "gainer," started with my standing on my right leg and swinging my left leg up and over to *gain* momentum for the following two back handsprings. The timing and direction had to be perfect. Steve was impressed I pulled it off because very few girls he'd seen could do three moves in succession. Still, I fell off the beam quite often in the beginning. I'm not sure I actually stayed on the beam during those first few years of competitions! It was all about learning. I would finally stick one skill, but another would suffer. I had to learn how to put it all together in that ninety-second period.

If Steve didn't think we were attentive when he explained the remedies to our troubles in competitions, he'd kick us out of practice and have us sit there until our parents picked us up hours later. Perhaps he grew impatient with the lack of consistency we girls on the small Dynamo team displayed, because he seemed to be exiling us to the lobby with increasing frequency. Some of the other girls didn't mind the breaks, particularly with Steve being so short-tempered, but not being able to practice was the worst punishment I could be handed.

On my tenth birthday my mother showed up early and found that there were eleven girls sitting in the lobby, including me—I was too excited by my birthday to fully concentrate that day. When we saw that my mother had brought a cake-size cookie for everyone to share, we couldn't help ourselves and we all started celebrating. Steve wasn't thrilled to find that the girls he was punishing were feasting on an enormous cookie topped with thick icing. If he'd denied us that cookie he might have lost us, so he grumpily stomped back to his office. Steve never stayed angry long, but I wasn't too interested in speaking with him right then. My mother encouraged me to take him a piece of cookie as a peace offering and apologize for not paying better attention. He tried mightily to keep that scowl, but it was too tough not to smile when a ten-year-old wisp of a girl was waving a piece of cookie at him as if waving a steak in front of a lion. He never stopped kicking us out entirely, but I think Mom helped him understand that if most of his pupils were in the lobby then there was a good possibility that they weren't the only problem that day.

Now that I was ten, Steve felt I was ready to compete with other girls in the gym in my first state competition, a Class 2 team competition held in Altus. On the first day, we did compulsories on all four events, and on the second day, we did optionals. Then both days' scores were added up to determine both the team winner and the individual all-around champion. For compulsories, every gymnast did exactly the same routines on the four events. Within that framework, we tried to find a way to set ourselves apart for the judges by showing we were superior on the fundamental skills and that we could make a standard routine look pretty. I loved compulsories. They were my strong suit.

On the second day, gymnasts got to show their individuality in the optionals competition. Optionals are more physically demanding than compulsories and each athlete's routine is unique. Gymnasts eagerly demonstrate the original routines they've conceived with their coaches, keeping in mind that completing skills with a higher level of difficulty, according to the Code of Points for the current four-year Olympic cycle, will garner the highest scores from the judges. I did well in the optionals, too, except that I fell on beam doing my back handspring layout step out series. In gymnastics, there's an intimidating adage: *You can't fall and win.* I'd heard this many times before and would for years to come. However, the only thing I knew to do after taking so many falls was to get back up, minimize the deduction, and finish the routine. That day I fell off the beam but got back on it and completed my routine. Because my beam routine had a high level of difficulty, I still received a solid score and, after doing well in the three remaining events, ended up as the Class 2 all-around state champion for my age bracket. *It was amazing.* I learned that day that the adage was wrong. Even more exciting was that my score helped my team take home the first-place trophy! Of course we loved the trophy, but what made it really special was that Steve had promised if we won, he'd do a standing backflip in the middle of the arena with everyone watching. He did it and landed on his feet!

I learned a major lesson about gymnastics competition that day: *If you fall, you still can win. So never give up. If you make a mistake, put it behind you and move forward while minimizing deductions as much as possible.* This was also a tremendously important and powerful life lesson. In fact, I would carry it with me through my life, including in major gymnastics competitions and in my life-or-death competition with cancer.

I applied this lesson that June at a USAIGC meet in Dover, Delaware. Steve was required to have six gymnasts compete, but he had only five Class 1 girls, so I was thrilled when he chose me from the Class 2 girls to fill out his team. I was excited that we'd all take part in each event of the team competition. This was the first time I had ever been a part of a televised meet. There were cameramen just feet from the equipment, which could be intimidating. I tried to pay attention to the older girls to see if they did anything different. I saw that they ignored the cameras and focused on their routines. I tried to do the same.

In the team competition, only the five top scores from each team were counted on each event, and I proved myself in the elimination round by never having the worst score and having it discarded. In the televised finals featuring the top four of the original twelve teams, I did well on the bars, but I fell on beam yet again. I saved my tears for after the dismount, then moved on to the next event, my fall forgotten. I scored the best on the team on floor exercise and got my first 9.0 ever in competition for doing a piked Tsuk vault—a roundoff onto the vaulting horse and then a piked backflip off—helping Dynamo win a bronze medal.

I often fell early at competitions, but I learned to put it behind me quickly. I seemed to thrive under pressure, particularly when I needed to redeem myself from a disastrous previous event. Turning a negative into a positive, I used my fall as motivation to do even better on the next apparatus. I had a dogged determination that rivaled that of more seasoned athletes. I was never the strongest, most flexible, or even most talented gymnast, but Steve was the first to say that I could outwork anyone and, somehow, turn it on in clutch situations.

My improvement and competitive fire convinced Steve that I was ready to move up. I had won Class 2, so it was time to do more. Instead of going to Class 1, which was the logical next step, I bypassed that level and moved straight to Elite. No, it wasn't because I was "that good." It was actually because I was "that short." In Class 1 there was a particular skill required during the compulsory uneven bar routine for which you had to move from the low bar up to the high bar. My torso and arms were simply not long enough for me to catch the bar. I would have to take the full deduction, the equivalent of a complete fall, every single time I attempted it. Instead of allowing me to face that frustration, Steve opted to toss me in with the higher-level girls and see if I could qualify for Elite, which did not require this particular move. He wanted a small group of potential Elites to train long hours in the summer on difficult skills.

To carry out this plan and expand Dynamo to accommodate an influx of new gymnasts, Steve realized it was time to move to a bigger space—his own. He rented a large warehouse in Oklahoma City, which meant that while my training hours would be longer, the drive time would be cut in half. Since my father was also chauffeuring Tessa and Troy to their various activities, he was glad not to be spending as much time in the car. However, Dad gave up much of his spare time to help build the offices in Steve's new facility. He also helped dig the foam pits. If that weren't enough, Dad helped out by running the scoring at our home meets.

I had a productive summer at Dynamo, working on new skills and refining old ones, and building bold routines that mixed athleticism and artistry. I could do some impressive skills, but my task was to put them together to make them seamless and beautiful, which would go a long way to setting me apart. On each apparatus, I wanted to tell a story and show my personality through my moves—even on vault. Preparing to become an Elite, I worked tirelessly on the Yurchenko vault, during which you do a roundoff onto the springboard and a back handspring onto the vaulting horse. After that, you spring off your hands to do a backward flip, hopefully landing on your feet. I made dramatic improvements on this vault that summer.

When I had free time in the afternoon, I swam at the community swimming pool in our neighborhood with Tessa and Troy. One day I was just playing around and treating the diving board like a balance beam. A local diving coach saw me do a double-twist off the board and told my mother, "I think she'd be a good addition to my diving team." Of course, I had gone into the water feetfirst. One day my mother took me out to the aquatic center to try out for his team. I wasn't sure what exactly I was supposed to do, so I performed the same skills I had been doing while fooling around at the pool. The coach seemed a little put out and finally turned to my mother and said, "That's great, but can she please do some actual dives? I need her to go in headfirst." That's where I drew the line. No matter that I was regularly performing multiple flips and twists in the gym; gymnasts land only on their feet. No way was I going to intentionally flip toward my head! I just couldn't fathom why anyone would choose to do that, even into water. So much for my diving career.

Fall arrived quickly and that meant I was back at school and on my weeknight and Saturday morning training schedule. Saturday afternoons and Sundays were totally gymnastics-free and my time to be a "normal girl." I was a voracious reader, so on Saturday or Sunday afternoons I got to relax with a good book, usually something that wasn't assigned in school. Or I spent time with my sister. Since Tessa and I were old enough to ride bikes on our own, we went riding together everywhere. For years they built new additions to our neighborhood, so we would pack our little lunches, and ride our bikes around and check out all the model homes. We were playing house in real houses! It was our fun adventure and no one seemed to mind. They probably assumed our parents were out looking for a home to purchase.

Also, Tessa and I might hang out with our father at his shop in our garage, or he'd take us to the one at his college. He wanted us to learn how to safely use saws, hammers, and other tools and to fix and build things. He taught us how to clamp things and cut things. It wasn't just my mother who wanted us girls to be self-reliant. We took pride in that. Today when I fix something around the house or do something substantial like put together our child's crib, I flash back to those times with my father. We were always building something.

Every time I open a box of tea and inhale the aroma I have memories of my dad making huge batches of sun tea in the backyard. It was an all-day process. I also have fond memories of shooting baskets with him in the driveway or working with him in the yard. Back in the house, we'd turn on the television and he'd try to explain professional wrestling to me. We really enjoyed watching basketball together and marveling at Michael Jordan and my dad's favorite, Larry Bird, and grumbling about an angry-acting player named Charles Barkley, never dreaming I'd meet them all a few years later when we were Olympic teammates. When I asked my dad about Barkley's demeanor on the court, he said, "Shannon, he's a good guy; he's just putting on an act. He's got his game face on, just like you do on the balance beam." My dad certainly didn't know Charles Barkley, but he made him out to be a teddy bear. And when I met him, that's exactly what he turned out to be!

Throughout my career I'd miss church occasionally because I was away weekends at competitions, but when I was home I went Sunday mornings with my family. Faith and prayer have always been a huge part of my life. Whenever I'd have a rough time, my mother put me back on track by reminding me that I needn't take all the stress on myself when I could put it in God's hands.

Sunday was also the day I spent the most time with my mother. After I'd cleaned my room, made the bed, and finished my other chores, I liked helping her in the kitchen. Maybe we'd bake cookies together. I inherited my sweet tooth from her. Sometimes just the three girls would go to the mall to window-shop or pick out one item. However, those were not leisurely strolls in the mall. My mother walked so fast that it was hard to keep up. Sometimes we had to jog to catch up or risk being left behind. That might explain why when I was really young she lost me a couple of times at the mall! Actually, one of those times, Tessa and I weren't lost but were just hiding in the racks of clothes. The other time, I had wandered off at eighteen months old. My mother was panic-stricken before finding me in the men's section stomping around in men's shoes.

Tessa and I weren't your typical shoppers. We certainly could not have been classified as "girly girls." Neither of us was into shoes, clothes, jewelry, or makeup at the time. All I wore were sneakers, jeans, sweat suits, and leotards, and I had not much use for anything else. There's one school photo of me where you can see my leotard sticking out from underneath my clothes. My mother was not pleased.

Weekend family meals were more leisurely than on weeknights. We might even have time for dessert! I was painfully shy at school but not at home, so I did my share of the talking, though Mom usually led the way. Dad contributed, too, though he was the quietest Miller at the table, waiting for everyone to finish so he could get to the dishes.

Knowing I had free time at the end of the week was important to me. I knew I needed some time to lead the life of a normal girl my age. I was very determined to keep my life in balance, and that's probably why I was able to avoid any real conflict during my gymnastics career. I felt pride that I had dinner with my family, did my chores, went to public school, and made good grades. My parents made sure I had the right priorities. Most important, I had long conversations with my dad in the car and my mother in the kitchen. When they felt I was having a hard time and not enjoying myself, we would talk about it. They made sure the lines of communication were always open. They were the same with Tessa and Troy.

6

For Steve, fall meant not the beginning of school but the beginning of a new competition season, one where he hoped I'd make significant strides toward Elite status. As he'd done in Norman, he began with his traditional Halloween meet for his gymnasts, when everyone would show up in a costume, including the coaches and parents. Steve didn't like us to eat candy all that much, but on that day he gave out candy prizes to the girl with the best Halloween costume. The year before I came as a ghost, but this year I asked my mother to help me come up with a more creative costume so I could win some candy.

I showed up at Dynamo in the most ridiculous costume of all time. My mother had saved egg cartons, cereal boxes, and paper bags and now she glued them together so that I could dress as a bag of groceries! My face was beet red from embarrassment, but nobody knew that because I wore a Ruffles potato chip bag over my head, with holes for my eyes. The other girls lined up in their expensive, store-bought costumes. The judges looked at my weird outfit and the spindly legs poking out underneath and gave me first prize!

I doubt if I wore that costume when I went trick-or-treating that Halloween. One year I dressed like a ballerina in a pink leotard and tights. I remember that costume because I slipped into a gutter and scraped my leg. That was par for the course. As graceful as I was on a balance beam, I was a clumsy mess just walking down the street.

Halloween was a lot of fun because my neighborhood was great for trick-or-treating and I always came home with a nice full pumpkin of candy. I enjoyed all holidays, especially Thanksgiving and Christmas. I would help my mom with shopping, preparing for the meal the night before, and setting the table. Thanksgiving was a big family event. We would invite a few friends, neighbors, and often Steve, who wasn't married yet. We'd always have a turkey with cornbread stuffing made from scratch and if we had many guests we'd also have a small ham. Tessa and I helped Mom bake sugar cookies until Troy was old enough to join in.

Naturally, my favorite holiday was Christmas. I loved being Mama's helper and polishing what little silver we had (until we realized I was allergic to silver polish), taking out the good china, and setting the table. I also relished my role as the gift-wrapper. I wrapped all the gifts for everyone in the family and extended family. The only gifts I didn't wrap were my own, but that worked out because on occasion, when the suspense was just too much, I'd unwrap an edge, peek, and then rewrap it. I'm pretty sure my mother knew but didn't mind so much since I was saving her quite a bit of time.

Tessa, Troy, and I would get up at the crack of dawn to run downstairs to look at the beautifully decorated tree and all the wrapped gifts below it. My parents always hid one present for each of us, and my mother wrote on slips of paper a poem or a rhyme that gave us hints as to where we could find them. We weren't allowed to go near the other presents until we found the hidden ones. We had a ball trying to find our gifts and that bought my parents a little more time to sleep. The trampoline had been a terrific Christmas gift. Getting clothes was kind of like getting a Tootsie Roll on Halloween—you hoped for something a little more exciting. Dolls were a much better present for me. Of course, I was really into Barbie and Cabbage Patch dolls were a big thing for a while. I also had a growing collection of stuffed animals.

No, I didn't train on Christmas Day. But my training over Christmas vacation was a big issue with Steve because competitions would be coming up in January. Over the years, my parents argued with him about whether he was overworking or putting too much pressure on me; about their diminished role in gymnastics decisions; and whether I should be resting an injury or, as Steve preferred, pushing through it—as I was doing with my aching hamstring pulls at age ten. But the most frequent dispute between them was about whether I should go on family vacations rather than stay home and train. Steve pointed out that gymnastics is a full-year sport, and if you don't train steadily it takes a long time to get back into form. My parents countered emphatically that I needed to get away from constant training and do what other girls did for a change. If asked, I would agree with my parents. I loved gymnastics, but gymnastics was not life. A family trip was life and a chance for me to enjoy being normal. A small break allowed me to miss the sport just enough to feel refreshed and ready to get back to it.

Steve would give in and say, "Okay, she can go, but here's a list of the basic skills and conditioning that I need her to do each day." My parents were good about compromise and would find me a gym or space wherever we went so I could do what was on Steve's list. It was a team effort through and through.

Trips were a big deal in our family. Throughout my entire childhood, we'd take two family vacations a year, one in the summer, even if my father taught summer school, and another beginning the day after Christmas. We didn't have the money to fly as a family, so we drove to places within a radius of about ten hours. Our road trips might take us to Colorado Springs or Branson, Missouri. We would drive nine to ten hours and then find a decent motel. If we saw one for twenty-two dollars a night, we'd drive around some more to see if there was another for twenty dollars a night. Then we'd spend four or five days there before driving home.

I feel a strong nostalgia for those long drives with the three of us kids crammed into the backseat. I don't recall any seatbelt laws in those days, and Tessa and I would lie on each side and poor Troy was relegated to the little nest we'd make for him on the floorboard.

As teenagers we mostly read during those long car rides, but when we were young we'd play games like I Spy and the License Plate Game. At other times, in those pre-iPod days, I'd keep myself occupied by listening to cassette tapes of movies I'd recorded. On one trip I had a new kazoo, and I have no idea how anyone in the car tolerated my playing it for ten hours straight. Dad always drove and Mom read or slept. I don't want to get Dad into trouble, but if we were on straight roads and there was no traffic, there were times he'd let me sit on his lap and gave me some driving instructions. I still recall his words, "You have to make *small* corrections; don't just crank the wheel." It was just a different time.

We were always very active on our trips. We went hiking, biking, and hang gliding on simulators at Pikes Peak. We also canoed down a river in Missouri. Once we rented a speedboat that I insisted on driving because, as usual, I wanted control, and I pulled Troy behind us on a big tube. My mother always joined in our activities, which were strenuous but not really dangerous. My dad usually took photographs, although he enjoyed skiing. Steve didn't know half of what I ended up doing on vacation (and I wasn't going to tell him), but I did make him a big concession in regard to skiing. Steve forbade me to ski and everyone agreed. So the only times we went on skiing vacations were before we met him, when I was five or six. My first time on skis, I stayed in the children's area. I did so well on the bunny slope that the people at the ski resort asked my parents for permission to take an 8 x 10 of me to use in their promotional material. I guess that was my first endorsement!

Our most frequent destination, always after Christmas, was San Antonio. I loved going there at whatever age because I was close to both sets of my grandparents, and we'd also get to visit with my aunts and uncles. Steve knew the owner of HUGS Gymnastics in San Antonio, and I'd go there to do some stretching, conditioning, and a few basic skills on each event so that I wouldn't lose too much ground when I returned to Dynamo in January. When I couldn't get to HUGS, I'd at least get some conditioning in at one of my grandparents' houses.

I enjoyed spending time with all my grandparents, and would bounce from one house to the other. My father's parents, Mabel Lee and Charles Miller, were a sweet couple who had a living room that was like a winter wonderland. There was a huge Christmas display that Grandpa built and Grandma decorated. The centerpiece was a gorgeous white tree with every imaginable ornament and a quaint electric train that sped beneath and around it through a village of miniature houses. Grandma was a great cook and always served incredible homemade tamales. I'd also nibble on the pecans that my sister and I would spend hours picking up and shelling from the big tree out back.

I often spent the night with my mother's parents, Rosemary and Chester Murff. Besides paying for my dance lessons when I was young, Grandma Murff unleashed my competitive instincts by teaching me to play gin rummy and other card games. I had so much fun with her. I also think about my grandpa often because when he wasn't sitting on his porch swing chewing on an unlit cigar, he so enjoyed walking his three grandkids down to Jim's Restaurant, a local greasy spoon, for hot cocoa. Those strolls are among my most cherished memories of my childhood, and are a reason I have always made it a point to take plenty of walks with my son.

I was always so sad to have to say good-bye to my grandparents each December because that usually meant I wouldn't see them for a while. So I was very excited when Steve announced that one of our competitions in early 1988 would take place in San Antonio, and they could all come watch me. Prior to that meet, we competed at a big one in Houston, along with the girls from the nearby Károlyi camp. I had a fair competition try-ing out new skills, but fell off the uneven bars going for a difficult move called a reverse hecht (or, as it is referred to these days, a Tkatchev). For this move I started in a handstand on the high bar and then swung down through the low bar with my legs piked. Before I completed a full 360-degree giant swing around the bar, I let go of the bar, rotated my body in a for-ward flip, and tried to regrasp the bar. My dad videotaped me, and later used the visual of my missing the bar with my hands and plummeting to the floor to teach certain physics theories to his students. (He did ask for my permission first and agreed to also show a fault-free version!)

My grandparents knew I was a gymnast and had seen me do some simple demonstrations, but they had no idea of my skill level until they at-tended the Alamo Classic in their hometown. It took place in March, soon after my eleventh birthday. I was too focused to look for them or my father in the stands, but I was so glad they could see me perform. Steve wanted his girls to compete in this meet because we could again test ourselves against the country's top gymnasts, including future Olympians Wendy Bruce and the powerful, up-and-coming Kim Zmeskal. Steve and my grandparents were impressed when I finished second to Wendy in the all-around. My dad was equally impressed that for the first time people lined up to get my autograph, as well as the other girls'.

It was important for me that I did well in the all-around and made three event finals. Beam was my best event at the time and what I am still known for, but from the start I wanted to be recognized as an all-around gymnast who was adept on all four apparatuses.

Was I happy with my scores? I had no idea what they were. I can't recall many of the details of even the major competitions Steve took me to from the ages nine to eleven. Competitions whizzed by so quickly that they blurred together. Unless I had completed my final event of the day, I almost never watched the other competitors or checked the scoreboard for scores. During a competition I tried to remain focused on the task at hand. My goal was to hit each routine as close to perfection as possible, and I didn't want to get sidetracked by scores that I could do nothing about.

I had great respect for the judges, especially because my mother was one, and let the chips fall where they may. We would often review my routines and scores after the competition because we needed to understand where mistakes happened and whether or not the judges were seeing something we weren't. Sometimes they gave a routine a higher score than I thought it deserved, sometimes a lower score, but the great majority of times, I agreed with their assessment.

My entire competitive career, whether in small local meets or at the Olympics, the goal remained the same. Hit, hit, hit. That's what Steve would talk about, not beating a particular girl, even if she was one of the highly publicized gymnasts from the Károlyi team. They would walk in with such confidence and hit their routines; they had clean lines and perfect hair. Once the dust settled, if you were still in the mix with those amazing girls, then you were doing something right. Even against such tremendous competition, Steve and I did our best to run our own race. He told me to do the skills we'd been practicing and let the routines speak for themselves. I did want to win badly, but I realized that it made more sense to try to do a good routine rather than try to get a high score because a well-done routine would get you the high score that made a win possible.

I was a fairly tough competitor because the other girls and the judges didn't typically concern me or make me nervous. I probably should have been intimidated, but I was ignorant about how I was supposed to feel. I would get lost in my own thoughts and struggles and barely notice what was going on around me. It was just me challenging the apparatus and trying to improve. My enjoyment came when I learned a new skill in gym and while I performed.

My competition in the gym and during meets was always with myself: *Did I beat myself? Did I do as well as I know that I can?* I wanted so badly to be perfect, in everything.

As I got better, I took victories in stride. My thinking was that since I wasn't flawless, rather than celebrating, I needed to get back to the gym to make corrections in time for the next meet. My mind was always on the *next* competition and the *next* goal and I rarely took time to pat myself on the back for a job well done. As a perfectionist, I was never impressed by my victories, even when I received high scores, because I always saw my weaknesses. I could be doing a dismount no one in the world has done before, but be dissatisfied with my inconsistency. Never being satisfied can get frustrating, but perhaps it was a major reason I became such a strong competitor. I was always raising the bar on myself, trying to get better. I can see that this mind-set came at a price. But it was a price I was happy to pay to become the best in the world.

I probably fell as much as any gymnast in history at the beginning, but what I didn't realize at the time was that I was falling because I was constantly stretching myself, going beyond what I could already do by adding new moves and skills for competitions. Our plan was for me to always be thoroughly prepared. As time went by I became as well-known for my consistency as my mental toughness at major competitions. My mother, aware of my vulnerable side, said I was "strong, but pliant." I took pride in being a fighter.

When a competition was going really smoothly and there was no adversity, I wasn't fully motivated and was more prone to making mistakes. But when I had my back against the wall, I fought harder on the routines that followed and often emerged victorious. I saw that gymnastics was like life in that everyone makes mistakes and everyone falls, so the key is to try again before the fear and doubt build up. That's the attitude I needed to become a successful gymnast and years later it would save my life.

There were so many extremely talented athletes that came through Steve's gym over the years, but many decided competitive gymnastics wasn't their thing. Maybe they were missing the mental game. Maybe they'd fall apart in competitions even though they always hit everything in the gym, or they faced injuries that were too challenging to overcome. Maybe they just didn't want to devote the time and effort needed to take it to the next level. Competitive gymnastics isn't for everyone, so maybe they'd like it for a while but just didn't want it *enough*. I did. That it never came easy for me made me want it more. I wasn't impervious to pain and I experienced extreme frustration, disappointment, and monotony. But still I plugged away.

Steve might send me home if I didn't feel well, but he'd boast that in all the years we were together, I didn't skip a day of practice. The idea that *every day matters* would inspire me during my cancer battle. Back then I believed what I did during training each day might affect what would happen years down the road. Maybe five extra push-ups won't matter that night, but what if you do five extra push-ups twice a day six days a week for a year? Or for fifteen years, as I did? Eventually you realize it does make a difference. I was one of those that did extra. If Steve said, "Do a hundred toe-raises and twenty pull-ups," I would do a hundred and five toe-raises and twenty-two pull-ups, while he counted. I never tried to skim; I was always trying to do a little bit more. Even on a day I wasn't feeling well and had to be sent home, if I could at least manage some stretching, it was worth it for me to come in. No doubt, the extra training paid off in competitions.

Competition to me was all about remembering lessons from practice; ideally I made my mistakes in the gym, not when there were judges watching. Steve always went over routines with me before an event. He knew I didn't need pep talks because I was eager to get out there. But he did like to center me, focus my thoughts. The green light came on, I saluted the judge or panel of judges and I was ready. Not that I didn't make plenty of mistakes, but I thrived on competition. I'd walk out there, my adrenaline pumping, and my fears and pain would disappear, and I suddenly transformed into someone I wasn't in normal life. How did this quiet bookworm, who had trouble catching a ball or walking down the street without stumbling, suddenly turn into this graceful creature? How did this wallflower, who was too scared to raise her hand in class, become such an intrepid performer?

I can't solve the mystery entirely, but I had an uncanny ability to compartmentalize and, for ninety seconds on beam and floor, thirty seconds on bars, and only a few seconds on vault, forget who I was outside the gym. I worked hard, playing mind games with myself, to reach that point. When I first became a competitor and walked through that threshold at the smaller competitions, I pretended that I was confident. I had to trick myself into believing that I was a good gymnast and that I belonged in the competition. And little by little I actually became supremely confident when I walked out onto the floor. I finally began to see myself as a talented athlete and competitor. I began to believe in myself.

I felt like mild-mannered Clark Kent going into the phone booth and emerging as Superman. I was so self-assured when I slipped on my long-sleeved competition leotard that I could perform in front of enormous crowds, folks watching at home, and austere judges, and not feel inhibited. Instead, I felt courageous, empowered, and all the things that I wasn't like off the gymnastics floor.

7

In his quest to get us Elite status, Steve took me and Gina Jackson, another girl at Dynamo and one of my best friends, to a practice meet for
Elites. I have no recollection of how I did, though my mother says I had a
pretty rough time. However, she also says I had a revelation about competitive gymnastics. I believed that you competed as you practiced, so if
you had a good practice, you should have a good competition. But I also
believed that if I had a bad warm-up before I competed that was enough
to negate all my solid practices. Watching an Elite gymnast have a terrible
warm-up and then nail her routine made me rethink this. I began to see a
rough warm-up as "getting the bugs out beforehand." It sounds simple, but
it was an important lesson.

Another benefit from going to that meet was that the judges authorized Gina and me to prepare for the Junior B competition at the 1988
American Classic. That was a qualifying meet for Elite status and inclu-
sion on the Junior Elite national team. I finished second and we both qualified, although Steve insisted on taking us to another qualifying meet in
Atlanta to boost our rankings.

I was now an Elite gymnast.

I was classified as Junior B Elite because I was eleven, but I was expected to be a Junior A at twelve, and Senior A at fifteen. Because of my coach, I would take an accelerated path and invariably push the minimum age requirement for each level.

It had been a major goal of mine, which I wrote down on one of Steve's index cards, to make the national team and be able to go to international meets and compete for my country. The way it worked was the U.S. Gymnastics Federation (now USA Gymnastics) would see how many Elites were needed at the various competitions, and assign girls to go to specific events. My first assignment was to compete at the Junior Pan-American Games that summer in Ponce, Puerto Rico. I was thrilled because this would be my first international meet, and for the first time I'd be wearing a uniform representing the United States of America.

I'd always remember the day a box showed up on our doorstep. My dad cut it open and I pulled out an amazing red, white, and blue uniform! Of course I tried it on right away, and I was so overjoyed that I would have worn it around the house the rest of the day and slept in it if I weren't so worried I'd mess it up. I was so proud to wear it. Even at that young age, I understood that this was not about me, my gym club, or even my state. I was going to represent my entire country. I understood I was part of something a lot bigger than myself.

If Steve had been the head coach or assistant coach for this team, his expenses to Puerto Rico would have been paid by the U.S. Gymnastics Federation. But I wasn't ranked one of the top two gymnasts traveling to the Junior Pan-Am Games, so he wasn't given credentials for the competition. Still, he was willing to go if my parents would split the bill with him. They hated not to be able to go themselves but raised the money for Steve because they didn't want me to travel alone and have to make connecting flights in Miami. They trusted Steve with me and knew that I would feel much better having my personal coach there when I didn't know the official U.S. coaches.

I also didn't know my teammates. The sport would change considerably, but at the time there was no centralized system in the U.S. Gymnastics, as a sport, is very individual in the sense that you are alone on the equipment. The girls who came together on occasion to form teams didn't know one another well because they often trained in different gyms spread across the country and saw one another only briefly during competitions.

I was among strangers, so I felt much more comfortable with Steve in the arena, even if he did have to sit in the stands as a spectator.

This is the first competition, aside from my Level 2 state meet, of which I have vivid memories, though not total recall. I do remember I did well, but it wasn't smooth sailing. For instance, I face-planted a full twisting doubleback while warming up for my floor exercise routine. And I will never forget what took place during the competition as I was about to vault.

I saw the U.S. coach, who didn't know me very well at the time, setting the springboard. Immediately, I realized the setting was completely off. At the same time, I got the green light indicating I was supposed to salute the judge and charge down the runway. But I knew my board was not set correctly, which could have resulted in not only a really bad score but also a bad fall and possible injury. It wasn't something to play around with. I knew enough not to go, but didn't want to get a zero for the team. I didn't look at the head coach but rather at Steve in the stands, to the left of the vaulting horse. All I had to do was give him a look, and he had such an understanding of me that he could tell something was not right. He knew the head coach and started yelling down to him to check the board. The coach didn't hesitate and checked the board, fixed it, and off I went. That all happened within fifteen seconds. It sticks in my mind because it exemplified how close the coach-gymnast relationship has to be and how important it is to maintain a complete trust. Steve and I had that.

8

I turned twelve in March 1989 and became a Junior A Elite competitor. Even so, I was still essentially an unknown in gymnastics circles, not even a dark horse. Steve hoped to change that by having me compete in the 1989 Olympic Sports Festival, which that year was being held in Oklahoma. Athletes from around the country would be coming to Oklahoma City to compete in all the Olympic sports, so it was a big deal nationally, not just a state or regional competition. The U.S. Gymnastics Federation decided that its two-day competition would showcase up-and-coming talent, specifically Junior A competitors who in 1992 would be Senior Elites and in the pool of possible Olympians. I wasn't counted among the Olympic hopefuls, which was fine because I still didn't really have Olympic aspirations.

The festival was televised and covered by media from coast to coast, and the big gymnastics story was that Béla Károlyi was coming from Houston with six high-caliber girls. The media had dubbed them the "Károlyi Six-Pack" and according to many they were going to sweep every event. The local girls, Gina and I, weren't even in the picture.

A pulled hamstring had hampered me at the U.S. Classic (a meet of the same magnitude as the American Classic) and was becoming more painful, but I increased my training for the Sports Festival. I knew it was important to do well so that I'd be invited to more major competitions. I was more nervous than I was for any previous meet because this was my first really big competition in Oklahoma and people I knew might actually be there. I couldn't block things out as easily as before because everyone seemed to know about this meet. However, the supposedly invincible Six-Pack didn't intimidate me. It's very difficult to intimidate someone who lives in blissful ignorance. Besides, I was so worried about classmates possibly seeing me compete that the Károlyi team was the furthest thing from my mind.

They had given all the girls special colored leotards; mine was black with a large white stripe with a red border diagonally down the front. Of course, I also wore my trusty white scrunchie. Steve made sure I didn't read the papers, and, since he was a big talker, was happy to provide the answers when reporters asked me questions. He didn't try to pump me up by telling me about my stiff competition. He never mentioned anybody I had to beat. As usual, all I tried to do was complete perfect routines.

I took part in the team competition and the all-around and competed in all four individual events, which, barring injuries, was my intention at every competition I entered throughout my career. What I remember most was missing a skill on my final floor pass during the all-around competition. I landed short on a double backflip and "covered" up by doing a forward roll. Not a terribly convincing act.

On the video you could see me roll my eyes, not like a teenager does when an adult says anything *uncool*, but in an "ugh, I can't believe I did that" kind of way. I lost my chance for gold in the all-around but still managed a bronze medal behind Kim Zmeskal and Erica Stokes, and ahead of the four other girls in the Six-Pack. The next day I came back to win gold on the uneven bars. The Olympic Sports Festival was a big deal, so doing well was a tremendous confidence builder for me.

My mother was at work in her office at her bank in Edmond that afternoon. Suddenly, her excited receptionist told her that TV reporters and people with "movie cameras" and equipment were outside. She asked, "What's going on?" She found out they were there because her daughter, this pixie from Edmond, had upset some of the Károlyi girls. It was big news around the country, but especially in my home state. That was a turning point for me. I was still a complete unknown in Europe, but in America I was now at least on the map.

In Oklahoma I got my fifteen minutes of fame. I received much media attention across the state, and most of all in Edmond. At Summit Middle School, my teachers and classmates had seen me as a smart but very quiet girl who kept to herself and ran a ten-minute mile if she actually made it across the finish line within the time allotted. They had little idea what I was doing outside of school, and I'm sure they were surprised that I turned out to be a nationally ranked gymnast. My sudden celebrity status led to my being asked to do a balance beam demonstration at my school for the parents. The press was there, and the next morning my parents cut out a photo of the event in the paper. I thought the media attention that day was neat, although I was too introverted to answer questions above a whisper. I enjoyed performing for the kids at school, but I was embarrassed that I was calling attention to myself, something I'd tried to avoid since the first grade. My talent wasn't something I was comfortable talking about. I wanted to do gymnastics, but all these other things that went with it were a bit terrifying.

However, it turned out that having my teachers know I was an Elite gymnast on the U.S. national team was a major benefit. They were receptive to my going off for international competitions and then catching up with any schoolwork I missed. I liked my teachers and told them about gymnastics if they asked. I was always more comfortable talking to adults than girls in my class. Boys? I couldn't converse with them at all. My friends, who had similar goals and dreams, were mostly at the gym, where I could let down my guard.

I believe my performance at the Olympic Sports Festival confirmed that I had the potential to be a very strong competitor in the future. For Steve, that meant I needed to start paying more attention to detail, particularly on dance and balance beam. That was a major reason he hired Peggy Liddick. It was one of the smartest moves he ever made. Peggy had been coaching in Nebraska and moved to Oklahoma to work with all the upper-level gymnasts at Dynamo. She was a very good coach on all four events but focused primarily on balance beam and floor choreography. Steve knew he needed her help with me, and he had the evidence: a photo of me doing a back handspring on the beam with my legs in a curled-up mess. He commented, "This is why I brought in Peggy."

Peggy was instrumental in helping me develop some finesse. Steve was a great coach on bars, vault, and floor, but once Peggy arrived at Dynamo he was rarely allowed in the beam area. That was Peggy's domain and she ruled it like a queen. Steve had been very focused on the tumbling on beam, but Peggy looked at the entire routine because she understood that leaps and turns are also critical components.

Like me, Peggy was a perfectionist, so it wasn't just "Do ten routines," but "Today you need to hit ten error-free routines in a row." I wouldn't forget the times I fell on number nine and had to start over. Some of the girls thought she was too demanding, but I liked the feedback and how straightforward she was when I didn't meet her expectations. She never danced around but spoke to me bluntly when I wasn't at my best. Once again, I'd found someone who had the same goal as I did for myself, which was to be the best I could be. I now had another strong woman in my life to look up to.

Peggy didn't spot girls on the high beam, even when she was doing something difficult, and I liked that philosophy. A gymnast should never need someone to spot on the high beam while doing a skill; she should know how to do the skill long before she gets the opportunity to be on the high beam. Peggy instilled in me the understanding that if you're not comfortable enough to do this skill on your own up there, you'd better not be attempting that skill. Instead, get down on the low beam, do thirty of them, and we'll try again.

Peggy and I were on the same wavelength in that we incorporated physics and geometry into our approach. She, too, was comfortable looking at the beam in terms of angles and degrees. At one point, she'd actually return to college to take additional physics classes so she'd be more conversant on the subject and be able to explain to me why moving my arm or changing an angle would help me stay on the beam. She loved to learn just like I did. She told me that to perfect my routines, I would have to hit the same angles with the same weight distribution on each skill every time. It made me think of gymnastics in a new way. Hard work was one thing, but if you worked hard *and* smart then you had a winning combination.

She and my father used physics examples to help me visualize and make sense of all the crazy skills. Gymnasts don't use tools (skates, helmets, bats, or balls) on any of the four apparatuses, so the physics was about where I positioned my hands, arms, legs, and head as I went through a particular movement. For instance, we discussed the importance of proper weight distribution (the conservation of rotational momentum) and how you tuck to spin faster and lay out to spin slower. We discussed running fast for vault (kinetic energy; KE) and then converting that to altitude (potential energy; PE) using the springboard and blocking off the horse. Swinging on uneven bars was discussed in terms of energy management. You can't do a bar routine at half speed; you must have the correct speed (KE) at the bottom of the swing so that you have the correct altitude (PE) at the top of the swing.

Boring? Not for me! I was enthralled when Peggy and my father talked to me about physics in relation to the beam, especially. As much as I loved that event, it was often my nemesis. Most young gymnasts think only about staying on the beam (or rather, not falling off), which is what I did early in my career, but the *process* became important to me because my goal was to improve. That's why I was a workhorse in the gym. But in addition to doing the work, I needed to understand the mechanics of my body in relation to the apparatus.

Of the four events, the one that gave me the most trouble was vault. I'd have a substantial number of high-scoring vaults in my career, but while I could understand the physics of it on paper, I just could not get my body to do what I envisioned it should do. It was foreign to me.

With the addition of Peggy, who was an outstanding coach and travel companion for me, our three-person team was complete and we were eager to move forward. The goal for me was to become Senior Elite. That was Steve's short-term goal, which he saw as a stepping-stone for me to be considered for the 1992 Olympics team. He didn't mention it to me, but my becoming an Olympian had become his long-term goal. I wasn't even sure that I was the best gymnast at Dynamo, so making the Olympics when there were exceptional gymnasts across America was just a fleeting thought.

I was more concerned that at this crucial juncture I was suddenly forced to stop practicing and competing gymnastics.

9

My hamstrings had become so painful that I was unable to train much of anything. Not only couldn't I run; it hurt to walk. Even sitting on a hard chair at school was uncomfortable. I was constantly using ice, a heat pack, or a TENS unit. We tried massage and therapy and anything else we could think of. The concern was that I could pull the hamstring off the bone by continuing to push it. This was the first time I'd faced an injury that I couldn't just push through. Pain was one thing, but further damage was a whole new ball game. A doctor and a trainer both advised me to shut it down and give my hamstrings a chance to heal.

As a kid, I didn't see the doctor unless there was a "real" injury. A broken bone or a pulled hamstring qualified. If I had a cold or something minor I didn't find it cause for rushing to the doctor; that meant time away from the gym. And it wasn't like I was going to stay home!

I was in such pain and was so distraught over not being able to fully train that Steve knew he needed to do something. So he arranged for me to spend time that September with Keith Klevin, the trainer who had worked with Bart Conner to get him ready for the 1984 Olympics. Steve and I flew out to Las Vegas to work with him in a last-ditch attempt to get through this injury. Keith told us that I needed to rest for four months minimum. Steve negotiated for three months maximum. We worked specific types of stretching and conditioning each day in an effort to keep up my strength without putting undue stress on my hamstrings. Two months later I did a modified beam routine exhibition in Oklahoma City, which was a stopover on the 1988 post-Olympic tour. By December my hamstrings, which had been bothering me since April, were almost fully healed and I agreed to start training for the 1990 American Cup.

I got back to form fairly quickly on all the events with the exception of vault, but by the time of the American Cup I could even pull off my Yurchenko full twist. I didn't medal in the international field but reached my goal of hitting all my routines.

This competition and others in Canada and Germany paved the way to the U.S. Championship in Denver, my first national competition as a Senior Elite. Steve had successfully argued with the U.S. Gymnastics Federation that I should be allowed to compete as a senior because I would turn fifteen the year of the 1992 Olympic Games, making me eligible. My eighth-place finish at the National Championship and subsequent solid national ranking allowed me to realize that dream at the young age of thirteen. I was the youngest gymnast ever to earn a place on the senior team! This meant that I would be invited to senior international competitions in Europe and become familiar to international judges. Steve knew that if I was going to be under consideration for the Barcelona Olympics, this was essential. I was oblivious to the fact that he had me on an Olympic path.

Naturally, there was a stumbling block: money. Gymnastics can become expensive at a high level. I helped out my parents when I could, even sitting at our sewing machine for hours and making my own workout leotards. (My home economics course in school paid off.) But expenses kept increasing, particularly because it was essential for Peggy to accompany Steve and me on trips. Often, I was the only Dynamo girl going to a meet, so other parents wouldn't be sharing the coaches' expenses. Furthermore, unless I was wearing red, white, and blue as part of the official U.S. team, my parents had to pay for even my hotel and travel.

It helped that Steve often deferred his travel costs and some training fees because, as he admitted, my newfound fame served as his advertisement to attract a wave of new girls from around the country to join his gym. Around then, Dynamo had eight to twelve Elite gymnasts and a growing team program and recreational side.

Though my parents never discussed it with me, I knew that the leotards, grips, travel, and coaching fees all added up. They couldn't afford to pay for my gymnastics indefinitely. I didn't realize they were dipping into their savings in order to keep my career afloat. I did know the reason my mother was working her tail off judging gymnastics every weekend for six months a year, in addition to a full-time banking career, was to make sure I could continue training uninterrupted.

It was at this time, I made the decision to accept my first commercial. I remember sitting down on a bench next to Ronald McDonald. McDonald's was a title sponsor to some of our most prestigious events and I was happy to have been asked to take part. I have no idea if it ever aired anywhere, but I figured I could use the small fee to buy new grips. Every little bit helped. It was a minor transaction, but it meant something major: I was giving up my amateur status. That meant I could finally accept appearance fees and prize money, which was modest in those days. I wasn't going to get rich, but the extra money would help alleviate my parents' financial difficulties. On the downside, I would be giving up an opportunity to compete in gymnastics at a collegiate level.

My decision was tied to a family decision about whether I should accept funding from the U.S. Gymnastics Federation, which was being offered now that I was on the senior national team and had a fairly high ranking. A gymnast's rankings for the year dictated the amount of funding for training she qualified for. I could now receive monthly checks to help cover training costs and some travel costs. Here, too, if I accepted money, I would instantly give up my NCAA gymnastics eligibility and the chance for an athletic college scholarship when I was eighteen.

My choice to accept money and give up my amateur status was predicated on my understanding that since female gymnasts peak at an early age, I had a very small window of opportunity to acquire whatever endorsements were available for gymnasts at that time. I also couldn't see myself still being a gymnast when it was time to go to college. Eighteen seemed ancient. Regardless, I saw myself going to college strictly to get my education, not compete in gymnastics, as if they were mutually exclusive.

So at the age of thirteen I chose to turn professional, a decision I have never regretted. My parents were grateful to the U.S. Gymnastics Federation and relieved to get some financial assistance. In my world it was a very easy choice to accept the financial support over leaving the sport. I was just getting started. I needed to give myself a chance and if I could do that while taking on some of the financial burden then it was a big win.

I would soon make another monumental decision about the direction of my career. The 1990 Catania Cup in Italy changed my life. I captured the all-around for my first international win. I stood proudly on the podium wearing my country's colors and watching the American flag being raised and hearing the sounds of my national anthem resound through the arena. It was as if a lightbulb turned on in my head. That was the moment when I *finally* decided I had to go, needed to go, must go to the Olympics and represent my country on the biggest stage.

That unforgettable moment was the culmination of a wonderful trip that made me understand just how much this sport could offer me. One day we rented a boat, and Steve and I and another gymnast and her coach ventured all over the islands. We had a great time boating and looking for shells on the shore. We also stopped off in Rome for a bit of sightseeing, and I witnessed historic sites, such as the Colosseum and the Sistine Chapel, that without gymnastics I may have only seen in a history book.

Steve was always great about making sure that I had the opportunity to get out and see these amazing places. Of course, the rule was "You focus first on the competition and we'll have time to see the sites afterward." I'm sure my parents never imagined that by age thirteen their daughter would have already traveled to Italy, Canada, Puerto Rico, Germany, and even Japan, where, in Yokohama, I rode on what was then the world's tallest Ferris wheel, the 353-foot Cosmo Clock 21. I was getting to experience the world through gymnastics. I began to fantasize about another nice trip to a beautiful European city—Barcelona, Spain.

Back at Dynamo, the next time that Steve had his gymnasts write down their long-term goals, I was among those whose goal matched their ultimate dream: "I want to make the U.S. team for the 1992 Olympics!"

"Sure," my parents said. "If you think you can make the Olympic team, go for it." They never placed limits on me and made sure I put none on myself. It was a lesson I took to heart for gymnastics, for life, and for ultimately battling a life-threatening illness. If I had wanted to be an astronaut and rocket to the moon, they would have given me their blessing. An Olympic gymnast going to Barcelona was what I wanted to be, and they supported me on my journey.

10

After returning from Italy, there was a change in me. There was an appreciable shift and it was no longer, "Okay, Steve, let's go to the next competition." Now I was driven to reach my new long-term goal—the 1992 Summer Olympic Games—and I was asking, "Steve, how do I get there?" Getting there was what we built our strategy around over the next two years. I was still young and fearless, so it never even crossed my mind that I might not make the team. The people around me—Steve, Peggy, and my parents—helped me to believe in myself, to the point that I just assumed that if I wanted to go to the Olympics, I could do it if I did the required work. I was a girl who was told not to have limits, so I was naïve enough to assume the impossible could be accomplished. I'm still that girl.

Steve, Peggy, and I had to work harder than ever. Today, I wonder how I got through that tough time of training seven hours a day, six days a week.

Our goal was the Olympics, but our eyes were set on the 1992 U.S. Championship and Olympic Trials, the two competitions that determined who made the American team that would go to Barcelona. We stuck to a plan that involved learning certain skills, working on the compulsories (one of Peggy's strengths), and building strong competitive routines. I could do quite a few high-level skills, and Steve and Peggy found smart and unique ways to string them together to form sensational routines.

It wasn't just a matter of building routines around what I could do but also took into consideration the expectations of judges. Steve and Peggy were both experts on the Code of Points, the little green book that lists every gymnastics skill, states what each skill is worth during the current four-year Olympic cycle, and says how many skills from each level of difficulty is required by judges to be in a routine. Our goal was to put together routines that had a balance of difficult skills—so that I would have high start values—and routines that I could consistently hit during competition. Why do a routine that has a maximum score total of 9.6, when it will take at least a 9.8 to win? Why do a 10.0 routine that you always fall on? We had to be strategic.

For my routines to stand out, difficulty was not enough. Artistry was also needed. Fortunately, I excelled at artistry. More than anything that would become my niche. Now was the time to upgrade pretty routines to beautiful routines. To accomplish that, we focused on details. *Are my fingers in the right place? Is my toe in the correct spot?* This was like it had been when I trained in Russia when I was nine, and I still loved it. It was all about squeezing out that extra tenth of a point.

Train like you compete; compete like you train. Although we rarely trained for the same competitions, it was nice to have other high-level girls to train with at Dynamo. There were usually five or six girls training on an event at one time. On vault we'd form a line and take turns bolting down the runway. As with all events, we'd work about an hour at a time. Each day, we trained at least ten routines on balance beam, both compulsories and optionals. Peggy had a clipboard with a lesson chart attached, and each of us girls would write down how many routines we hit and missed. Then we'd repeat the skills we'd missed, five or ten times. Other days, if we fell during one of the ten routines, even on the first skill, we finished the routine and then did it over from the beginning. Peggy made us finish the routine because that's what we'd have to do in a competition. And you didn't get to take it easy on the first few routines and use them to warm up. The first routine was every bit as important as the last and each skill, whether it was the highest difficulty or lowest, deserved our complete focus and respect. It reinforced the idea that every performance, whether or not the judges were watching, truly matters.

I assumed that the top gymnasts around the country were also being taught to finish their routines after falls. However, I later came to realize that the opposite was true. Many gymnasts who fell during practice would stop in the middle of the routine, get a drink of water, wait for their next turn, and try again. You don't get to do that in competition. You don't get a five-minute break in the middle of the routine; you have only thirty seconds to get back on the beam to finish your set. Peggy made me think of every routine under competition circumstances. She knew I'd suffer falls in competition because it happens no matter how hard you train, and she wanted me to be prepared. *How are you going to continue when you've fouled up?* Being told to carry on after a big fall and even emerge victorious was an instruction I couldn't hear enough. It would be a life lesson I'd rely on time and again as an adult, pre- and post-cancer.

The pressure of trying to get through ten routines without falling so I didn't have to start over resulted in my development into a very efficient gymnast. I didn't want to take twenty-five tries to get it right. If you're going to do it, do it well, from the start. It forced me to pay even greater attention to detail.

In the best beam routines there are no stops because every single breath has a place and every pause is built in. You breathe at exactly the same moment each time you do a skill. You breathe and then go. It's the same every time. That has to be taught, and a lot of athletes don't learn that early on. Every breath, every beat, every pause, and every element, even if it doesn't look like an actual skill, must be choreographed into that routine. When you do have a stumble or a wobble, you have to get quickly back into the rhythm of your routine. On beam, if things are a little off, you quickly make the small adjustments you've learned to help disguise the problem. You then carry on as if nothing untoward happened and hope the judges missed it. *Minimize the damage.*

How Peggy worked with me on balance beam flowed over to how I approached the other three events with both my coaches. During a bar workout, I didn't specifically write down my errors in a notebook. However, my thought process was, "Okay, how many bar routines did I hit? Well, I missed that move, so I need to do it again a few times." On bars, especially, I'd have a plan B and even a plan C, so that if I missed a skill in the heat of competition, I could maintain my composure and complete the routine with minimal deductions. Floor was the same. There were times in competition that I didn't quite complete a required 360-degree turn. So I'd finish stronger and with more emotion, hoping to pull the judges' attention to my arms and face and away from my feet.

If I faltered on a tumbling pass or dance move, I'd finish my routine and then make sure to practice that skill a few extra times. I was not an athlete with much aerobic endurance, so for me a ninety-second floor routine was a killer. My legs would be like Jell-O and I could hardly breathe by the end, so I needed to take a good ten minutes between practicing floor routines. As I waited for the other girls to do their routines, I'd work on my dance, and when my turn came around I was rested and ready.

My planning was all very specific, particularly with regard to my hair. People didn't realize how much hair I truly had. When I was really young, I had a big frizzy ponytail and Steve would joke that it looked like I had two heads when I was out on the floor. At my first international competition a judge told Steve that it was so distracting that I could be deducted points for aesthetic reasons. From then on my ponytail was braided and tucked under with a whole packet of bobby pins that held it in place.

I felt I needed my hair in place for a good competition. I didn't want a side ponytail because I would have felt lopsided, especially on balance beam. Also, for some of the skills I performed on beam—like the backward extension rolls that required I grab the beam right by my head—if my hair wasn't tied perfectly and in the right spot on my head, I could have been thrown off. My hair was less about look and more about function for routines.

Fans still talk about my big white scrunchie, which became iconic in its own right. I loved that scrunchie and its little sparkles that Peggy glued on herself. Without my scrunchie, I wouldn't have felt ready to compete. (Yes, I still have it.)

I was more obsessive-compulsive than superstitious. I had certain rituals I needed to perform. I put on my leather grips and taped my toes in the same way every time, and I went through various routines before I felt ready to salute the judge.

I still would get frustrated when trying to learn a skill and didn't think

I was progressing quickly enough. Steve and Peggy forced me to think about it logically, which worked well because that's how I was wired. I could understand that getting upset wore me out and stopped me from improving as fast as I wanted. There were still plenty of times that I shed tears out of frustration or disappointment, but I was learning how to rid myself of negative thoughts quickly and move on. I needed a positive attitude as I took part in a number of competitions in 1991, in America and Europe.

My father loved being able to go to many of my meets in the States. He almost always went to ones that were within driving distance (and would later travel to major championships). He usually didn't stay in the host hotel with the Dynamo team but in an inexpensive Sun Motel or an equivalent. I often didn't see him for the entire competition, but I liked knowing he was there with his trusty camera. The guys at the various TV networks came to know him and understood he was taping only my routines to bring home for my mother to look at later.

On rare occasions, Mom saw me compete in person. However, even when she wasn't able to be there physically, she remained with me. She continued to send me off with a small stack of note cards, one for each day, filled with loving phrases from the Bible. When I was missing home and family, her cards gave me courage to get through even the roughest days. Somehow she just knew exactly what I needed to read each day.

The highlight of my European competitions that year certainly included receiving a perfect 10.0 on balance beam at the Swiss Cup. My first 10.0! I was proud and ecstatic, but I knew I had covered up an imperfect dismount.

During my career, I became an expert at covering up flawed landings on certain skills, including my dismounts. I had really bony knees and when I tried to land with them side by side on my full twisting doubleback dismount off beam or bars, they'd bang together and I'd come away with huge purple bruises on the insides of my knees. I found myself hesitating because I knew the blow was coming. Hesitation can be disastrous in gymnastics. It got so bad that I began taping a piece of foam around the inside of one knee to cushion the blow during training.

How could I protect my knees and also give myself better odds of sticking? I understood the importance of body position and balance and decided to start landing my dismounts with my left foot about two inches in front of my right foot. They were still parallel, which was important aesthetically, but were a just a few inches apart. I needed to keep the judges happy, so when I'd lift my arms at the finish I'd slide my heels together like Dorothy in *The Wizard of Oz*.

This seemed a more natural position for my body on the landing, with one foot slightly in front of the other. At the angle the seated judges would be seeing this, it looked like a perfect stick! It worked, and no one ever tried to correct it. I'm sure every gymnast has at least one little secret, something that they feel sets them apart and gives them an edge. This was mine and I never told anyone. When we'd have contests at the gym to see who stuck the most dismounts, this was my secret weapon.

Just days after the Swiss Cup, I received another 10.0 on balance beam at the Arthur Gander Memorial utilizing my special landing technique. Moreover, I won the all-around and tied Kim Zmeskal's recently established American women's record for points scored using the traditional 10.0 scale. I wish I understood then, even when I received the two 10.0s, that it's not about perfect but making the full effort. I was happy of course and offered a modest smile to the cheering crowd, but I was rarely impressed or satisfied when I got high scores or medals. As my harshest critic, I always thought I could do better, even when I got a 10.0. Even after I came off a great routine, my coaches, after giving me bear hugs, would immediately tell me the corrections I needed to make for next time. I wouldn't have had it any other way. That's what I wanted, what I knew I needed.

Though I didn't fully appreciate my achievements then, I would always relish the memories of those European successes. Peggy and Steve were thrilled with how I was progressing as the Olympics rapidly approached. We realized that it was to my benefit that I was now gaining a reputation internationally.

11

In non-Olympic years, the top gymnastic competition is the World Championship. I was thrilled to qualify for the 1991 Worlds in Indianapolis. This meant that I was considered one of the top female gymnasts on the national team. Competing on this world stage was part of our strategy that would have me peaking at the U.S. Championship and Olympic Trials the following year. However, simply representing my country at Worlds, where the best gymnasts from around the world gathered, and trying to hit all my routines was enough for me to think about. I was fourteen years old and competing at the World Championship. It just didn't get much better.

This was the biggest, most important competition I'd ever been to and rather than letting that intimidate me I used it as motivation. When I'd feel overwhelmed, I'd tell myself to calm down and try to forget about its size and remember I'd be doing the exact same events as I'd done at minor competitions. The small cards my mother gave me also helped.

The girls competing for the U.S. were a team, but there wasn't much interaction among us because at each event we were alone and being judged on our own merits. It was the same at every team competition. A team competition in gymnastics is different from other team sports in that you don't go head-to-head with an opponent and you're not waiting for your teammate to pass you a ball or give you a block so you can run for a touchdown. Instead, the best way to help your team is to get the highest score you can. For the most part, the teamwork took place behind the scenes. It was the words of encouragement at the chalk bowl and the cheering during your final routine of a long workout. It was the older girls setting a good example for us young ones, helping us understand what to expect when we walked out onto the floor for the biggest competition of our lives so far.

Camaraderie was important, but when the competition began we were all in our separate zones, focusing on our own performances. Our personal coaches helped us to do that. We learned that after a great performance a teammate could give off a good, positive vibe to those watching her, but what if she had a poor performance and broke down afterward? For some, that might be motivation to try harder, and for others, it could be intimidating in a team situation. Steve and Peggy wanted me thinking through my own routines and to give 100 percent regardless of how anyone else performed.

I'm sure I created some buzz at my first Worlds. In team competition, I actually placed second to the Soviet Union's Svetlana Boginskaya in compulsories. I finished fourth during the optional round and the rest of our team was strong, so we came away with a silver medal. This was huge because no American women's team had ever won a medal of any color at a World Championship. Kim Zmeskal also made history when she became the first American to achieve the World all-around gold medal, which further solidified her standing as not only Béla Károlyi's top gymnast but America's as well.

I was ecstatic when I was informed I was the first U.S. gymnast to ever qualify for all four event finals. I later won another silver medal, tying Soviet gymnast Tatiana Gutsu for second place in the individual uneven bars. It was a tremendous competition and a critical stepping-stone for me and the U.S. team leading to the Olympic Games the following year.

To keep me grounded and focused, Steve and my parents sheltered me from the media as much as possible. I was never interested in reading my own press or anyone else's, so I had no problem not reading gymnastics magazines or the sports pages in the newspaper. I was still a kid and these things were not on my priority list. I didn't watch gymnastics on television; I didn't have the time. I was too busy balancing school, my training regimen, and family life. While I knew that these competitions were a big deal in the gymnastics world, I didn't realize that people outside the sport were noticing—at least until I began to be inundated with requests for interviews. All of a sudden, I was being written about as a new Olympic hopeful and being asked by reporters about any Olympic aspirations. Being reticent, and confused by all the media interest, I wasn't comfortable talking about my successes or my failures, as my two-word replies reflected. I wanted my efforts to speak for themselves: *Don't talk about what you're going to do; just do it.*

I was blindsided with questions about a heated rivalry developing between Kim and me. A rivalry? Kim and I didn't know each other well enough at that time for there to be good or bad blood between us. We were competing for perfection, not against each other. Maybe people assumed there was a rivalry because we were both winning medals at the time, or because we had contrasting styles—she was known for power, I for artistry—and public demeanors. Or simply because she trained in Texas and I trained in Oklahoma. In fact, as Kim and I saw each other in more competitions in 1991 and early 1992, our friendship grew and we'd joke, "How's it going, rival?" Our relationship was one of mutual respect when we were young and that never changed.

Competition-wise, I was very pleased with how I did at Worlds. I had shown that I belonged and had the potential to beat the elite of the Elite if I was on my game. As we had hoped, I had made an impression leading into the Olympic year, perhaps moving me up in the rankings. I was peaking at the right time. I remember thinking, "Oh goodness, I did well at Worlds, so maybe that means I *do* have a legitimate shot at making the Olympic team." I just had to stay the course, keep healthy, and remain focused. I had never wanted anything so much.

Then it happened. I got hurt.

And it was serious.

On March 31, 1992, while training for the Individual World Championship in April, the U.S. Championship in May, and Olympic Trials in June, I was working on my compulsory uneven bar routine. On the dismount, a flyaway full twist, my timing was off and I rotated around and struck my feet on the high bar. Suddenly, I was falling headfirst toward the ground from ten feet in the air. Every coach tells you that when you fall you need to keep your hands in, "don't reach out." The goal is to absorb the impact on a larger, more padded part of your body. Unfortunately, my natural reaction was to throw my arms out to break the fall. We always had an extra crash pad on the top of the primary mat, but Steve had just removed it for my last routine of the day so I could work on sticking my final landing on what would be a competitive surface. This wasn't an odd request by Steve because it was a fairly simple dismount and I needed to practice the stick.

I landed hard but felt no pain. There was no popping sound, so I assumed everything was intact. But I didn't move because we were always taught to stay down until the coach did what we called a "body check." He would come over and make sure that it was safe for you to get up and move around. So I remained in a heap on the floor while Steve ran over from about twelve feet away. I noticed that he had a concerned look on his face and that he was peeling off his jacket. Then he threw his jacket over my left arm in an attempt to hide it from me. But he was too late and just before it was covered I saw that my arm had been bent completely the wrong way. Not good.

Steve was being protective and stayed calm as he said, "You're okay . . . but it looks like you've dislocated your elbow." He knew I needed a play-by-play; I needed him to talk, just talk.

I was beginning to feel the pain, but it didn't occur to me that I could have a career-threatening injury. It didn't dawn on me that in that instant my Olympic dream might be over. A friend at the gym had dislocated her elbow on bars years before, and I had seen Steve pop it back into place. I don't know if I said it out loud, but what crossed my mind was, "Steve, can you please just fix it?"

Another teammate ran over with ice and I thought, "Maybe I'll ice it tonight, but I'd hate to miss beam practice." I wasn't really thinking clearly. I kept telling myself that I had to practice beam to be ready for the Individual Worlds coming up. My mother had purchased expensive airline tickets to go to Paris to see me at this huge competition, so there was no way I was going to miss that. I just wanted Steve to hurry up and put my elbow back into place so the pain would go away and I could move on.

Steve said very calmly, "I'm not going to move it back into place. I don't know how your nerves are being affected. We need to get you to a doctor." He put me in the backseat of his car with my arm surrounded by ice packs and drove me to the hospital. With every jolt of pain, on every pothole, I realized more and more that this injury might be devastating to my future in the sport—*if* I had one.

In the span of three seconds everything had changed. It was the biggest injury of my career, and the timing couldn't have been worse. Prior to my injury, I may have been "in the mix" to squeak onto the Olympic team because I'd done well at Worlds in 1991. But I needed to train in order to qualify at the U.S. Championship and Olympic Trials. The injury may have squelched that opportunity.

As we headed to the hospital, Steve's office assistant called my parents and Dr. David Holden, who was our team doctor and an orthopedic surgeon, and they met us at the hospital. Dr. Holden was able to put my elbow back into place. That was extremely painful, but it was better to have my arm facing the correct way. He studied the X-rays and explained, "Shannon, you've dislocated your elbow, but you have also broken off a piece of bone. I can put you in a cast for six weeks and let the bone reattach and heal."

Then he started talking about the therapy that would follow, but my brain had stopped listening after the word "cast," and I was thinking, "Six weeks, are you kidding me? Oh, no, you're not putting me in a cast." I knew that after six weeks in a cast, my arm would have atrophied and need even more time to get back to normal. A cast seemed like death to my sports career. I was ready to pounce!

Dr. Holden must have read my mind (or noticed I was giving him the evil eye), because he said, "I didn't think you'd go for that. Well, plan B is to go into surgery right now. We'll put a screw in to hold the bones together and I'll put you in a splint."

"Sounds great!" I said. "Let's do it; let's go!"

But he continued, "You'll have a screw in your arm that will hold the bones together. You'll be in a splint for a couple of weeks, and only after that can you slowly start working on getting strength back in that arm. If you do not follow my rules, as far as not putting weight on it and making sure it is sturdy before you train, I will slap a cast on there faster than you can imagine."

"Yes, sir, I will go by the rules, but please don't put a cast on." I was a rule-follower as long I'd agreed to the rules beforehand, so I fully intended to follow the protocol. I knew Dr. Holden and understood that he wasn't going to put me at risk for further injury. He also understood what was at stake short term.

Less than an hour later, I counted backward from a hundred all the way to ninety-eight, and the next thing I knew I woke up in my hospital room. The surgery had been successful, but that didn't guarantee I'd be able to do gymnastics anytime soon. I was wheeled out of the hospital the next morning, feeling groggy as the anesthesia wore off. In the light of day, I began to have more questions I didn't know how to answer: *Now what? Do I take a break to wait for my elbow to heal? Do I just stop training and give up my dream?*

Steve greeted me at the hospital doors and looked down at me in my wheelchair. He could have said, "Shannon, I'm so sorry." He could have said, "Maybe after you heal we can resume training for the 1993 World Championship. Then in another four years, maybe you can try to make the next Olympic team." He didn't say any of those things that would have been completely realistic. Instead, with a nonchalant attitude, he said, "Okay, we've got some work to do now. See you in the gym tomorrow." That was exactly the right thing to say.

It was April Fools' Day, but he wasn't fooling. Steve knew that I needed him to be strong and help me believe that making the Olympic team was still possible if I put in the effort. He put me back into work mode and I did very well in work mode. The next day, with my parents on board, I went back to the gym. My faith in Steve had been reaffirmed and I was relieved to be denied a feeling-sorry-for-myself moment after leaving the hospital. My attitude was, "Yeah, it stinks, but it happened, so deal with it and move on."

The decision to continue training was the biggest turning point of my career.

12

I was disappointed not to be going to France for Worlds. However, I insisted my mother go forward with her trip, because I didn't want to be the reason she lost her opportunity to travel to Paris. She shouldn't miss her one chance to visit the City of Light. I was delighted that she had a wonderful time despite my absence, watching the competition and seeing the sights. Perhaps she still could watch me in Barcelona and bring the entire family. I wasn't giving up my quest to go there just yet. The odds were heavily against my coming back in time for the Nationals, but that was the kind of challenge that made me want to get to the gym early and stay late.

I had a new obstacle to face. How was I going to train with my left arm out of commission? I always looked for a way to put a positive spin on a difficult situation, but how could I do that when I had to deal with the most serious injury of my career? Back in the gym and smelling that familiar mix of chalk and sweat so soon after my bad fall was exactly where I needed to be, mentally and emotionally. But it was frustrating not being able to train my routines and being forced to sit on the sidelines watching the other girls get better. I felt stymied. Could I really do this?

Fortunately, there were people around me who had faith that I'd figure it out and urged me not to give up. Encouragement came from unexpected places. Only a few days after my injury, I received a call from Bart Conner. I was surprised he'd take the time to contact me, but he wanted to speak to me about the injury he sustained prior to the 1984 Olympics. While competing at the Chunichi Cup, he tore his left bicep during his still rings routine. As a gymnast I understood how devastating that particular injury was. His odds of making the 1984 Olympic team were slim to none. But following surgery and intensive physical therapy, he snuck onto the team. That year he won gold with his team and later scored a perfect 10.0 to take home Olympic gold on the parallel bars.

Bart was proof that other gymnasts overcame seemingly insurmountable difficulties, which made me think that if they could do it, so could I. He helped me see that what I faced was not an *insurmountable* obstacle but rather a stumbling block on the road to success. As Steve did in his own way, Bart urged me to focus on the future rather than the past. By being there for me, he reinforced what others kept telling me: that I was not alone. That "we're here for each other" theme has been a constant in my life. I have welcomed help from others as I have dealt with injuries and illness, because it's not a weakness to accept a helping hand; it's a strength. There would be times I would forget this important lesson and need to be reminded. But at that time, it felt good to know that there were others pulling for me.

As Bart advised, I moved forward and came up with a simple solution to getting past my injury. I would allow it to sidetrack me a little but not entirely. While I wasn't going to take the most efficient route from A to B, nevertheless I was determined to get there. I conferred with Steve and Peggy and we came up with a smart alternative to performing my routines, which was to work on other body parts and focus on my weak areas: strength, conditioning, and flexibility. That was precisely what I needed to do and I wouldn't have done it if I hadn't hurt my elbow. Once my arm healed I would be a stronger, better-rounded gymnast and a more formidable competitor than I would have been otherwise. By my transforming something catastrophic into something productive, my injury forced me to move forward in a new way that actually improved my chances of making the Olympic team.

It was a struggle and some days were brutal, but Steve and I felt our way through my recovery process. We just needed to take it one step at a time. *Baby steps!* I was glad Steve didn't have me just sit in splits so that he didn't have to worry about me and could work with his other gymnasts. Sure, he had me work on my flexibility because that was not something I could let slide. But he also focused on strength and I had more time to work through my routines mentally. We were both tempted to push the envelope because we were fighting against time. Sometimes Steve had to slow me down and other times I'd say, "I don't think I'm ready for this." It was safety first. We didn't want to overstep and derail the progress that we were making.

Not every part of recovery happened in the gym. One of the biggest issues I faced had little to do with strength and flexibility. Without constant use, my hands were getting soft. I needed to keep my calluses or I would lose precious time healing rips on my hands once I started working bars again. My dad knew just what to do. He found a piece of wood and cut and shaved it down to the circumference of an uneven bar, then smoothed it to about the same feel as the bar. Every day I would work for at least an hour making sure I kept my hands in shape and calluses intact! I imagine there weren't many girls my age whose biggest issue was making sure she kept her calluses, but this was my life. (Taking care of my hands during my career was essential, so I put Bacitracin on my hands every night as if it were lotion, with socks covering the ointment. I concocted a surefire recipe for ripped skin—two days of zinc oxide, then coat it with Bacitracin; dry the fresh wound to ease the pain, then keep it moist so it won't crack.)

We relied a great deal on physical therapist Mark Cranston, who had helped me with my hamstring problems and other smaller issues from time to time. He saw me nearly every day. Dr. Holden also came by to check on my progress and make sure we were following his rules. After a couple of weeks, I was thrilled that he removed my big splint.

At first my arm didn't even feel like part of my body; it was pretty much deadweight. I hadn't expected that it would be so stiff or that it would have atrophied as much as it did. Dr. Holden instructed me not to put weight on my arm until I could straighten it to a complete 180-degrees and bend it enough to touch my shoulder. At the beginning it was stuck at a ninety-degree angle, not something I had anticipated.

I could do plenty without using the arm and that was a good thing because I now realized it was going to take a lot more time than expected to fully heal. While I did conditioning and flexibility exercises, I continued to work the rest of my body. It would have been disastrous to sit out for four or five weeks and then start from scratch because I was out of shape. After I got the heavy splint off, I could do some running and one-armed skills. Bars was a problem, but I did one-armed back handsprings on beam and floor, diving backward toward my head but landing on my right arm and springing off it and back to my feet. I even attempted a few simple one-armed vaults so that I didn't forget what it was like to barrel down the runway and hit the springboard.

The time came for me to work at straightening my arm. I had to stand by the vaulting horse, put my arm up on it, and hold a ten-pound weight for twenty minutes. I felt foolish doing this while everyone else in the gym was training their skills, but it worked. Slowly my arm got closer to 180 degrees. After that, I was allowed to hang on the bar. I wasn't allowed to swing, just hang there like a monkey on a branch.

Those were my big arm workouts, stretching and hanging. When my arm was finally perfectly straight and I could also touch my left shoulder with my fingertips, I was allowed to begin implementing a few skills. I admit I was nervous about putting weight on it for the first time. I worried that it might not be strong enough or might lock up. I wasn't sure if it would ever work the same as it had before. But I knew I had to believe that it would, because during training or a competition it was too dangerous to be hesitant. I would need to go full out, which meant I had to convince myself that I was fully recovered. If I tried to compensate for my elbow, things could go drastically wrong.

To recover from the type of injury I suffered would have taken two or three months under normal circumstances. To be able to compete at Nationals in only five or six weeks, even at less than 100 percent, was beyond belief. My prayers were answered.

To earn a spot on the Olympic team I needed to do well at Nationals in mid-May as well as the Olympic Trials a month later. At both competitions during that era, gymnasts were required to do compulsories as well as the more creative and taxing optionals. Fundamentals were a strength of mine, so compulsories were to my benefit.

At the U.S. National Championship, which was held at Ohio State

University, I did very well in each of the four events in compulsories and won that portion of the competition. Our plan was to compete only the compulsory round. We believed that a strong performance in that round after the solid training of my optional routines was enough to prove *readiness* and allow Steve to petition me to compete at the U.S. Olympic Trials.

Of course, I was extremely competitive, so after my success in the compulsory round, Steve and I briefly considered doing the optional round. I had been training routines, but we both knew they weren't quite 100 percent. During the warm-up on bars for optionals, I could tell I wasn't ready. In the end we decided not to chance it and to stick to the original plan.

Steve immediately petitioned the U.S. Gymnastics Federation to allow me to compete at the Olympic Trials based on my solid performance in the compulsories and the fact that my injury was healing. Petitioning was not unprecedented or a Hail Mary. In fact, Michelle Campi and Betty Okino ended up petitioning all the way onto the Olympic team that year. So while my participation at the Nationals was over, my Olympic dream was still quite alive. I had faith that Steve understood the process and, as expected, our petition was accepted.

At the time, the Nationals counted for 30 percent of the total score and the Trials counted for 70 percent, but for me the Trials would count 100 percent. My entire career would ride on that one performance. I would be under extreme pressure, knowing one bad move could offset years of training. But I prided myself on being my best when under the gun.

There was still a screw in my arm, but I felt it was fully recovered by June 11, when the Trials began in Baltimore. It was just ten weeks after I dislocated and broke my elbow. Upon arrival at the Baltimore airport my small wristwatch had stopped. When I mentioned this to Steve, he said, "It doesn't matter; it's Miller Time."

For me, it was the same as at other competitions. I couldn't allow the magnitude of this event to shake me. I let Steve do all the scoreboard watching and kept focused on my routines.

Coming off her 1991 World Championship victory in the all-around, Kim Zmeskal was the favorite to win at the Trials and the Olympic Games. I was regarded as an underdog at the Trials, which is how I liked seeing myself in every competition. I didn't try to compete against Kim, Dominique

Dawes, or anyone else in the strong field. As always, I stayed focused on hitting the routines I'd done a thousand times in practice, and I ended up winning the Olympic Trials. The scoring system, which took 100 percent of my score from the Olympic Trials and Kim's combined score from both the U.S. Nationals and the Trials, gave me the slightest lead. There was a little controversy over the outcome due to the weighted scoring, but it didn't really matter because we both made the team. The adults felt the need to haggle, but Kim and I both understood that while the Trials were vital to the selection process, Barcelona was where we both needed to focus.

I had secured a spot on the 1992 U.S. women's Olympic team!

It was mind-boggling that out of all the girls training in gymnastics in America I was one of only six chosen. I was a skinny, timid fifteen-year-old high school freshman from Oklahoma who wasn't even surefire Olympic material before she got hurt. I had many accomplishments during my gymnastics career, but I believe coming back from that severe elbow injury as a better gymnast than before and making the Olympic team was the biggest.

13

After the Olympic Trials I went home for a few days and packed for an entire month. Steve, Peggy, and I would first travel to Florida for a training camp and then find our way to the south of France, where we'd continue to train prior to going to Barcelona. While my parents focused on raising the $25,000 necessary for the whole family to travel to Barcelona, I headed to Tampa for the most intense training camp I'd ever participated in. There a final determination was to be made as to which seven girls would travel to Barcelona. The alternate would be chosen, from those seven, prior to the competition.

Injuries forced Michelle Campi and Betty Okino to petition directly to the camp, which meant there were eight girls invited to Tampa for only seven available spots on the team. At the end of the camp, Kim Kelly was sent home despite finishing in sixth place after the Olympic Trials, causing some controversy. After my finishing in the top spot at the Olympic Trials and proving readiness during the Tampa training camp, my position was secure. Steve continued to keep me focused on training and nothing else.

The final 1992 women's Olympic team—Wendy Bruce, Dominique Dawes, Betty Okino, Kerri Strug, Kim Zmeskal, Michelle Campi, and I—headed to Europe for the final stretch. (Michelle, suffering from a hip injury, would be named alternate prior to the start of competition.) As the personal coach of three out of the seven girls on the team, Béla Károlyi was named head coach. Steve became the team's assistant coach. This was an incredible benefit to me because I would have my personal coach, along with his comfort and expertise, on the floor with me through-out the team competition.

We landed in France, where we trained for two weeks while getting acclimated to the time change. I had missed the Worlds in Paris, so this was my first trip to France. But sightseeing was not part of our agenda. All we wanted to do after an exhausting morning of practice was quietly eat lunch and nap before getting ready for the next practice. By the time the evening workout was finished, we wanted only to eat dinner and fall into bed so we'd be well rested for the next day. Because of our full train-ing schedule, we really didn't have the opportunity to socialize with each other. Kim, Kerri, and Betty knew each other really well because they'd trained together every day at Béla's gym. The rest of us trained at our own facilities in different states, so we knew the other girls only slightly from competitions. I would get to know some of the girls better in a less intense environment during the post-Olympic tour.

The one teammate I got to know fairly well at the time was my room-mate, Dominique Dawes, from Silver Spring, Maryland. "Awesome Dawe-some," as she was known, was indeed awesome. She was also fifteen, really nice, and the perfect roommate because we had a similar mentality when preparing for competition. We liked to have our space and be in our own heads. We also both liked to read and rest. We conserved our energy off the floor so that we could prove ourselves during competition.

I think Dominique and I had an understanding between us that our paths were similar and unlike those of the other girls. We weren't part of the Károlyi team and were the only girls in our respective gyms training for the Olympic Games. Everyone else in our gyms would be learning new skills and taking downtime from the monotony of repeated routines while we were hammering out endless sets on every event, twice a day. On that Olympic team, Dominique and I were too green to be leaders, and though we wanted all of our teammates to do well, we weren't cheerleaders. We focused on listening to our personal coaches and training the way we had always done to get to this point. We would run our own race.

The main reasons we went early to Europe were to become accustomed to the time change and to the European equipment. Equipment could be very different from what we were used to in the United States. We were always informed which types of equipment we could look forward to at international events, and the Olympic Games were no exception. Balance beams could be very different in touch and feel and spring, so my coaches at Dynamo had actually brought in a European-style balance beam for me to train on. The uneven bars were often too tight or too loose and bouncy, or they might have been chalked differently. Peggy covered one of our landing mats with carpet so it would be more like the landing surfaces we'd experience in Barcelona. We also took into account that the floor exercise surface would be slipperier than what we were used to in America. When the floor exercise surface was placed on top of concrete it would often have less give, and we regarded these as "dead floors."

You'd hear in the gym coaches and athletes calling out, "How is the floor?" If the reply was, "It's dead!" chills went up and down your spine. Those two words meant you needed to adjust. You'd need to work a little bit harder on takeoffs and be prepared for a bit more pain on the landings. On vault, it was imperative to figure out the amount and configuration of the springs in the springboard and the feel of the runway under your feet. So we were given two weeks in France to get used to such things.

However, I wasn't getting used to the floor mat in France because the exercise surface had no give. My foot was aching and one reason I was looking forward to the Olympic competition was that floor exercise and the other events would be on a giant podium, so there would be more spring. Raised surfaces have so much spring that gymnasts who aren't used to it often bounce out-of-bounds on tumbling passes. I couldn't wait for the extra help! The other good thing is that the podium setup, including the location of the stairs, was the same at all large competitions, so there wouldn't be additional surprises.

I had the most trouble training on the floor exercise because my foot was becoming very sore, just what I didn't need after my arm was finally in good shape. I was used to doing most of my training on soft surfaces and then gradually transferring to a competition surface. However, during the training camps in Tampa and then in France, we were often asked to show our routines on the harder landing surfaces to help prepare us for competition. My foot bothered me, but I had no choice but to push through. I wouldn't find out until after competing in the Olympics that it was broken.

Finally training ended and we flew to Barcelona. I felt a wave of exhilaration as we got off the plane. I had actually arrived at where the Olympics were being held and the competition was only days away! My excitement was augmented as we rode the bus through the lovely city toward the Olympic Village. I was looking out the window and enjoying the sights and as we entered the Village I spotted a security guard with a machine gun. This was serious security, unlike anything I'd ever seen. As a fifteen-year-old, I found that unsettling, but Steve quickly reminded me that the security was there to keep us safe.

If that weren't surreal enough, as soon as we walked inside the facility to receive our official credentials, we came face-to-face (actually face-to-stomach) with the Dream Team! I recognized Charles Barkley, Larry Bird, Scottie Pippen, and seven or eight other basketball superstars that I'd watched with my father play on television. So for a few minutes the shortest and tallest members of America's Olympic team mingled.

I was so excited and a little bit nervous for the opportunity to know what it's like to stay in the Olympic Village. I was curious about all the athletes around us from different sports and from all over the world, although I wasn't terribly outgoing and was too intimidated to start a conversation with people I didn't know. However, the first time Steve and I went to the cafeteria for lunch, a young American sitting next to me began to ask me questions. He turned out to be a wrestler named Kendall Cross, who just happened to be from Oklahoma. It was one of those small-world moments. And it came at just the right time. I needed to feel a little closer to home.

I soon realized that it didn't matter who they were or where they were from; everyone competing at the Olympics had the same hope as I did. We all wanted to show what we'd been practicing and do it well. We wanted to enjoy the experience of a lifetime.

While I didn't get to see my family much before or during the competition, it felt great knowing they were there in Barcelona with me. This would be the first time that my mom, dad, sister, and brother were together to see me compete in a major competition. They'd raised the money in various ways for the flight, accommodations, and tickets to see me perform. A local gas station held a car wash. Mom's bank made a large financial contribution and paid to have some Olympic T-shirts made up for sale at special rates. Three local TV stations held a benefit baseball game. And others in the community made significant donations. With so many people helping out, my parents actually accumulated more money than needed, so they donated the surplus funds to the Special Olympics. I was thankful to my community for being there for my family and me each step of the way. Having that support and knowing I was never alone was essential to my success.

My parents, Tessa, and Troy stayed by the sea in Salou, which was an hour's bus ride from Barcelona. My mother knew I was a picky eater and worried I might have run out of snacks, so one day while I was busy training, she managed to sneak me a survival package through Steve. I was the envy of all the girls when my coach handed me a huge bag filled with crackers, peanut butter, Nutra-Grain bars, and even Vienna sausages.

I did run into my father the day of the Opening Ceremonies. He was standing just outside the Village gate in the sweltering sun, peeling an orange. He had raced around town on a day the trains weren't running trying to track down the person with the family's tickets for the ceremony that night. He'd been standing there for several hours waiting for information about the tickets, and the orange was all that he had to eat. He'd picked that spot because he hoped I'd pass by, and finally I showed up, on my way to a workout! I had to hold back my tears seeing him there. This had been the longest I had ever been away from my family, and it had been nearly impossible to connect with them because in those days there were no cellphones, e-mail, or other easy ways to reach anyone.

The women's gymnastics team did not march in the Opening Ceremony that night because our competition began the next morning. It was critical to prepare for the next day by resting and staying off our legs. In addition to the typical "get horizontal" instruction from my coaches, I also needed to take care of my injured foot. That night, the whole team huddled around the television and watched until the arrow was shot to light the Olympic flame. It was inspiring. Not only did that moment reinforce in me the idea that *anything is possible*, but it also lit a fire within me to go out and represent my country as best I could, injured or not. That night, I slept like a rock.

14

Heading into the Olympics, I had great expectations. I believed that the women's team could medal and, based on the Trials, I could qualify for all-around and possibly some of the individual event finals. I tried not to think too far ahead, but it was difficult. I wanted very much to help my team earn a medal, but my overall goal wasn't to win medals of any specific color for my team or myself. When I disappointed reporters by saying, "All I want to do is my best," I was being completely honest. It wasn't a glamorous, intriguing, or fascinating quote, but it was to the point. Of course, my expectation for doing "my best" was perfection, a pretty daunting task.

I needed to hit every single routine. That was Steve's goal and mine. I had trained hard, done the repetition. If I didn't absolutely believe I could hit every set then there was no chance I'd do it. I wasn't going to accomplish every goal I had set for myself, but failure could not be part of my thinking. I had learned that it was most important to get up each day and look for a win. Maybe that meant acing an exam or learning a new skill. Whatever it was, if I gave it my all then I was a winner. So now, staring down the most important athletic competition of my life at that point, I wanted to win the day. *Do your best and medals will follow.*

I assured the media that my elbow was fully healed, though the screw wouldn't come out for another three months. I saw no reason to mention I'd injured my left foot landing on the hard surfaces during training in France. What did it matter at that point? At the time, I didn't realize it was so serious, that I had fractured my fourth metatarsal. That explained why my takeoffs and landings were extremely painful. I could deal with running and do most of my skills despite the bad foot, but it was hard not to wince during the tumbling runs and on balance beam dismounts. However, I was not anxious about it because my experiences had taught me that when the green light came on and the adrenaline kicked in I would feel no pain on any events. I could barely walk in the warm-up gym and had to muster all my determination before each pass. Yet I had no doubt I could compete without a problem. With God's help and a bit of ice, ibuprofen, and adrenaline, I'd make it through. Doing four routines in a night of competition was easy compared to training ten or more routines on each event on a daily basis, sometimes twice a day. I never would have put my team or myself at risk if I thought that I couldn't be 100 percent during the competition. I was ready to go, no excuses.

I have vivid memories of stepping into my leotard on the first day of competition, July 26, and thinking, "The next time I come back to this room I'm going to be really happy or really sad depending on how my performances went." There would be no medal awarded that first night after compulsories, but this was the start of our Olympics and our team was thrilled. As I walked into the Palau Sant Jordi, my stomach was tied in knots. I was excited but scared.

We walked toward the left side of the arena and high up in the stands I focused on two U.S. soldiers holding a huge American flag, one on each side, and cheering at the top of their lungs. At that moment it hit me: I wanted so badly to treat these Olympics like any other competition. But it wasn't. It was the same four events, and I could focus on that, but this meet was different. Here were these soldiers who fought for our freedom every day, and they were there to cheer *us* on. I felt my chest tighten up and had to hold back tears. If I was looking for motivation and inspiration, they were it. If they could do what they do, I could certainly get through some gymnastics routines.

I was reminded of why competing in the Olympics was so important for me. It was not only about feeling good if I hit my routines but about the uniform I was wearing. I never felt burdened by the worry that I had to do well for my country. I could have felt the *weight* of millions of Americans who were going to watch my every move, but I chose to feel their support instead. They would carry me through the competition. Only at rare moments did I think, "What if I let them down?" I never wanted to let anyone down—parents, siblings, coaches, the Gymnastics Federation, or Oklahomans—and certainly not the entire country!

Although expectations weren't quite as high in those days for American gymnasts to win Olympic medals, there was pressure on our team to come through. The Unified Team—consisting of Russia, Ukraine, Georgia, Belarus, and eight other countries that had been part of the former Soviet Union—Romania, and China were very strong. So while gold was a long shot for us, we still felt we had a real chance to stand on that medal podium.

The team competition spanned two days. I always felt like the team portion was more difficult and nerve-wracking than the individual competitions. When you miss a skill during all-around or an event final, you are certainly disappointed. But feeling lousy about missing on an individual routine isn't nearly as devastating as when your mistake affects an entire team of girls who had invested years of hard training for this opportunity.

Although Béla Károlyi was the women's head coach, Steve and Peggy remained my personal coaches and were the ones who I looked to during training and competition. As the assistant coach, Steve also helped Béla with the other girls, and that worked out for everyone. They had coached together on many occasions and seemed to respect each other. Not that this stopped them from bickering at times, mostly when it came to the media. They would both pull for their own athletes because that was their job. It's what you want from your coach, someone to stand up for you.

At these Olympics, many people saw Steve and me together for the first time. They saw this big, burly bear with an intimidating mustache and this sixty-five-pound pixie working in unison. Before each performance, he'd put his hands on my shoulders, stare into my eyes, and I'd feel instantly calm and grounded. He didn't tell me to go out and win a medal or beat another gymnast. As always, he said, "Do what we worked on and show what you can do. Go out and have some fun." That was our ritual and I was grateful that Steve hadn't changed it or his persona for the Olympics. It was hard to remember that this was his first Olympics, too, because he always seemed to have everything under control. Naturally, Steve and I had our dicey moments over the years, but during competitions we were always in sync.

Steve talked to me right up until I had to salute the judges. I think he did that partly to keep himself calm and partly to keep me focused on him rather than allowing me time to be distracted, overthink my routine, or get negative "What if I fall?" thoughts about the upcoming routine. Some may have seen me as stoic when he talked to me and when I competed because I rarely changed expression, even after doing well on an event. That was my game face. I was in the zone. Sometimes fans saw my look of steely determination and just knew Steve was giving me a brilliant bit of instruction. Sometimes that was the case, and other times I'd be thinking, "Enough already. I've got it. I need to go salute the judges." I hadn't competed on a podium that often, and I was always worried the judges might salute me and I'd still be talking with Steve.

That never happened. What I eventually realized was that Steve always watched the judges and timed it so I didn't have to stand on the raised floor for a long period of time and get cold—because if I tried moving around too much before the green light I'd actually get a deduction. He watched the judges and even the television cameras, because he was aware that if I was high up in the standings, I may be forced to wait until the television cameras were in place to film my routine—that was something that hadn't even dawned on me. Whereas I may have wanted to get up there quickly, he was determined that I not get up there too soon. There was always a method to his madness.

As soon as I came down the steps of the podium, Steve or Peggy would be there to give me hugs . . . and corrections. There wasn't a lot of time for high fives because I was usually one of the last to compete in the lineup our coaches devised. The lineup for each event was all about strategy, and typically those with the best chance to throw a high score were placed toward the end. Going late in our lineup, I would finish my routine and then have to immediately get my stuff together, get my uniform on, and prepare to march to the next event so I could warm up and get refocused. Before the next event my coaches would constantly talk to me to get me back on track, even if I had just completed a good routine. There was no mention of my score. It was simply, "Okay, good job, but forget about it and think about what you're going to do now." They would go through each element in the upcoming routine, even if it was a vault. That is how we always worked. I was performing consistently at these Games and we didn't want to mess with the recipe.

Our team really wanted to be in the medals. We had to get on that podium. As in past competitions, I wasn't really aware how I was doing on the scoreboard, or how we were doing as a team. *Compete your best every time up.* I was only aware that Kim had fallen off the beam during her compulsory routine because I overheard one of the coaches mention it. I couldn't believe it. Kim never fell. My heart ached for her, especially since she had so much pressure on her coming into these Games as a favorite to win several medals. She was a hard worker who never complained, and I had tremendous admiration for her. Steve told me to focus. He was right; there was nothing I could do but try to score well to help the team.

I hit each of my four routines during the compulsory round and another four during the optional competition. Kim rebounded from her fall, the rest of the girls put up good scores, and when it was all said and done, Team USA finished on the podium! We landed in third place behind the Unified Team and Romania. Getting a bronze medal was a huge achievement for us. In the 1988 Olympics, the American team had finished in fourth place, just out of the medals, so when our bronze medals were placed around our necks we were very happy to have done our country proud. It was the best finish for the U.S. women's team in a nonboycotted Olympics.

It surely surprised quite a few people that I ended up with the highest all-around score among all gymnasts in the team competition because I wasn't even supposed to finish first on the American team. It surprised me, too.

It was a thrill to stand on the podium with my team as I received my first Olympic medal. I looked for my parents and Tessa and Troy in the crowd. Peggy and I were the same in that we contained our excitement; Steve showed enough emotion for all three of us. Of course, we all realized I had little time to celebrate or relax because there were new pressures ahead. In addition to qualifying for the all-around, I had become the first American gymnast, male or female, to qualify for every event finals at an Olympics. For some of the girls, their Olympic competition was over, but mine had just begun. With eight routines remaining, I couldn't go sight-seeing or spend time with my family; I needed to go back to training twice a day. The team competition was the cake, everything else was the icing. However, I was still wearing red, white, and blue, and I wasn't going to let up.

15

My scores had put me in first place after the team competition, but they no longer mattered. For the first time in Olympic history, a gymnast's scores in the team round did not carry over to the individual all-around competition. The "New Life" rule meant that all the athletes who had qualified started from scratch in the all-around and that my advantage was gone. At the time, I didn't realize Tatiana Gutsu was the one to watch. I remember sneaking peaks at Svetlana Boginskaya, "the Belarusian Swan." Svetlana commanded everyone's attention with her skills, artistry, and beauty. I envied her style and her confidence. She was nineteen years old and still at the top of her game. It was Svetlana who helped me get past the idea that gymnastics had to end at fifteen or sixteen. Yes, we were competitors, but I had great respect for her, Tatiana, and the other athletes.

Gutsu—whose nickname was "the Painted Bird"—and I were these skinny little girls with blond hair and big scrunchies, and people commented that we looked like sisters. We were both shy and quiet yet in the all-around, we provided what is still considered one of the most dramatic competitions in Olympic history.

That night was spectacular! I was fortunate to compete in my favorite rotation order—starting on bars and then moving through beam, floor, and vault. I was very pleased with my performances on the first three events. On floor exercise, I competed what became my favorite routine of my entire career. The music, a Hungarian rhapsody, and choreography were a perfect fit with my personality. With only vault to go, I didn't know where I was in the standings but could tell by Steve's excitement that I was in the medal mix. He gave me last-minute corrections, and I climbed the steps to the podium.

Tatiana had only vault to go, as well. Perhaps she knew what I didn't: that I was the only one who stood between her and gold. I wasn't sure about scores, but I sensed tension in the arena. Even coaches from other countries were watching me intently. The back of the vault runway was lined with the Romanian coaches. I was thrilled to execute my first vault well; NBC commentator Tim Daggett, who had won two medals for the U.S. at the 1984 Games, described my first vault as "the most perfect piece of gymnastics that I have ever seen." When I landed, Steve went nuts on the sidelines, yelling, "That's the one; that's the one; one more time!" As I turned to salute for my second vault, he shouted, "Keep it open all the way and nail it!" My score for my first vault flashed on the scoreboard: A 9.975. There was no way to avoid seeing it. I wasn't sure how I could top that vault.

So I had one in the bag and one chance to top it. My second vault was good, but the first had been better. Steve went crazy on the sidelines once again, hugging me, lifting me up, and then offering me to the audience. He instructed me to wave; I smiled on my own. I couldn't have been happier in that moment. I had hit all four routines about as well as I ever had. I left it all on the floor that night.

I had done two excellent vaults, but Gutsu got the score she needed to edge me for the most coveted gold medal in women's gymnastics by the closest margin in Olympic history: .012. I wasn't crushed—far from it. I had just won an Olympic silver medal! I wanted to cry tears of joy and jump up and down, but instead I settled for a shy smile and a feeling of gratitude for one of the greatest nights of my life. Yes, I would have loved to have achieved a gold medal, but I knew there was nothing more I could have done that night. I had no regrets. My ambitious goal going into the Olympics was to hit every routine and I had just hit all four events again, making it twelve for twelve so far. My coaches were thrilled, too. Their little-known gymnast had just finished second in the all-around at the Olympics!

Backstage was pandemonium. I was being pulled in all directions, and poor Peggy had to jump over some barriers, risking possible arrest, to reach the staging person who had walked off with my bag, not realizing I needed my uniform for the awards ceremony. Then I was furiously trying to get on my pants and jacket and get things together. It was surreal. *Am I really here? Did the competition really go by so fast?* At the time, I didn't realize just how close I'd come to winning gold. Facing the media later, I was asked about having the best placement by an American in the all-around at a nonboycotted Olympics, but I hadn't had time to think about that, either, or anything else. I was still in a bit of shock.

After my performances in team and all-around, I was inundated with media attention. I was no longer a secret, the dark horse. Steve kept me sheltered the best he could and I managed to get through the interviews we couldn't avoid. It wasn't that I disliked interviews or reporters, but that I just wasn't always sure what to say. I was used to Steve doing all of the talking, but he had begun to back away and let me take the stage. He knew I needed to learn to talk to reporters and the best way was to get out there and do it.

My emergence at the Games may have been unexpected to some, but it was the plan that Steve, Peggy, and I had begun formulating after my success in Catania, Italy, in 1990. All the training we did was geared to my peaking at the right time. We didn't want to be in a situation where I had to "rise to the occasion." There were times in my career when I had to do this, but it was much better to go into a competition, particularly the Olympics, when you are already performing at the highest level. I much preferred steady-as-she-goes to throw-caution-to-the-wind—although I became adept at both because of happenstance. You never *want* to be in a position where when the green light goes on, you have to turn it up a notch. One of the cardinal sins of gymnastics is to practice one way and compete another way. You practice your routines without holding anything back, just as you will do in a competition. You don't rise; you remain consistent.

The most grueling competitions, team and all-around, were now finished. I had a couple days' rest before event finals began, and I'd be competing two events each day for two days. Steve knew I needed rest and actually canceled practice one morning, opting for some light conditioning on the beach instead. I needed an easy day and some fresh air. I had been practically living at the gym, and Steve didn't want to chance my burning out with four events left.

On the first night of event finals, I began with vault. My first vault was my typical Yurchenko full twist, and I hit it. Each gymnast had to compete a second vault that was different from her first. Unfortunately, my second vault did not have as high a start value, so I knew it was unlikely I'd be a contender. It was a front handspring front somersault. I landed with a large forward step, which meant landing out of medal contention. I hadn't expected to medal, but I wanted to at least give it my best shot. Next, I headed to uneven bars. I hit my fourth bar routine of the Games and earned my second bronze medal, behind Lu Li of China and Tatiana Gutsu.

With only two events to go, I had now hit fourteen of fourteen routines. Fourteen routines with no major breaks! The second night of event finals began with balance beam. With only one credential between the two of them, Peggy and Steve acted like a tag team and Peggy was, as always, my coach on this event. Steve had to remain behind the barricade. I performed what I thought to be a very good routine and finished tied for second with Lu Li, behind Tatiana Lysenko of the Unified Team. I now had two silver medals and four medals overall, quite a bounty. However, I couldn't bask in the glow because I needed to focus on floor exercise, which was coming up momentarily. They held the award ceremony after each event, and I was still very much in competition mode as they hung the medal around my neck. I was happy to be part of the ceremony, but at the same time I was reminding myself that I needed to keep warm for floor.

It seems strange with hindsight, but while climbing the podium stairs to do floor exercise, I didn't consider that it might be the last Olympic event of my life. I didn't wonder if I was going to make another Olympic team or even still be a gymnast four years later. I was busy trying not to think of my injured foot or the fact that I'd be finished soon and able to rest. *Let's go hit this routine and be done.*

The tumbling was painful on my foot, but I loved floor and telling a story through dance. I was first up in this event, which was not my favorite draw, but it was nice to get finished and watch the other athletes. Steve helped me find my family in the audience as we waited for my score to come up. I waved to them. I'm sure my parents were relieved it was over, too.

I'd finished my last event of the competition, so for a rare time, I watched the other girls and even looked at the leaderboard. Lavinia Miloşovici of Romania would win the gold, and Henrietta Ónodi of Hungary would capture the silver, but I couldn't imagine my score holding up for a bronze medal after going first on the event. It did. I finished in a three-way tie for third place, sharing the bronze with Tatiana Gutsu and Cristina Bontaş of Romania.

Steve yelled out, "You've got another medal!" I was stunned.

Five medals! It was the most medals taken home by an American in any sport from Barcelona. Nobody predicted that.

It was a clean-hit Games for me, sixteen mistake-free routines in a row. That had been my focus. The media understandably emphasized the five medals, but to me going sixteen for sixteen was even more phenomenal than winning them and was arguably my greatest achievement in gymnastics competition.

Looking back, not winning the all-around might have been the best thing that happened to me at those Games. Would I have retired if I had won the gold? Maybe I wouldn't have had that fire in my belly to train and compete for four more grueling years to try for the 1996 Olympics. My gut feeling is that I would have continued in the sport for at least a year because I wasn't through learning. I still had moves that I hadn't yet perfected. But who knows? Of course, it was never really about medals but rather seeing what crazy feats I could learn to do and how *well* I could perform them. It was still, for better or worse, about achieving perfection— not in the judges' eyes, but in my own. I had no idea if I'd be doing gymnastics at eighteen, which seemed so old, but I knew that I'd continue in this sport I loved once I returned to the States, and at the time that was enough.

After the competition concluded it was chaos; I had never answered so many questions or seen so many cameras pointed at me. Afterward, I was happy to let my game face fade away and finally see my whole family. I was glad I had a chance to spend a day with them enjoying sights in Barcelona and adding to my memories. Then we all headed home.

16

My family flew back to Oklahoma, but I took a detour to Washington, D.C. The whole U.S. Olympic team was invited to the White House to be congratulated personally by President George H. W. Bush. Arnold Schwarzenegger, who served on the President's Council on Physical Fitness and Sports, was also present. Olympians and coaches gathered around, shaking the president's and actor's hands and posing with them for pictures. We planned to picnic on the White House lawn, but it stormed, so we took cover inside, eating hot dogs and hamburgers along the White House hallways. It was fantastic!

Steve, Peggy, and I then flew to Edmond on a private jet, a first for me. Steve said it was the only way I could get home "in time." In time for what? I assumed a much-anticipated day off. I stepped out of the plane and there was the governor, the mayor, and thousands of people from all over Oklahoma to greet me. I was astonished and more than a little embarrassed. I was oblivious to how people were reacting to my Olympic success. Although I had done plenty of interviews, I didn't think about the sheer number of people reading or watching them.

I was whisked away to meet more dignitaries, do more interviews, and sign autographs. Tessa and Troy happily signed autographs, too. Then

Edmond threw me a parade! Seriously, what fifteen-year-old gets her own parade? It was incredible. I couldn't believe how many people lined the streets, many holding placards expressing sentiments like CONGRATULATIONS! WE LOVE YOU SHANNON! and GO USA! Fifteen thousand people were there to welcome me home. I was in one car, followed by a car with my family, and another with Steve and Peggy. The band from my high school marched and played, cheerleaders chanted my name, and local gymnasts cartwheeled down the street like I used to do when I was at Adventures. Hovering overhead were helicopters from local affiliates of the three major networks. Video clips from the parade would be broadcast across the country.

As the ceremony concluded, I was presented the key to the City of Edmond as well as the key to a bright red 1992 Saturn. Bob Moore of the local Saturn dealership told me that the car was being loaned to me for a year, but since I was too young to drive and hadn't even taken driver's ed, it was later decided that it was mine to keep. Tessa enjoyed being in the parade and I knew she was proud of me, but she didn't quite understand why I got a free new car while she had to work babysitting and doing other jobs to earn enough money to buy her own. And *she* was old enough to drive. Mom had to remind her that when she was waking up late in the summers and on all those Saturdays, I was going to the gym to work.

In fact, I was back in the gym three days after I returned from the Olympics. It was what I knew. I didn't know that you were supposed to retire after winning five medals in the Olympics. My mother said nothing to me about it, but she thought I'd retire after my first Olympics, like most gymnasts did, and move on to something else. She tells me now that she hoped I'd delay making any decision because she believed I was only then coming into my prime. I felt the same way. I was only fifteen and, although the next Olympics were too far away to consider, there were skills I still wanted to learn.

It was comforting to be back home with my family and to get back into a familiar routine. Little did I know that those days were gone. Things were different now. Yes, my dad would continue to drive me to school each morning and to Dynamo in the late afternoon, often in my new car. But my schedule otherwise was busier than ever.

My parents had been devoting their time and effort to helping others for many years and they made me aware that now that I had some popularity and fame, I needed to do something good with it. It wasn't a hard sell because they had instilled those values in me from an early age. I had done plenty of charity work prior to the Olympics, and that intensified after I came back home. I was happy to help in any way I could, lending my time and efforts to worthy causes like the Children's Miracle Network, the Red Ribbon Campaign for a Drug-Free Youth, and many other organizations. From 1992 to 1996, in addition to these activities, I continued with my training and handled endorsements and appearances. All of a sudden I was balancing more than gym and school.

Still, I made time to answer fan mail. Thousands of letters were pouring in from around the world. They came from every age group: I received crayon drawings from preschool children and a lovely handwritten letter from a ninety-seven-year-old great-grandmother. The letters were interesting and often incredibly moving, and I did my best to respond personally and with an autograph, particularly to kids. My parents had made it clear that there were a lot of young girls who looked up to me, and it was my obligation to be a good role model. Nearly all of the mail was friendly, but my parents screened it because of the few that weren't. That included my first death threat. It was an alarming moment. This person had never even met me, and I couldn't fathom why he was so angry at a gymnast. The FBI came to our house several times. I tried to put it out of my mind and carry on with all my activities. Fortunately, I had plenty to occupy my thoughts, between workouts and going back to school that fall.

I attended Edmond North High School. It may sound strange, but I didn't know what anybody at school thought of me then. I don't remember anyone making a fuss over me, and as far as I know, nobody said, "Wow, that Olympic medal winner goes to *our* school!" In addition to the parade, I was honored by the Chamber of Commerce as the "Edmond Citizen of the Year," and Edmond erected a sign at the main entrance of town that read HOME OF SHANNON MILLER, WINNER OF 5 MEDALS, 1992 OLYMPICS. But I didn't know how many kids at school realized I was that girl.

I wasn't the type to wear my medals around town and certainly not to school. I liked to keep my two worlds fairly separate. However, I was an Olympian after my freshman year, so my teachers and high school principal understood that training and international travel were necessary for me to represent our country. They graciously approved of my missing home-room if I had morning practices, gave me homework assignments ahead of time, and let me take tests at special times if I was going to be away for competitions.

I worked hard to keep up my grades to earn this special treatment and be able to pursue my career in gymnastics. I still wanted to be like my crazy-smart sister and spent a lot of time studying. I loved math and sci-ence, but I also loved to read and write. I was the type who read entire assigned books *plus* the Cliff's Notes in order to do well on tests and make the honor roll. I had only one speed and it was full throttle. *Do it right or not at all.*

I loved my teachers and school and had a thirst for knowledge, but I was not outspoken in the classroom. I continued to dread getting called on in class for fear of giving the wrong answer. I'd feel that panic, that cold sweat. I would battle that anxiety for years. I had become accustomed to answering questions in a room filled with reporters from all over the world, but it was different in a classroom, where nobody was asking my thoughts on gymnastics.

Because I was used to being around adults, I felt more comfortable with my teachers than I did with my peers. In those few minutes between classes when I was free to socialize with the other kids, I didn't have any idea what to talk about. I knew gymnastics and my language was that of Tusks, Shaposhnikovas, and handsprings, not of boys and upcoming dances. I dove into work to avoid those awkward moments. That meant eating my lunch in the library while getting a jump on my homework. This was my way of dealing with the stress of finding kids to sit with in the cafeteria.

I didn't think about boys; they were so alien to me. I was petrified at the thought of going to dances or parties. I wouldn't have gone if I could, but I enjoyed the excuse, "I think I have a competition that day." I didn't want to put myself in an uncomfortable situation. I liked my neat and tidy world and did all I could to remain in my comfort zone. Now I wish I wouldn't have been so timid because I think some kids wanted to reach out, but I didn't give them a chance. I was too busy burying my head in a book and trying to go unnoticed.

I was four foot seven and weighed between sixty-five and seventy pounds my freshman and sophomore years. I didn't know how to put on makeup or what to wear. I didn't feel like I fit in with any particular group. It could have been awkward, but no one ever treated me badly at school. My size alone could have been an issue in high school with cliques and bullies, but no one cared about my size because I was a gymnast. (Maybe they knew after all!) I could have been a tiny, bashful girl who withdrew inside myself because I had self-image and self-esteem issues, but gymnastics let me sidestep all that. In those areas where things could have taken a wrong turn, I was saved by my sport. Instead of feeling bad about what I didn't have to offer, I would head to the gym, where I could display my God-given athletic talent. I spent a tremendous amount of time training and competing in gymnastics, but I never felt I had to sacrifice anything, especially my childhood. I loved my sport and it was such a positive in my life.

I did have friends at school, although the majority of my closest girl-friends came through gymnastics. The girls on my team at Dynamo were friendly, supportive, and a lot of fun. I'm not sure Steve would have allowed it, but there was no boy talk, although we all watched *21 Jump Street* and had crushes on Johnny Depp—who didn't? When we had time off we would hit the water park or Frontier City, or go to a movie or hockey game. But most of our time was spent together in the gym, until late in the evening. We rooted for each other and made each other laugh, which got us through the rough days.

TOP: Me with my big sis Tessa and brother Troy. I used to push Troy around in my doll stroller! *Shannon Miller's Personal Collection.* BOTTOM LEFT: Here I am at six years old, loving beam already! *Shannon Miller's Personal Collection.* BOTTOM RIGHT: Very focused as Steve gives me corrections during the 1991 McDonald's American Cup. We were always a great team. *Dave Black.*

Previous page: TOP LEFT: Balance beam during the 1993 World Gymnastics Championship All Around competition. This was my moment of calm before the storm of skills would begin. *Dave Black.* TOP RIGHT: During my all-time favorite floor routine (1992 Olympic Games). I adored the choreography and music of this routine. *Dave Black.* BOTTOM: Floor exercise during the 1992 Olympic Games. My fifth and final medal of this Games was won on floor. However, I still feel my biggest accomplishment was hitting 16 out of 16 routines. *Mike Proebsting.*

Current page: TOP: Taking the bronze medal was a huge accomplishment for our team! Three of us would utilize the experience four years later to bring home the gold. *Dave Black.* BOTTOM LEFT: Found myself surrounded by amazing athletes at the 1994 James E. Sullivan Award ceremony. (Left to Right: Michael Johnson, Shannon Miller, Tiger Woods and Bruce Baumgartner). *Shannon Miller's Personal Collection.* BOTTOM RIGHT: Peggy (Liddick) is one of the true treasures of the gymnastics world. I was incredibly fortunate to have the opportunity to work with her and learn from her throughout my career. *Dave Black.*

TOP: This is it! The pressure was on for our team to bring home the first ever women's gymnastics gold medal for the United States of America! I can still feel the butterflies! BOTTOM: Our team mugging for the camera after a tough training day at the Georgia Dome prior to the start of the 1996 Olympics. *Both photos Dave Black.*

Me and Rocco, my sweet, sweet boy. He kept me going on the bad days. He was the constant reminder that I simply had to push through. *Liliane Hakim.*

In 2011, after my cancer diagnosis. This is where I spent the hours during chemotherapy. I am so thankful for the wonderful nurses who took such great care of me. *Shannon Miller's Personal Collection.*

I was humbled to be honored as the Look Good, Feel Better "Dream Girl" in late 2011. (Left to Right: Robin Roberts, Giada de Laurentiis, Kelly Ripa, Shannon Miller). *Shannon Miller's Personal Collection.*

NANCY OWENS
MEMORIAL FOUNDATION

Nancy Owens
Memorial Foundation
Luncheon

Previous page: TOP: While I had been involved with health and fitness long before my battle, my cancer journey brought renewed passion to my mission to help women make their health a priority. *Matthew White.* BOTTOM: Commentating Men's and Women's Artistic Gymnastics during the 2012 Olympic Games in London with Stephen Robilliard. (I had trouble keeping my wig on straight with those big headphones!) *Shannon Miller's Personal Collection.*

Current page: TOP: Here I am with my team from Yahoo! Sports in London as an expert analyst for the London Olympic Games. *Shannon Miller's Personal Collection.* BOTTOM LEFT: Fitness post cancer involved walking, swimming, and yoga. Moving my body was empowering. *Sable Tidd.* BOTTOM RIGHT: Still feels like a dream! I will forever be thankful for all of those who helped me fulfill my Olympic dream. *Renee Parenteau.*

TOP: Our sweet baby girl, Sterling (or "Sister Bear" as Rocco calls her). BOTTOM: We are so blessed. My hair has grown back although other scars remain. I will always have a reminder to stop and appreciate life and all that it has to offer. *Both photos Renee Parenteau.*

17

Before I left for Barcelona, Steve advised my parents to find me an agent in case I did well in the Olympics. He introduced my parents to a few options including ProServ, an agency that represented athletes. Two representatives from its office took me and my parents out to dinner and explained how things worked. I signed with ProServ, becoming the first American gymnast to sign with an agent *prior* to an Olympic Games. Once I had arrived home with my medals, they booked me for some exhibitions and autograph signings at malls and auto shows and got me a commercial for Trivial Pursuit and an appearance on *Live! with Regis and Kathie Lee* in New York.

Steve negotiated with ProServ and Bill Graham Presents for me and Vitaly Scherbo of Russia, who won an unprecedented six gold medals in Barcelona, to headline a gymnastics tour. It featured Olympians from the U.S. like me and Kim Zmeskal and Unified Team stars Scherbo, Tatiana Gutsu, and Svetlana Boginskaya. A second tour sponsored by USA Gymnastics (formerly the U.S. Gymnastics Federation) and the U.S. Postal Service piggybacked on our tour. The Postal Service had helped offset the cost of expensive event tickets for some parents who traveled to Barcelona in exchange for the athletes agreeing to do a post-Olympics mini-tour.

Through this arrangement we were able to perform our show in thir-teen additional cities.

It was a professional tour, the most extensive to date, and provided me with an unbelievable opportunity to experience a different side of the sport. Steve was pleased that I had decided to tour and that he was able to go with me as one of the coaches. For the duration, he would help me train and also help all the athletes stay in competitive shape.

We had about two weeks of rehearsals before hitting the road. Being in the gym from 8:00 A.M. to 8:00 P.M., for two solid weeks, was actually a blast. My foot was beginning to heal and it helped that these weren't the rigorous workouts that we had had prior to the Olympics. As we learned new dances, we had the opportunity to bond with each other. It was par-ticularly nice getting to know Tatiana, Svetlana, and all the other girls and to establish friendships with them. Although we didn't all speak the same language, we were able to "converse" and learn about each other, which we didn't have the opportunity to do as competitors. At the same time I felt I had gained a team of big brothers in Vitaly, Grigory Misutin of Ukraine, and the members of the U.S. men's team who performed with us.

The tour was coast-to-coast, hitting most of the major cities. We would typically perform on Thursday night, followed by an autograph session at the arena, and then the cast would get on the bus at around 11:30 P.M. and arrive at the next city between 2:00 A.M. and 5:00 A.M. At the new hotel you might sleep a little, then freshen up. You'd get to the arena around 2:00 P.M. for warm-ups or a full run-through, eat an early catered meal, perform the show that night, and then get back on the bus. We often did shows on three or four consecutive nights. If there was a show on Sunday and not another until Thursday, some of the cast might jet home. Others would remain in the city for some sightseeing or, depending where we were, hit the beach.

I would have liked to have traveled with the rest of the cast by bus, but I typically had to fly ahead to the next city on our tour. There I'd train for a couple of hours each day with Steve at local gyms, do advance me-dia, and make sure I kept up with my schoolwork. It was a challenging schedule, but I wasn't training as hard as I did at Dynamo. I trained enough to keep in good shape, so that when the end of the tour came, I wouldn't have to make up too much lost time.

The tour was a lot of fun, but it was by no means easy. People paid their hard-earned money to see the show, so we wanted to deliver fun and excitement to them. In addition to my training, I performed my full-out Olympic beam set and uneven bar routine during every show. Steve wanted me to think of these performances as practice for future competitions.

One of my favorite parts of the show was when Tatiana and I did the compulsory floor routine from the Olympics together. Because we looked similar, wore identical leotards, and were doing the same moves in unison, it was a really cool thing for the audience to see. We showed that there were no hard feelings.

Different things were expected from each gymnast. I did two or three group routines, which were a bit nerve-wracking because I couldn't stick to my traditional and classical dance background. But they turned out to be great fun. We had big opening and closing numbers with the whole cast out on the floor together to do a tumbling routine and a group dance. We also had rhythmic gymnasts with us and some gymnasts performing acro, an acrobatic form of gymnastics. It was the first time I really saw gymnastics as more of a performance, complete with costumes and music. At times, I'd practice doing different acrobatic skills with the acro gymnastics stars on our tour, like handstands on top of their hands. (It was so much fun that for a time I thought I may switch from artistic to acro.)

I was pushed to try new things that were out of my comfort zone, and I grew as a performer. I learned how to do my routines no matter what the situation. It could be ice cold in the arena or the lights could be flashing on and off, but we were prepared to perform every single night. I became a better competitor because now I could do my Olympic routines even if it was pitch-black in the arena with only a spotlight to light the beam. It's not easy doing a flip on balance beam with the light shining in your eyes. In future competitions, I wouldn't care if music was blaring or anyone was using flash photography because I had basically done balance beam in the dark!

My biggest issue on tour was that some of the arena floors were on ice. I didn't have very good circulation in my feet and, as I stood on the floor prior to doing balance beam, my toes would turn completely white and go numb. I really needed to feel my toes on the beam, so before I went out, I'd go to the nearest restroom and run my toes under hot water for a couple minutes. (On the 1996 tour we knew to carry industrial-size heating pads with us everywhere.)

It was amazing for a fifteen-year-old to perform in front of five thousand to twenty thousand people almost every night. It was a nice change that there were no judges with hovering pens, and I felt no need to block out the fans so I could stay focused. I was now able to experience firsthand the reactions of fans to what I was doing. At times, they would be sitting only feet away from the equipment and I could actually interact with them. After a routine, we were allowed to give high fives, shake people's hands, and give hugs. Fans could see me smile. Ultimately, the tour also helped me come out of my shell a bit. It was an opportunity to let my hair down and show more of my personality, because this was a celebration for all the years of hard work.

Steve kept an eye on me and made sure I was getting enough sleep and ate properly. It helped me during my gymnastics career that I could doze with a band playing next to me (although I wasn't real happy when Troy got a drum set one Christmas), so sleep was no problem. On the tour I just ate what I ate, as always. I was warned that I had to be more careful while traveling because I wasn't going to be getting those nice meals my mother prepared. I just tried to make good food choices, and mostly ate chicken and rice, fruit, and even some vegetables.

Since I couldn't attend school that fall, the tour agreed to provide a tutor, Terri Thomas, who was the daughter of my algebra teacher. She was my roommate and chaperone during the tour, and we became good friends. "Terri the Tutor," as she was known on the tour, tutored me in every subject and even gave exams. So in addition to traveling, performing, and training, I was doing my homework and making sure I didn't fall behind. It was still three years away, but I was adamant about graduating with my class.

18

Even before I returned home after the tour, I had decided against retiring from gymnastics. I don't remember having a specific conversation about it with my parents or my coaches, but I immediately went back to Dynamo and kept going. I filled out Steve's new index card. I didn't think to set my long-term goal as the 1996 Olympics in Atlanta. Now that the 1992 Olympics were over, the goals I wrote down were less ambitious. My short-term goals included doing a full twisting back handspring on the beam. Because I'd never done it before, it was at least as important to me as my long-term goal of performing well at the 1993 World Championship in Birmingham, England. The next Olympics were too far away for me to consider.

I had a new training and traveling partner. Béla Károlyi had retired (for the first time) after the 1992 Olympics, and though the Károlyi gymnastics center was going strong under Bela's wife, Márta, Kerri Strug, my Olympic teammate, decided to move to Dynamo. Gym hopping happens frequently in the sport for better or worse. Gymnasts often look elsewhere to find the most positive and productive work environment. Because there is not one coach who is right for everyone, they seek coaches they can trust completely, and often it's a game of trial and error. What makes it really difficult is that a *great* coach might not be the *right* coach for your individual needs and personality.

In 1991, an Elite from Károlyi's gym, Erica Stokes, had shifted from his gym to train under Steve with mixed results, culminating with her sudden retirement. Steve expected better results with Kerri because she and I were closer in age and could really push each other. In fact, Kerri beat me out for first place in our very first competition together, Steve's annual Dynamo Classic. I then managed to overtake Kerri to win the all-around and all four events in the prestigious American Cup. The competitive atmosphere seemed to work. It helped me to know that I was not necessarily the best in the gym. It's much easier to remain driven if you have someone pushing you each step of the way.

A month before the American Classic, I had turned sixteen. That meant I could take my driving test and finally get my license. I had taken a driver's ed class and my parents had given me lessons in one of the high school parking lots, so I felt I was ready. I passed the test the first time, even though I had to parallel park behind a boat! Really? How many boats was I going to run across in *Oklahoma*?

At last my parents handed over the keys to my Saturn! I didn't think of the car in terms of my gaining independence, because I'd been traveling all over the world without my parents since I was a kid, but I knew getting a license meant I could drive myself to and from the gym and to school each day. I'd be giving back to my parents a substantial amount of time. It felt great to finally give them a break.

At sixteen, I also became a businesswoman—one who wore leotards and tights instead of a suit. Through ProServ, I was introduced to Sallie Weaver, the owner of Elite GK. Many of my leotards during my gymnastics career had come from her sportswear company, so I jumped at the chance to be its first celebrity endorser and start my own signature sportswear line of leotards, bike shorts, and warm-ups. I was the opposite of a fashion plate when it came to teen attire, but I sure knew leotards. I had strong ideas about design, fabric, and what was comfortable. Tessa sketched a logo I liked and we were off and . . . tumbling.

This period of time after I turned sixteen, when I grew several inches and put on some weight, learned to drive a car, and started my sportswear line, is what I look back on as my "rebellious" period. With more people demanding my time and more obligations, I wanted to make more decisions about my life. That included at the gym. In truth, it was a pretty innocent period because I was not one to buck Steve's authority or talk back to him during competitions or threaten to quit the gym if he didn't give in to one of my ultimatums. I made no ultimatums. "Rebellious" for me was what I now did when I got into trouble and Steve said, "Go sit in the lobby." His expectation was that I would sit in the lobby and wait until the end of practice to do conditioning with the others. Steve had realized long ago that this was the best punishment strategy: no fun stuff, just work. But since he had not specified for me to wait, I defiantly charged through the lobby and got in my car and drove home. He completely forgot I had a license! I was testing him, showing what happened if he kept telling me what to do. I was no rebel, but I wanted to remind him I was growing up.

I had been so quiet all my years at Dynamo and had basically done everything Steve asked of me. When I had an opinion, I kept it to myself and allowed him to be autocratic. But around this time, I became more assertive about everything gymnastics. In kind, Steve and Peggy allowed me a little autonomy and more say about my training. It became even more of a team effort now that they were even asking for my opinion on occasion. There was no need for drastic change. I simply wanted some acknowledgment that I was an equal part of the team. Instead of talking about me, they could talk *with* me.

Steve had likely seen my shift in attitude coming. In fact, since the Olympics, he had given the media more access to me because he saw that I was becoming increasingly comfortable doing interviews. (As long as the questions were about gymnastics, I was fine.) Steve never told me to smile or felt the need to prepare me for tough questions, and he never suggested that I put on makeup, fix my hair, or wear anything but sweats and jeans. Looking back, I kind of wish he had.

Steve and Peggy allowed me to assert my independence in what, I now realize, were carefully monitored situations. Steve continued to bring in many different clinicians to help with specific skills or choreography. One time, a clinician worked with our whole group of six or seven girls, and she wanted us to wear ankle and wrist weights while practicing on the balance beam. To me, it seemed dangerous to practice skills while weighed down, and I couldn't comprehend how it was going to help any of us. I needed to give Peggy only a slight glance, and with a nod she gave me the okay to go off and train on my own—without the weights.

Another time they brought in a choreographer who decided I should change my classical style. She wanted me to shake things up . . . and shake my shoulders and hips. She insisted that cutesy, jazzy routines were all the rage and said, "You've always done ballet; let's try something different." In the past, I had been reticent to object when I was told anything by an adult, particularly a visiting coach or choreographer. But I felt I had earned the right to stand up for myself. I would give almost anything a try, but then if it wasn't working I wasn't going to do it. The whole point of a floor routine is to express one's personality and *peppy* just wasn't my style. While they both insisted I give it a good try, I appreciated that when Peggy and Steve saw it wasn't working, they backed me on the decision to ditch the "new" Shannon and stick with the tried and true.

I had automatically qualified for the 1993 World Championship by winning individual medals at the Olympic Games; Kerri and Dominique Dawes earned invitations with strong performances at the American Classic. So with the previous all-around World champion Kim Zmeskal taking a break from gymnastics, Kerri, Dominique, and I were America's representatives against an impressive field of gymnasts from Romania and the former Soviet Union. I had missed the 1992 Worlds due to my elbow injury, so I was excited to compete again at this event. The 1991 Worlds in Indianapolis had been my biggest competition prior to the 1992 Olympics, and I had drawn from my experiences there on the big stage to get me through the Olympic Trials and the Olympic Games.

I was still on a roll that began with the 1992 Trials and continued through the Olympic Games. I showed extraordinary consistency during the World all-around competition and qualified for all four events finals once again. After I won every event during the preliminary round, broadcaster Kathy Johnson, a former Olympian, stated that she hadn't seen a gymnast so dominant since Nadia Comăneci in 1976. During the all-around final, I hit clean routines on the first three events, but it wasn't until beam that I slipped past Romania's Gina Gogean to finish in first place. The gold medal I wore that night at the award ceremony, as "The Star-Spangled Banner" played and the American flag was raised, signified that I was the women's world gymnastics champion! I could picture my mother jumping up and down when I called her with the good news.

After hitting all my routines once again and winning the gold medal in the all-around, I was fired up to compete in the next four rounds of competition. But I woke up that night violently ill. This was a shock to me because in my whole life I had never been this sick. We had a day or two before the event finals began, so I prayed this was just a twenty-four-hour bug. The trouble was I could keep nothing down. I couldn't eat and I couldn't work out. The team trainer got me a bottle of Tums, and I tried eating a small amount of plain rice and crackers.

I was so determined to compete on the day of vault and uneven bar finals that I managed to get my leotard on and hair up. I was representing my country, and I felt I owed it to the girls who hadn't received a spot on the team. I never scratched (opted not to compete), except when it was done well in advance of a meet, but Steve gave me a much-needed reality check. We felt we had no choice but to scratch vault. It made sense because we knew I wasn't going to compete vaults that were strong enough to win a medal unless several girls fell—and that wasn't how I wanted to win a medal anyhow. By scratching vault, I would have to do only uneven bars that night. We hoped I could muster enough energy to get through a thirty-second bar routine and then rest for beam and floor the next night.

I did make it through bars that night. In fact, I captured the gold medal! And my teammate Dominique Dawes took the first of two silvers she'd win at Worlds. It was certainly a boost that the USA took the top two spots.

I got some sleep that night, but on the final day of event finals, I still felt horrible. Was it a bug or something I ate? Steve thought it may have been a reaction to the ibuprofen that I was taking for my back. Maybe I wasn't eating enough while taking the medication.

That night I got to the arena and felt dizzy warming up, which is not a great feeling when you're attempting fairly dangerous skills on a balance beam that is four inches wide. Peggy wanted me to scratch both balance beam and floor exercise. But I was already too upset about missing vault. I kept thinking I could pull it together. Plus, I wanted to redeem myself after a far from stellar performance on beam during the all-around final.

However, this was different from powering through an injury—I could hardly see straight.

Warm-ups concluded and finally it was time. I marched out to the arena and up onto the podium in a daze. On my first tumbling series my feet completely missed the beam and I slid off, scraping my left side on the beam, bouncing off my rib cage before I hit the floor. I was a bit stunned but regrouped quickly, thinking, "Okay, get back on the beam; finish with some dignity." I made it through a couple of skills before doing an easy back handspring quarter turn to a handstand. I hit the floor for the second time. I found myself getting on the beam for the third time in less than sixty seconds. I would have preferred to crawl under a table.

I chose to look for a silver lining, and if there was a saving grace it was that I successfully completed "the Miller." An amazing skill that Peggy dreamed up one Saturday morning, the Miller was a back handspring with a quarter turn to handstand, hop half turn, landing in a handstand with a 180-degree split. A new skill is named after a gymnast only if she or he competes it successfully during World or Olympic competition. No one had ever performed this difficult move before, so after I executed it mistake-free during the World all-around competition, it was named for me. Now I did it again and though it wasn't perfect I was relieved to stay on the beam. Falling is bad enough, but falling on a move named for me would have been the height of embarrassment that night.

I completed the rest of my skills and thought, "Oh, please let me land on my feet on the dismount." Hoping not to land short, I pulled it a little too hard and landed on the backs of my heels and rotated onto my bottom. I saluted the judges and headed for the stairs. One part of me wanted to race to the nearest bathroom and hide; another part was terrified to face Peggy at the bottom of the stairs. She was not happy that I had pushed to compete when I wasn't at full strength. Competing at well below 100 percent was not acceptable. We gave each other space.

I was supposed to go into the warm-up gym and then immediately march out for the beam award ceremony with the other seven competitors, and then I was to return backstage and then march right back out for floor exercise finals. Instead, Steve told me to sit. He did not want me getting sick at the award ceremony or on the floor exercise mat before everyone competed. He found me half a banana, and Peggy got me some water. They both insisted I get something into my stomach. Kathy Johnson came over and offered me a PowerBar. I took a bite of the banana and a few bites of the bar. I worried I wouldn't be able to keep it down but swallowed anyway. Meanwhile, Steve was deciding whether he should tell the officials that I needed to withdraw from floor exercise finals.

By the time the girls returned from the award ceremony, I was feeling a little better. Everything had stayed in my stomach. Steve asked me to make my final decision about competing on floor. I wasn't sure what to do. Then Steve asked me to listen to something. I heard my name being called. It was a surreal moment. The crowd had been amazing throughout the week and now they were calling my name! Steve could see in my eyes that I was going to compete. He said, "All right, we're looking for a little redemption."

At that moment, I couldn't imagine even making it through one tumbling pass. But I figured it would be easier to stay on a forty-by-forty-foot floor than a four-inch-wide balance beam. So I forced myself to focus the best I could.

For ninety seconds the anger and frustration over my truly horrendous beam performance overshadowed my nausea and empowered me to fight through each tumbling pass. I knew that night I had to leave it all on the floor, and the crowd helped carry me by clapping along to the music. As I hit my final pose at the end of the routine, I was ready to collapse. I had pushed my body to the limit. That night I was rewarded for my efforts with a medal: a gold medal!

The lesson I took away from my improbable victory on floor was that when mistakes happen and you take a fall, if you dig down deep and get back up, good things can happen. I had just been crowned the new World champion in women's gymnastics when, in front of the same crowd, I fell three times on one balance beam routine. What happened at Worlds reaffirmed my belief (a similar lesson) that no matter how bad your mistake is you must put it behind you and move forward. You can't win if you aren't in the game.

I didn't feel well on the victory stand, or for at least a week after. Yet despite my mystery illness, I was very pleased with my overall performance in Birmingham. Winning the all-around gold medal at Worlds was certainly one of the highlights of my career, but I was equally excited that I had qualified for all four event finals. True, I had done it in the Olympics as well, but I knew it was a rarity for gymnasts to qualify for all the events. People tend to remember me as a beam specialist, and sometimes I do that myself. But over the years at major competitions, I finished first in all four events, even vault. Back then, I felt it was important that I be successful on all four apparatuses. Today, when I look back at what I accomplished at the 1993 World Championship, I am reminded that I was by definition "an all-around gymnast."

19

I went on to win the all-around and again qualified for all four event finals at the Olympic Sports Festival, capturing three golds and a silver. That meet took place in San Antonio, so I was glad to do so well in front of my grandparents. I had come a long way since that Alamo Classic in 1988. I truly appreciated they were proud of me. Grandma and Grandpa Miller would even raise the Olympic flag in their yard whenever I was in town.

The Sports Festival proved to be a great tune-up for the U.S. Championship in Salt Lake City. Having sat out the optional portion the year before because of my elbow, I hoped to put in a good showing. I did better than that, as I won the all-around, beating out Dominique Dawes and Kerri Strug to become the U.S. champion. I leaped into Steve's arms. The microphones picked it up as he was complimenting me as we walked off. Instead of saying, "You're the queen," for some reason he said, "You're the president."

My dad is correct when he says that I did things backward by winning medals in the Olympics, then the all-around at Worlds, and then the all-around at Nationals, instead of doing it in reverse order. At Nationals, I won two more gold medals on bars and floor, a silver on vault, and, despite a fall, a bronze on beam. I was performing better than ever and racking up medals and titles. By this time, Kerri decided to leave Dynamo and train at home in Arizona, and I was back to being the sole Olympian in the gym.

Meanwhile, Tessa was planning on leaving home. In the fall, my scientifically inclined sister would be attending Caltech in Pasadena. It was hard getting used to that idea. I loved my sister dearly, and her going off to college seemed to creep up on me. I fear that I dealt with it by focusing on my gymnastics goals and school, protecting myself from how much I was going to miss her.

I had never really considered how Tessa and Troy felt about my so-called celebrity after returning from Barcelona. I didn't notice if or how it affected them because I was always at school or in the gym. While I was doing my gymnastics, Tessa was focusing on academics or off swimming, running cross-country, or horseback riding. And Troy was busy doing karate, tae kwon do, or soccer. Looking back, I realize Tessa was very proud of me and was always ready to defend my skill and accomplishments; however, at times, my having an income at such a young age must have made life a little frustrating for her. With part-time jobs and some help from my parents, she was able to purchase her own car, but she did not have much extra spending money and it was hard for her to head off to college in California with so many expenses looming. In fact, a laptop computer (almost essential by the time she got to college) was not something within her budget. When I overheard my mom and dad discussing how they could afford to either buy her a computer or visit her in California, but not both, I realized this was a time when my "income" could benefit Tessa. My parents kept my earnings separate, and I wasn't really aware of how much was there, but I asked if I had enough to afford her computer. She was happy and grateful to have a new computer for school, and I was glad that my gymnastics ability could also help my sister.

Now it would be just Troy and me. Unlike Tessa, he'd grown up with me already in the spotlight, so he didn't have to make as big an adjustment to my newfound fame. While he may have gotten tired of people asking if I was his sister, he was happy for me when I did well and eager to focus on his own endeavors.

But all was not well with me. I was so pleased by my performances at Worlds and Nationals that I should have been energized to train for the next competition, but instead I sunk into a mysterious funk that summer and was going sideways rather than forward. For the first time, I was unenthusiastic about gymnastics. That was probably reflected in how many times Steve kicked me out of the gym for lack of effort or attentiveness. My back was hurting really badly, and I was suffering from horrible shin splints. I was coming home from the gym in agony every day. At night, the pain in my shins was so excruciating that I cried myself to sleep.

I attended Steve's annual picnic for his gymnasts and coaches. I played volleyball and other outdoor games that had nothing to do with gymnastics and had a good time. When I got home, I walked in and told my parents, "I'm finished with gymnastics. I'm done!" I was dead serious.

One great thing about my parents throughout my career is that they never overreacted to anything. They didn't try to talk me out of my decision; they wanted to wait and see if that was what I really wanted to do. Of course, they were concerned about my pain, but they weren't the type to allow their kids to quit something just because the going got tough. It was an issue of commitment and of follow-through. Every person at some point in his or her life thinks about quitting something. They wanted me to understand that there was a significant difference between quitting and following a new path. Which was I trying to do?

So my parents invited Steve and Peggy to the house to see if they could help me figure this out. They didn't want me to make a rash decision that I would come to regret. I thought, "Sure, let them come, because there's nothing they can say to change my mind." The five of us sat around the dining room table where we had Christmas and Thanksgiving meals together. My parents and Peggy let Steve take the lead.

He just looked at me and said, "Okay, what's going on? Tell me why you want to stop training."

I looked back at him and said, "Well, my back hurts, my shins are killing me, I'm coming home from practice crying every day, and I just don't want to do it anymore."

So he said, "Okay. So why do you want to quit gymnastics?"

I was thinking that he must be thick. Didn't he hear me? "I just told you what's going on. My back hurts; my shins hurt; I'm tired of being in such pain."

He said calmly, "I understand the pain, but you know these are not career-ending injuries. Your back and shins are going to stop hurting and we can make sure that happens fairly quickly. So forget about the temporary pain and help me understand why you want to stop gymnastics."

I couldn't really explain my reasoning beyond the pain, so I just said, "It's just something I need to do."

Steve finally said, "If you truly want to stop, I have no problem with that. But I want you to give yourself the benefit of just making sure that this is really what you want. I don't want you to quit cold turkey, so do something for me. Come to the gym for three hours each morning, four days a week, for the next three weeks. You can work on new skills while allowing your back and shins time to heal. Then after three weeks if you still want to quit, I won't stand in your way."

After all the training I had done, I felt I could do three hours a day in my sleep, especially since the first hour at the gym was just stretching and warm-up. So I agreed, halfheartedly. He knew better than to make it a competition of wills because he had no way of winning. He was well aware of my stubbornness.

So I returned to the gym, fully planning on training for only three weeks. Steve rearranged his schedule so he could work with me each morning during that time. Like he promised, we didn't train anything that would aggravate my back or shins, which meant I spent most of my time on uneven bars. After the first week, I had learned a new bar skill, and my back and my shins were beginning to feel a little bit better. By the end of the second week, my injuries were feeling okay. In the third week, they were feeling good and I was doing a second new skill on bars, one that would end up being named after me.

Steve had not made much of an attempt to steer me back to the sport, other than to make sure I completed my three-week obligation. However, in that third week, he began to drop a few bread crumbs, like, "Hey, I heard Dominique Dawes signed on to do the Goodwill Games. That's great news, Shannon, because you can sit on your couch and cheer for her on TV." That was completely fabricated, but I admit it was an artful way for him to push exactly the right buttons at the right time. He needed to gauge whether I still had that competitive fire. He didn't want to talk me into something that I wasn't truly, in my heart, completely on board with.

All good coaches know how to manipulate their athletes. It's not always a bad thing. It's that pep talk they give them before a big game or a reminder of all the hard work they have already put into their dream. At various times, coaches need to find positive forms of motivation, something that speaks to that particular athlete. For me, during that third week, I needed help realizing that my desire to quit was not about injuries or a need to move on to something different. Instead, it was about a lack of goals.

Goal-setting had always been such a huge theme in my life, but after winning five medals in the Olympics, the all-around at the U.S. Championship, and three gold medals at the World Championship, I had forgotten to set new goals. I had become bored training routine after routine with no specific competition in mind. When you have precise goals, you're often able to overlook nagging pains and fatigue and not lose focus and motivation. I was a forward thinker, so when there was nothing to look forward to I didn't know what to do with myself. Quitting shouldn't ever be an option; changing lanes can certainly be a valid option, but I had no scenario in which I left one career for a more exciting one. I had no true plans to replace gymnastics with anything else.

I'm not exactly sure when I decided that I didn't want to leave gymnastics after all. I never said to anyone, "I've decided not to quit." I just kept driving myself to the gym after the three weeks were up. The hours got longer and the skills more difficult, but Steve and I had a shift in our mental approach to how I trained. Steve was forced to take into account and always remember that I was not a machine and needed to be nurtured along the way. And I realized that it was critical for me to write down new goals and create a plan of attack for how I'd accomplish them. Steve gave me time to work on new skills, realizing that this had always been one of my favorite reasons to do gymnastics.

I was able to focus on the future once again. I rededicated myself to the sport, with mind, body, and soul. *You give it 100 percent or nothing; there is no in-between.*

At the end of the three-week period, my physical condition was no longer a factor. I may have still felt pain, but it was of no concern. In the past, I had worked through jammed ankles, pulled hamstrings, and broken bones for the simple reason that I had something specific I wanted to achieve. Goal-setting was now back in play. But what goals? *Hey, the 1994 Goodwill*

Games are coming up in Russia, and of course the 1994 World Championship will be in Brisbane, Australia. And though it could only be considered a "long long-term" goal, in the back of my mind, and the minds of my coaches and parents, was that the 1996 Olympics would be held in the United States. By creating those dreams, I had something to work for again.

20

Some gymnasts retire after one Olympics due to injury. Others, who are now four to eight years older than they were when they began their Olympic quests, want to move on to the next part of their lives. A third, rarely mentioned reason that these young female athletes don't often pursue multiple Olympics is that not all coaches think to adjust the training as these girls mature. I give tremendous credit to Steve and Peggy because they understood that I couldn't train at seventeen to nineteen in the way I did when I was ten to twelve. The biggest difference in my training after the 1992 Olympics is that I didn't need to do as many repetitions of the skills I'd been doing for a decade. Instead of doing fifteen routines, as the younger, less-experienced girls did at Dynamo, I'd now do ten or twelve really good ones. Our new focus was on quality over quantity.

We continued to do an hour to an hour and a half of stretching and conditioning at the start of practice and then usually an hour on each apparatus. Some days we'd do three events, other times four. We would rotate events, depending on the day. There was a consistency to the training, but Steve and Peggy tried to keep it from getting boring. That was my regular routine and little changed heading into a big meet. My larger goals were written out, but it was imperative that I never lost sight of my daily goals as well.

In the back of my mind, I always wanted to be five feet tall. I was happy when that eventually happened, but I always assumed it would be after I retired. When you're a gymnast you don't really want a growth spurt. All of a sudden, here I was with a different height and weight distribution; I felt different and my timing and balance were off. Skills I had been doing for years were suddenly giving me trouble. I believe my significant four-inch growth spurt had a lot to do with my back and shin pain. I was taller and heavier, and my center of gravity had shifted. We were back to physics. It simply takes more force and energy to move a greater mass; and the change in rotational inertia affects the timing of each trick.

Steve and Peggy weren't concerned that I grew so much so quickly or that I put on weight as a result. It was life; I was going to grow. But it was something we had to take into account. They reminded me, "Hey, it's natural that you're going through this; we're going to work with it." Steve would try to turn my body's changes into positives when I began to get aggravated. On bars, he pointed out that I had improved because of my added inches. It was true that I now had longer lines, which were more aesthetically pleasing for the judges. On vault, he'd say, "Because you have a little bit more weight, you can actually bend the springs on the springboard. You can do a bigger vault now!" He was correct here, too. I'd always had stick legs and couldn't get a whole lot of spring off the board, but with added inches and a bit more weight I had gained power. So I adjusted to my new body by appreciating the positive side of the changes, and it never became an overwhelming issue.

Another adjustment I had to make was to the new Code of Points. Every four years it changed as the sport progressed. That meant the value of skills on all the events went up or down. Some skills that had a high value when I was training for the 1992 Olympics had lesser value as we moved toward the 1996 Olympics. So moving through 1993 and into 1994, I had to upgrade the difficulty level in all my routines. A few moves could be left as they were, but the makeup of my routines changed significantly. It was just the way the sport worked, and I didn't find it daunting because my training had been continuous. There was never a question of "Can I do it?" As a gymnast you learn to roll with the punches. You get the new Code, the rules for your routines, and then you get to work. (You even take it in stride when they change the equipment!)

The new Code wasn't really about easier or harder; it was just different. My intention was to have the highest amount of difficulty in a routine that I could hit. I didn't want to throw everything and the kitchen sink into a routine if I was going to fall four times. It was a tricky balancing act trying to devise a routine I could perform flawlessly while knowing I had to risk a certain amount of difficulty for mine to stand out.

On beam, there might have been some different choreography. I might have added a skill to a series or taken one away or done a couple of different jumps. The routine in essence would change, but some of the more foundational skills might have stayed the same. I added a new mount, but there was no need to change the dismount I had been competing for over five years, because it had the highest difficulty value. I was the only American to compete a full twisting doubleback at the time, so it was a great way to set my routine apart from others.

I also kept one of my favorite skills, a back extension roll, in my balance beam routine. When people saw that extension roll I heard a gasp: "Ahhhh!" No one else did that skill, so it really made my routine stand out.

My uneven bar routine changed, too. For the most part, you compete the same uneven bar routine for the Olympic cycle. Tweaks are fine, but if you're going to do a complete overhaul you'd best do it toward the beginning of the four years. It wasn't as easy as adding a skill or taking one out. Maybe you'd work a new release move and then decide to throw it in. Then you'd have to ask yourself if that new release move changed your direction so that you now needed to add another skill to ensure you're swinging in the right direction. You'd have to look at the routine in its entirety.

Early in 1994, I tried out a new skill during competition, a one-and-a-half pirouette on the high bar to a handstand on the low bar. But I'm not sure if I ever completely understood this skill. I thought back to around 1990 when I was learning, also with great difficulty, another bar skill called a Gienger, a formidable release move named after Eberhard Gienger, an Olympic gymnast for Germany in the 1970s. For this skill, the gymnast swings upward and releases the bar with her hands, and then completes a backward flip and half turn before grasping the bar. I was used to visualizing skills and routines. If I could picture it in my head, I could usually do it. But bar skills were often difficult for me to *see*—I had to feel my way along—and I just couldn't visualize doing this skill from the release of the bar to the catch. I kept working it but would be frustrated that neither my mind nor my body seemed to adjust. When I was successful it seemed more like luck than anything else.

At one point, Steve invited a clinician named Valeri Liukin to help his team with skills on each apparatus. Liukin had won two gold and two silver medals while competing for the Soviet Union in the 1988 Olympics. He would eventually become well-known in America as the coach of Olympic champions Carly Patterson, and his daughter, Nastia Liukin, but at the time I understood him to be one of the most technically proficient, elegant gymnasts in the world. One Saturday I stayed after gym working, while Steve and Valeri talked. All of a sudden, Valeri, with no protective grips or a warm-up of any kind, jumped up onto a *girls'* single rail bar and performed a flawless Gienger! I stared in awe. He then explained to me that sometimes you don't have to *see* it; it's enough to trust your instincts. He said, "Focus on the takeoff and the regrasping of the bar; the rest will happen. Don't force it." For the rest of my career I never again tried to visualize that particular skill, and I rarely missed it. It was yet another critical lesson. In the world of gymnastics, with all the high-speed flips and turns, and the need for split-second decisions, I had to learn to trust my instincts and not overthink it. So on the Gienger and my new pirouette move, I focused on my hand placement and let the rest happen.

My uneven bar dismount changed completely. I had one dismount in 1992 at the Olympics, and then I changed it the next year for the 1993 World Championship. I'd competed a full twisting doubleback dismount for years but changed it to the double layout, two flips in a straight body position. My routine needed a little facelift, something that the judges had not seen before from me.

I was known for being fearless, but at times almost every gymnast is going to come up against something that makes him or her uneasy. For a time, I developed a mental block and could not let go of the bar on one of my releases, the Tkatchev. It's a familiar issue for many young gymnasts, but I'd been competing the skill for seven years. I'd already competed it more than once at the World Championship and at the Olympic Games. I was sixteen or seventeen and knew that it was illogical for me to suddenly have this fear, but I could not talk myself into doing the release. Luckily, at this point in my career, I was able to walk up to Steve and say, "I have no idea what's wrong. I know this is ridiculous, but I cannot let go of the bar. What can we do about this?"

I won't say that Steve was happy about it, but he had been around long enough to know that such things happen. It's far better to work with the athlete on his or her issues than to simply make demands or dole out punishment. We went back to "timers" for a week, which is like doing a partial skill. I worked the mechanics of each segment as if I were learning the skill from scratch. At first we focused on the first portion of the skill, the release, without worrying about catching the bar. Steve spotted me on every try. On the third week, it was time for me to go it alone. I released the bar successfully a couple of times and the fear was gone as quickly as it had appeared. We were able to work through a difficult patch through teamwork, the hallmark of our relationship.

Vault scoring had also changed, and I knew I could no longer rely on the vault that I competed in 1992 because it had been devalued from 10.0 to 9.8. I had to continue to grow and change with the times. The Code of Points listed all the vaults and their new values. Unless you created a new vault, you had to pick one. At the time there wasn't a lot to teach on vault. You could add a half twist, or you could add a full twist, forward versus backward. I had competed the Yurchenko full twist in 1992 and parts of 1993 while training a higher-level vault. And I'd worked on and even competed a Yurchenko double twist in the American Classic, but it still wasn't quite strong enough for a big score. With more difficulty demanded, and my Yurchenko double twist not quite up to par, I began to work on a Yurchenko half twist front layout. I typically earned a spot in the finals and scored high enough to win medals, but those were at competitions that required only *one* strong vault. It was not so easy for me during the individual vault finals where you had to perform two strong and completely different vaults. Vault was not my finest event, but in 1993 I was still one of the best in the world when it came to my first or primary vault. Throughout my career, I struggled to maintain a second vault with a high start value that I could perform well during the few competitions two vaults were required. By 1996, the vaults became outrageous in their level of difficulty. Suddenly, many girls were competing a one-and-a-half or a double twist. I don't feel I went backward; other athletes simply passed me by.

In my younger years, I competed different floor routines almost every year, but as I got older, I kept them for at least two years. I might have changed my tumbling passes or a nuance here and there. Or I might have felt the need for completely new floor music and choreography. If I was doing a routine, I wanted it to be something that I loved and felt I could *perform*. I wanted it to reflect my personality. I didn't want to dread the dance part to the point that I couldn't focus on the tumbling, which was the more difficult part. The two fabulous choreographers who helped me through most of my career were Nancy Roach and Geza Pozsar. They knew I preferred violin, and I favored a more artistic, classical side in my dance. It was through that music and style that I felt I could tell a story, *my* story.

When I was very young I performed to music from *Cats*. In 1991, I danced to an upbeat piece, "When the Saints Go Marching In." At the 1992 Olympics, the music was by Sandor Lakatos. I absolutely loved that routine and competed it again at the 1993 and 1994 Worlds. In 1995, Peggy and Steve decided to try new music, a new routine, and that's when they brought in the new choreographer who wanted me to try some out-of-the-box moves. The routine she came up with was a jazzy number, and the music choice startled me at first. Where were the violins I adored? At one point while learning the routine, I was told to shake my hips, my shoulders, and my head and "be unruly." I wasn't sure if I should laugh or cry. I could have sworn I was being "punk'd," had that term existed at the time. I was a color-inside-the-lines type of gal and for choreography, especially, I liked to be *in* the box! The music just didn't fit me. I gave it a try during a couple competitions, but my heart was never in it and that routine did not last long. Soon I was back to my beloved style with a dramatic version of *Cocher Ralentis Tes Chevaux*. At the 1996 Olympics it became "Two Guitars," another routine I truly enjoyed.

The new routines I was doing in 1993, 1994, and after were under different rules than the ones I competed in 1992. All of a sudden forward tumbling was en vogue. In addition, I now needed to complete four tumbling passes instead of three. That reflected a significant change in the sport. While my front tumbling pass was much easier than some of the ones I performed in 1992, I now had to add an extra pass. That new pass would take time away from two things I cherished in my routine—dance and artistry.

Steve, Peggy, and I went over the new Code of Points a little bit at a time. We'd think about reconfiguring my routines, deciding what to keep or discard and what to add because of the different values placed on the skills. Steve also brought in judges to look at the new routines and make sure we had all the elements needed.

I was getting older, but I felt I was still learning from Peggy and Steve, be it technical aspects of the sport or life lessons. The three of us were a great team, and even though we would have some minor tiffs as we trained, we all had the same goal and worked through them. We were each strong-willed and stubborn, but somehow we made it work.

At times, I sensed my parents felt left out of the decision-making, particularly my mother. When watching workouts, Mom would on occasion want me to do one thing and Steve would have me do another. It was tough being in the middle, listening to my coach but knowing my mom was an astute judge. Steve respected her insight, too. One day during training she went into his office and said, "Shannon's missing a C on floor exercise." In routines, elements are graded A, B, C, D, and so forth, with A being the lowest value. A gymnast needed to have specific amounts of each letter value in each routine. Steve was in no mood to hear about this possible mistake and declared, "No, no, no, she's not." So there I was caught between two people I loved and respected, while they both proceeded to write down my floor routine and go through it element by element. And yep, I was missing a C!

Mom had to walk a fine line. She was supportive as a mother and helped me in my career by giving her insights as a high-level judge, but she was also expected to back off and let a coach I trusted have full control of my gym life. When Mom and Steve had disagreements, I had to explain to her that when I was in the gym, Steve was my coach, period. She didn't like that so much, but that's the way I had to train. I was so grateful to both my parents for their efforts in trying to build a person, not just an athlete. I also appreciated that my coach was helping me become a well-rounded person. Everyone played their part on this team. Steve's job was not to help me with my math or remind me to clean my room. And I didn't want my parents to spot me on uneven bars. I needed them all to do what they did best. *We all have the same goal, so let's stay on track!*

21

I was training hard with the 1994 Worlds in my sights. I had been battling significant back pain for over a year, forcing me to water down my routines during various competitions, but we were getting past it. Then there was another setback. About a month prior to leaving for Brisbane, where Worlds would take place, I tore a stomach muscle. A doctor examined me, and I worked with a physical therapist, but the pain wouldn't go away. I could get used to competing with jammed ankles and severe shin splints, but this was different. Working through this pain was not an option. For other injuries I was still able to work on conditioning and flexibility during the healing process, but this tear was at my core, literally. It's not like I could tape it or slip on a brace. The tear would only get worse if I didn't rest. It would take time to heal, so there was genuine concern I wouldn't be able to perform at Worlds, even at far less than 100 percent.

My coaches and I had to decide quickly whether to give up my spot on the U.S. team so another gymnast would get the chance to compete. Ultimately, we decided I should soldier on and we'd work around my injury as best we could. Not that it was ever easy, but I always felt that I could get past an injury or rough time if I worked hard enough. Of course, my faith always played a critical role in my thinking. I knew that God was there with me every step of the way.

Training with a stomach muscle tear was a constant battle. I was shocked to discover how much I depended on those muscles for *everything*! As the competition grew near, I went all in, doing as many repetitions as I could manage without backsliding on any recovery. I knew that if I could get through training, the competition itself would be easier. In competition, I knew I could rely on muscle memory and be confident in the knowledge that I had the numbers behind me. When the green flag went up I would feel no pain.

Worlds turned out to be fun yet difficult because of the torn muscle. I wasn't terribly surprised that in the preliminaries, the one event final for which I didn't qualify was uneven bars. My lack of training showed in my shaky performance. Fortunately, I was able to get it together during the all-around and compete my full bar routine without a hitch, including doing the newly christened "Miller"—a one-and-half turn on the high bar to a straddle with flight to the low bar.

I was the defending champion in the all-around, but by thinking of myself as the underdog I was able to push through as I battled Romania's Lavinia Miloşovici down to the wire. Miloşovici, who won two individual gold medals in Barcelona, finished on beam while I was competing my vault. Each of my two vaults was clean in the air, but I took a forward hop on both landings. Would the deductions cost me a gold medal or were my scores high enough to put me in first place?

Pictures taken afterward on the victory podium of me, Lavinia, and bronze medalist Dina Kochetkova of Russia showed me as the girl with the widest grin. I'd become the first American to win back-to-back World all-around titles!

Two days later, I moved on to the event finals. Because I didn't have to train on uneven bars, I wasn't in as much pain. Vault was the first event, as always. I was excited because I had been working on a new second vault that brought my start value up and gave me a better opportunity to medal. My first vault went well. For my second vault I attempted a Tsuk half-front layout, also known as an "Arabian." This new vault would come to be called the "Phelps." It was named after Jaycie Phelps, who, in 1996, would become my Olympic teammate and good friend. We both competed it, hoping to introduce the skill as our own and have it named after us. But I fell on my bottom at this World Championship and Jaycie would hit the skill at the 1995 World Championship in Sabae, Japan, claiming the Phelps as her own. She beat me to it.

During the second day of event finals at the 1994 World Championship I competed on both balance beam and floor exercise. I would not medal on floor, finishing fourth after stepping out-of-bounds on my first tumbling pass. But prior to that misstep was the balance beam. I did so poorly during warm-ups that Peggy considered scratching me. But after my humiliating three-fall 1993 balance beam performance at Worlds, which was by all accounts the biggest disaster of my career, I wasn't about to pull out. I knew I could stay on the beam. I knew I could make it through. I was determined to prove to myself and everyone else that 1993 was a fluke.

I loved performing skills that few others were competing, and my beam routine at Worlds was filled with difficulty. Many people contend it was *the* best beam routine of my career. I know it was one of the best. When I stuck my full twisting doubleback dismount, it sealed the deal for a huge score and World balance beam gold! *Redemption.*

Yes, it was a bit of redemption from the previous year, but during the routine that was the furthest thing from my mind. In the heat of battle, you live in the now and take it a step at a time. *Don't look back; just keep moving forward.*

After some sightseeing with Peggy that included holding koalas and petting kangaroos, I left Australia and returned home with my mission accomplished. I had won my second all-around World Championship. Worlds also served as a huge stepping-stone to the 1996 Olympics. It showed people that I was still there and was up to Code and doing exciting and difficult routines. I had to be included in the mix heading into the next two years.

My stomach muscle was fully healed by the time of the next major competition in 1994: the Goodwill Games in St. Petersburg, Russia, from July 23 to August 7. Two thousand athletes from fifty-six countries competed in the sixteen-day event, the third edition of Ted Turner's creation to promote international harmony through sports. The host country won the most gold and overall medals, but the U.S. was a strong runner-up and I did my part by taking home five medals. It was disappointing to finish fourth in the team competition but, aside from me, our four-girl team hadn't much international experience. This competition was a way for the other girls to gain significant exposure.

The all-around final was tight and I was narrowly defeated by Dina Kochetkova, but I later won gold medals in the balance beam and floor exercise, along with silver medals on vault and bars. I felt I had done exceptionally well considering I was exhausted after competing in numerous meets with little downtime. Other top American gymnasts had stayed home for just that reason. I was pleased to have won five medals, but many were focused only on the color of my all-around medal, and it wasn't gold. When asked by the media how I was dealing with my *loss*, I was confused. Hadn't I just won a silver medal? And I'd won two gold medals and two more silvers in the event competitions. I'd finished in the top two in five events!

Steve and Peggy talked to me at length during the long flight home, helping me understand that these questions were not truly about a *loss*, but were about my previous success. This was the first time in a year and a half that I had not won gold in the all-around. *Was it over? Was it time to hang up the leotard?* It was difficult to hear the whispering.

Of course, I probably could have reversed that backward thinking by winning the all-around and other gold medals at the Nationals in late August, but I arrived in Nashville more worn out than ever. My legs were beat, and my painful shin splints had returned. During training at the arena, I went for a skill on the balance beam and my Jell-O legs gave out. There was nothing I could do to stop myself from landing hard on my head. I was lucky to come away with just a headache and bruised ego. It was a very distinct moment in time for me, when I was shocked by the realization of "I cannot push myself anymore." I'd been training like crazy and competing when I should have been resting. I was known as a workhorse and didn't want to admit that I had hit my limit, but I finally voiced my concerns to Steve and Peggy. It was too late. Here we were the day before the meet began, so my only attempt at rest was to put my feet up until the next night.

The compulsory competition, held on the first day, counted as 60 percent of the overall score. I did well during day one with the exception of beam, on which I had a large balance check, a big wobble. My score reflected that error. Overall, I ended the day with a slight lead over the competition. During the second day, optionals, the dreaded beam struck again. I got another large deduction when I underrotated my dismount and touched my hands to the floor. On that night, Dominique Dawes was clearly the better gymnast. During that week she would take the all-around gold medal and gold in all four individual events. I was left with silver all five times. This time I didn't see winning a silver medal as a victory. I knew I hadn't competed the routines I was capable of doing. I was happy for my friend but not pleased with my performance. I wasn't supposed to be peaking at this competition, but I was troubled that I had gone in not fully prepared. You can't plan for injuries, but taking time to rest and recuperate *is* something you strategize. We had not planned well.

Having had no first-place finishes at the U.S. Championship, I was now fielding questions from the media about my supposed decline on a regular basis. *Shannon, do you feel you're getting too old to stick around for two more years? Shannon, do you think you should retire and make way for the new crop?* I guess to some degree I understood their thinking. After a substantial period when I was winning, winning, winning—including back-to-back Worlds—everyone thought that I'd never stop winning. When I finished anywhere but first place, they were shocked and assumed it was all downhill from there. *Whoa! I touched my hands on a dismount; I didn't fall off a cliff.*

Hearing negative reactions to my second-place finishes was difficult at first, but in a way it reenergized me. I had that moment when I stopped feeling sorry for myself and realized that I could turn this around. *You think I'm too old? You think I'm burnt out? You think this dog doesn't have any more new tricks? Just wait!* My entire career had been a testament to "talk is cheap." I wasn't one who talked a big game. I preferred action. I would use anyone's negative perception of my abilities to fuel the fire. The words "no" and "can't" always motivated me to prove otherwise. *Watch me!*

My coaches were not terribly happy with my results, but they were also looking at the big picture, which had me peaking at the 1996 Olympics. Although it would have been nice, none of us expected me to win every single meet I entered. But I was still up there as one of America's top two female gymnasts, and that was a secure place to be. We remembered that in Barcelona, the girls who won medals weren't necessarily the favorites going into the Olympics. Not only was I okay with being the underdog; I thrived on it.

In 1994, there were actually two World Championship events: the individual Worlds that took place in April in Australia, and the team Worlds that were held in November in Dortmund, Germany. After Nationals, USA Gymnastics began putting together a U.S. team to go to Germany, and both Steve and the federation were eager for me to participate. But I wasn't going to make the same mistake of competing when I was collapsing from fatigue. I told my parents that I needed to draw the line because I needed to rest until at least January, when the 1995 season would begin. I felt the need to assert myself and was adamant that I was staying home and taking a break.

Eventually, USA Gymnastics, Steve, and I came up with a compromise. I would travel to Germany as part of the team, but I would do *only* compulsories and then go home to rest. That would be fairly easy for me because compulsories were already part of my "downtime" training regimen. I had to take it up a notch, but without having to train or compete the more strenuous optionals, this would be like a vacation for my body.

But prior to leaving for the event, I suffered another injury. While a sore Achilles tendon is not something to brush off, I was thankful it wasn't something worse. I was limping when I competed in the compulsories in Germany, yet I performed solid routines on beam, vault, and floor exercise. The only imperfection was my feet slipping off the high bar during my dismount. I was embarrassed to make such a simple mistake, but I came away with a respectable score.

I had competed compulsories. I had followed the plan. Naturally, whether real or imagined, I felt pressure to compete optionals as well, "as long as I was there." It's too easy to get excited and want to compete; it's too easy to start thinking of medals and what-ifs. And that was exactly why I had been adamant about *not* training optionals at all. This was rest time and I needed to stick to the plan. I had done my part and I knew I was leaving the team in good hands. Kerri Strug and Dominique Dawes had been on the 1992 Olympic team with me and Amanda Borden; Amy Chow and Jaycie Phelps were incredible gymnasts. Dominique had our best scores on all four events in optionals as the U.S. captured a silver medal behind Romania and in front of Russia.

Upon arrival in the U.S., I was greeted with an onslaught of media asking me why I'd left the team. Apparently, no one had explained the circumstances to the press. People back home had read the papers and, not seeing my name among those who excelled at optionals, presumed I had a poor meet. The confusion over my departure contributed to speculation that I was on the downturn.

It was difficult to hear negative comments about Dortmund. I thought I was helping my team and my country by agreeing to do compulsories when I should have been at home taking care of my injuries and preparing for the next year. I had never expected a thank-you, but it hurt deeply that anyone would even consider that I'd left my team high and dry. I did my best to move beyond it.

My spirits were raised when I had the honor of receiving my second of three consecutive nominations for the Sullivan Award as the nation's top amateur athlete. I was also presented with the prestigious Dial Award for being the National High School Athlete of the Year. I flew to Washington, D.C., to accept the large Dial trophy. I had been feted often since the 1992 Olympics, but it was special to be appreciated for my academic work as well as athletics.

22

Some of the new girls at Dynamo who had moved from other states to train in our gym were being homeschooled. So it wasn't a big surprise when Steve strongly suggested that I be homeschooled in my senior year of high school. I wouldn't consider it. I could see the slippery slope ahead. Because I attended public school, I could train only for a limited amount of time in the morning before school and from the late afternoon into the evening. Having very specific times in which I could or could not train worked for me. It allowed me to take a break physically and mentally from non-stop gymnastics. I feared that if I switched to homeschooling, Steve would see I had flexible hours and decide I should work out for three hours in the morning, three hours in the afternoon, and three more hours in the evening. It would be a free-for-all and I would not have a life outside of the gym. I refused to live and breathe gymnastics.

At times, it felt as if I were a visitor to my high school because I was away so much. It could have been construed that gymnastics was what I did and school was my extracurricular activity, instead of the other way around, although I didn't feel this way. Oddly, I learned that I actually got more work accomplished when I was away than when I attended my classes. I was a ridiculously efficient person when I wanted to be and managed to do two weeks of schoolwork in three days, which gave me a little extra time to relax. I admit that gave me incentive to miss more days of my senior year of high school than I truly needed to for gym and competitions. It wasn't difficult to keep up, particularly because my father was such a good tutor.

I didn't go to my senior prom. I wanted to fit in but was too nervous to go. I analyzed the pros and cons of going to the prom and eventually decided that if I was fretting about it that much, it probably wasn't something I needed to spend the time or money doing. My mother reminds me I had three invitations but turned them all down. I didn't know the boys at all, and I'm not sure I could have said hello to them without turning bright red. Fortunately, I had a built-in excuse for not going to the prom with anyone: gymnastics. I didn't have to explain why I wasn't at prom because everyone assumed I was at a competition, even if no competition existed. In truth, it was my fear of the unknown that kept me from going.

There was never any doubt that I'd go to college, but even in my senior year I rarely broached the subject other than to ask, "Should I go to the University of Central Oklahoma or the University of Oklahoma?" Those were the only options I considered because I was going to be training for the Olympics during my freshman year and needed my college to be close to home and Dynamo. My father taught at UCO, about ten minutes from our house, so I knew that if I went there I wouldn't be homesick as a freshman. But I needed to look beyond my first year. I knew that eventually I would need to have a bit more separation. So the University of Oklahoma was where I set my sights.

I took the ACT and surprised myself and shocked my parents with my score. Tessa was the brilliant sister and I was the gymnast, so no one expected me to score almost as well. Now I had the test scores and the grades to get into college.

It was my goal in high school to match Tessa's 4.0 grade-point average. My chance to do that had ended quickly in my freshman year when I got what would be the lone blemish on my report card in four years. My dad had been helping me with my math homework whenever I had to miss school for training or competitions, which was quite often leading up to the 1992 Olympics. For years he'd taught physics to college students. Many of the young women who entered his class were brought up appreciating English and fearing math, so he made it a point to have his own daughters see that math was fun. I enjoyed geometry and on my homework assignments I got all the answers correct. So I stared in disbelief when I received my final grade—B. To the ultimate perfectionist that was unacceptable.

My teacher was a large, burly man with a full beard named Darrell Allen. My father went with me to speak to Mr. Allen, who explained that I got the B because on my assignments I didn't write out the questions from the book, only the answers. Apparently, I had been out of class when Mr. Allen hammered home the "need" to write out the questions. My father had been teaching me the math concepts and never considered the need to do such busywork. I offered to do extra credit assignments or whatever it took to show that I understood the concepts and deserved a better grade. There was no budging him.

I had always liked Mr. Allen; he was a wonderful teacher, even if I didn't always agree with his methods. I was very upset when he was later diagnosed with leukemia. My senior year, I helped my parents organize a silent auction at the Adventures in Gymnastics facility, which Steve had purchased from Jerry Clavier to supplement Dynamo Gymnastics in Oklahoma City. I'd met numerous sports figures during my travels and was humbled at the autographed items that came pouring in from such luminaries as Bart Conner, Nadia Comăneci, Bonnie Blair, Steffi Graf, Tiger Woods, Janet Evans, Nancy Kerrigan, Boomer Esiason, Tracy Austin, Oksana Baiul, Nolan Ryan, Kim Zmeskal, Dan Jansen, Gabriela Sabatini, Brian Boitano, Barry Switzer, and even Béla Károlyi. With the help of so many, we raised about $5,000 for Mr. Allen's family to cover medical expenses. He passed away just days later.

At 9:02 on the morning of April 19, 1995, I was walking to my car to head to class when I heard a huge thundering noise. I looked up, thinking it was odd to have a beautiful blue sky and hear thunder. I turned on the car radio and heard the breaking news that something had happened in downtown Oklahoma City but nobody knew what. At school it was all anyone was talking about. We would eventually learn that a truck bomb exploded at the Alfred P. Murrah Federal Building, leaving 168 people dead, 680 injured, and 324 buildings damaged or destroyed. This act of domestic terrorism devastated the entire country, but the way the people of Oklahoma rallied together and gained strength through tragedy was inspiring.

Days after the explosion, rescue crews from FEMA, law enforcement, and the fire departments and public safety continued to sift through the rubble looking for survivors. We prayed and prayed and prayed. My mother, who had been in northwest Oklahoma City at the time of the explosion, helped us pack food, water, and other supplies to take to the rescue workers. It was a difficult, confusing time, and Troy and I asked a lot of questions that our parents were unsure how to answer. We just tried to help in any small way we could.

My high school graduation on May 18, 1995, should have been a happier occasion, but the entire community was still reeling. Still, I was proud to be one of five hundred students wearing a cap and gown that day at Edmond North High School. I thought it peculiar that Tessa, Troy, and I would graduate from three different high schools as a result of expansion in our area.

Academically, I was thinking about going to college in the fall. As a gymnast, I was focusing on the Olympics that were only a year away, but in my subconscious I was probably considering that my career was nearing the end. Although, for now, I was still competing at the highest level. I was back in form early in 1995. I won the all-around at the Peachtree Classic in Atlanta, the site of the 1996 Olympics. I won another all-around at the American Classic, which qualified me for the Pan-American Games in Mar del Plata, Argentina.

Taking place right after I turned eighteen, the Pan-Am Games was a huge event that brought together athletes from forty-two nations to compete in thirty-six sports. Argentina served as the host country for the first time since the inaugural Pan-Am Games forty-two years before. After we won the gold medal in team competition over Cuba and Argentina, I led an American sweep in the all-around, with Amanda Borden winning silver and Amy Chow taking bronze. I went 1-2 with Amanda Borden on floor. Then I went 1-2 with Amy on uneven bars. Then Amy and I reversed our order to take gold and silver in vault finals. Although I didn't medal on beam—Amanda won gold—I was told I had won more medals than any other American gymnast in the history of the Pan-Am Games.

I was elated that my mother was able to take off time from the bank where she was vice president and, with the help of USA Gymnastics, book an affordable flight to Argentina. It was comforting knowing she was there to watch me perform and afterward spend some quality time with me. She came with me to a beach picnic that the coaches threw for the gymnasts and we got to talk and hike through the woods until there was a downpour. The heavy rain continued and we weren't sure our bus could make it to the gym that afternoon. The arena flooded and there was worry the meet was over.

It did move forward and the competition was a good one for me although it was not exactly smooth sailing. I recall my leather hand grip breaking during warm-ups. Taking care of your grips is paramount. They take at least a month to work in properly, so it was standard to carry an extra pair in your gym bag at all times. I had the extra pair but hadn't had time to work them in. Peggy grabbed them and tried to quickly flex the leather and shape it to surround the bar. It was the best we could do. From then on I switched off grips every couple of days to make sure I always had a competition-ready second pair.

The naysayers who had been documenting my decline temporarily disappeared while I won those three all-arounds. But they reappeared at the next big competition, the U.S. Championship in New Orleans, in mid-August. It didn't matter that I won three medals, including a gold in vault, because I received a silver in the all-around and was outscored by the Károlyis' new sensation, Dominique Moceanu. At thirteen, the diminutive Romanian-born gymnast was the youngest all-around champion ever at Nationals. Dominique Dawes won golds on bars and floor, ahead of Dominique Moceanu and me. So now a "rivalry" was growing among the two Dominiques and me.

I have been reminded so often that Dawes won all firsts and I won all seconds at the 1994 Nationals that I'll never forget the results, but I had to look up the all-around results at the 1995 Nationals to remind myself that Moceanu finished first and I second. I do clearly remember that I fell off the beam, though. I rarely forget my mistakes.

That fall, I enrolled at the University of Oklahoma in Norman. Steve was perturbed that I was starting college while I was training for the 1996 Olympics. He wanted me to delay college until after the Games and to have me train full-time, which I knew would not work. I needed balance.

So Steve and I talked, I looked to my parents for guidance, and we all reached a compromise. I would not move to Norman or go to school full-time; I would continue to live at home and go to OU part-time, taking only a few classes. It would be difficult commuting, but I arranged my schedule so that I had to do the forty-five-minute drive only a couple of times each week. That left me with plenty of time for both workouts and mental breaks.

At OU, I felt a little bit lost, as the majority of freshmen do, but it was good for me to go to a large school where I could walk around and do my thing. In the real world, I was still withdrawn, very shy, and lacking in confidence, particularly in social situations. I went to my classes; I drove home. I didn't go to the school library to study or join a study group. When I went to competitions I took homework with me so I kept up.

Meanwhile, the media was really playing up the typical "old girl makes way for young girl" story because I had finished second to Dominique Moceanu in the U.S. Championship in August. Of course, I would have liked to have won every all-around in 1995, but I was satisfied that I was competing well and still in the hunt. I had made some mistakes along the way, but I was still refining routines and overall I was on a good path.

The only meet from which I came away truly disappointed that year was the 1995 World Championship in Sabae, Japan, in early October. I was elated that my second vault allowed our team to sneak into third place for a bronze medal, but after snaring five individual gold medals at the previous two Worlds, I was shut out. Unfortunately, I had landed badly on a beam dismount during training, spraining my ankle. It wasn't a career-ending injury, but it became difficult for me to run, punch the floor, and handle hard landings. I had qualified for the all-around final and all four event finals, but now I could barely walk. How was I to compete? I finished twelfth in the all-around. With my right ankle getting worse, I was forced to withdraw from both vault and floor exercise. I had the best chance to medal on the balance beam, but a few slight bobbles dropped me into fourth place and I went home empty-handed.

It wasn't the way I would have liked my World Championship experience to go, especially with the media seeing it as further proof that my championship days were over, but my focus had to be forward. It was the next year that mattered most.

23

I wouldn't say I was more injury prone as I got older. Injuries were spread out fairly evenly during my years of competition. If they seemed more prevalent in later years it was because they usually coincided with major events, of which I was doing more than when I was younger. Injuries, as well as fatigue, might have kept me from attending a minor meet, but rarely something major. Although pain invariably accompanied injuries, injuries and pain were different. Competing with injuries could be very precarious, but competing with pain was a constant. I wasn't alone. All of my teammates and competitors had a litany of physical issues that rivaled my own. No athlete is complacent about injuries, but as long as we knew we could push through them or could give them time to heal, we didn't worry.

So while I was terribly disappointed that I couldn't give 100 percent at Worlds, I wasn't worried that I had gone off track on my journey to the Olympics. It was merely a sprained ankle that I knew would heal soon. After that happened, I needed to figure out how to stay healthy while training my Olympic routines. Physically, nothing was out of the ordinary. However, I was about to enter unfamiliar territory.

Soon after returning from Sabae, I started to feel a piercing pain in my left wrist. It made doing even the simplest skills, like handsprings and grabbing the bar, almost impossible. I couldn't hold a glass of milk without wincing. I began icing my wrist after practice, praying the pain would go away. Steve, who honeymooned in Hawaii that November, thought I may have hurt myself by compensating for my ankle injury at Worlds.

X-rays were taken, doctors were consulted, and my trainer continued with physical therapy, but we couldn't establish the cause of the pain. I believed the cause was overuse, and seemed to confirm this when I did only light training during our annual Christmas trip to Texas and the pain decreased. When I returned to Dynamo in January and resumed training full throttle so I'd be ready for U.S. Nationals and Olympic Trials, the pain returned with a vengeance.

With no more time to rest my wrist, we tailored workouts to try to put less pressure on it. Icing my left wrist alone wasn't working, so I also began taping it to train on all the apparatuses but uneven bars. My grip already acted as a support for that event. I then taped my right wrist because I noticed I was compensating for my left wrist and was in danger of further injury. I started wearing a brace to give my wrist added support on vault. The brace was a soft neoprene wrap with Velcro that I could get pretty tight so my wrist wouldn't bend much more than thirty degrees. I was not a gymnast that felt comfortable wearing a brace for beam or floor. Particularly on balance beam, a brace prevented me from getting the necessary grip on the types of skills I was doing.

The pain continued to worsen during the spring, so there were more X-rays and an MRI was done, and more doctors were consulted, each more of a specialist than the previous one. We tried to figure out if icing, bracing, and physical therapy was the right course of action or, as some doctors advised, more drastic measures were needed. Surgery that would require months of recovery time was, of course, out of the question. One doctor said, "It's seems like severe tendonitis, but if you can get through workouts with the least amount of harm, we can give you cortisone shots before major competitions." I understood that this would help with the inflammation, so it was tempting to say yes. But my parents and I were very concerned that this injection could weaken the structural soundness of the area and further damage the weakened tissues.

With that option on the table as the Nationals and Olympic Trials neared, my mother and I visited a hand specialist and surgeon. He checked the X-rays and MRI and examined my wrist. He then told me that I would be risking "severe injury and even death" if I ever competed again. As I sat there in shock, he explained in graphic detail how the tendon could snap on a vault, which would allow my head to crash into the vaulting horse; or snap as I was swinging around the bars, allowing me to soar into outer space with horrifying consequences.

I was thinking, "Wait, you're joking, right?" I was waiting for the laugh, but he was totally serious. He obviously wanted me to understand the critical nature of the injury, but scare tactics don't work well with me. As he continued to talk about the perils I'd risk if I ever put on my leotard again, I tuned him out. Now I was thinking, "Ah, I need a better opinion, because this one doesn't work for me."

The doctor then left his office, letting us mull over what he said. My mother recalls that she sat in stunned silence trying to muster the courage to look at me and was perplexed because I was completely serene after this devastating news. She recalls, "I asked you what you thought about what the doctor had said. You responded that God had gotten you this far and you didn't think He was planning to abandon you now." Apparently, I simply declared, "I'm competing!" She says, "You were so calm and confident that I could not doubt your decision."

I'm not sure how serene or confident I truly was, because the doctor's opinion had frightened me. In truth, I did not think his diagnosis was necessarily incorrect. Perhaps the odds did favor something going terribly wrong if I continued in my sport. I took everything he said into account and realized I had a potentially career-ending injury. But I knew my body and had experience training when hurting. Perhaps I was naïve, but I truly felt I could push forward. I decided to resume my workouts and receive the injection if absolutely needed. *You hope that's the right decision, but you never really know.*

At home, I discussed my decision with my dad. He is tranquil and thinks things through fully, so it was calming for me to be with him at that time. He assured me that I had made an informed decision, not a rash one. He said, "That was just one doctor's opinion. You've decided to instead go with another doctor's choice of treatment. Let's get all of the information and sit down with Steve, and we'll figure it out."

I'm sure we all knew from the outset that I wasn't going to stop.

I took no time off from training, not even to see more doctors because I felt that would have been pointless. I was now back at full force, in the thick of things. Steve and Peggy were doing their best to work around the injury so it wouldn't flare up, but there was no "Sugar, do you want to rest your wrist?" It was very frustrating for all of us because something outside our control was preventing me from doing the numbers. *How do I work around it while still getting done what I needed to?* Sure, it was comforting to know that when I'd soon compete at the Nationals and Trials, the adrenaline rush would vanquish the pain, but if I didn't put in the repetitions my positive attitude would be for naught. Then I wouldn't be able to hit my routines and qualify for the Olympics.

I could rest my wrist after the Games.

The adrenaline didn't kick in at the gym as it did when I performed in an arena. I hurt every day, all day. Obviously my wrist hurt more on specific skills. Scariest was how hard it was to grip the bar. It was a frustrating time. I didn't like to be held back for any competition, but this was the Olympic Games!

The pain was excruciating even when doing simple acts like drinking from my water bottle and trying to sleep. I wore a heavy-duty metal brace at night and during the day when I wasn't at the gym. It was a silver bar that was placed in a full hand wrap that extended from the bottoms of my fingertips to the forearm, keeping my wrist stable. I even tucked magnets into the brace at night. I would try anything.

At times the constant pain took its toll on me mentally. I kept asking myself, "Is my hand going to work when I need it to? Will I be able to let go of the bar and catch it during a competition? And on vault, if I push really hard, what's going to happen?" Fortunately, such negative thoughts didn't stick around long. *Surround yourself with positive energy.* I pushed aside the doubts and kept plowing forward. I couldn't afford to second-guess my decision to keep training for the Olympics.

Considering I hadn't competed in any of the meets that were on our schedule before my injury, the Olympics was probably an unrealistic goal. But I was undeterred. *Shannon, you don't allow others to place limits on you, so don't place them on yourself.* I wasn't counting the days and months to the Games or even the qualifying meets. I kept my eyes not on the prize but on our plan to get me there.

I never considered myself the most talented or exciting gymnast, but I could outwork anybody. That workhorse attitude helped me during difficult months leading to the qualifying competitions. We continued to focus on quality, but we also understood that quantity was needed as well. *How many routines can I do?* Our strategy was to get enough repetitions in without overdoing it and further damaging the wrist. I would also focus on conditioning and flexibility so that the rest of my body could endure the rigorous competition schedule. *When everything goes up in flames at the competition, rely on the repetitions already completed.* I needed to do the work. That was my insurance.

My wrist didn't get better, the pain didn't go away, but after dealing with it for six months, I was ready to compete.

A month before the Nationals, I entered the U.S. Classic. It was part of our plan to use this meet as a tune-up, where I could test the wrist and get back into a competitive mode after months on the sidelines.

Steve, Peggy, and I were concerned that even if I did well at both the Nationals and Olympic Trials, the toll the two competitions would have on my fragile wrist might force me to withdraw from the Olympics. So we made the big decision to compete only in the U.S. Nationals and skip the Olympic Trials. My score from the National Championship would now count 100 percent. It was all eggs in one basket yet again. In 1992, I had petitioned to compete at the Olympic Trials after sitting out the optional round at the National Championship. This time we flipped it and chose the Nationals over the Trials because that would allow my wrist more recovery time before the Olympics began.

This was our strategy, but you never knew what could happen, so we didn't share the plan in case we needed to change it up on the fly. We did know that if I was forced to compete at the Trials, there was little chance I would be able to muster through the actual Olympic competition. My wrist couldn't take it.

24

The 1996 U.S. Championship took place in June at the Thompson-Boling Arena in Knoxville, Tennessee. The media was focused on Dominique Moceanu, but there was a strong field of competitors vying for a spot on the team, including Dominique Dawes, Kerri Strug, Amanda Borden, Jaycie Phelps, and Amy Chow. It had been so long since I'd competed in a major competition that I didn't think anyone considered me more than a long shot to make the team. I couldn't ignore the pain in my wrist, but it was heavily taped and I knew that once I was in front of an audience I could push through it. My main concern was that I'd lose my grip on uneven bars.

I hit four solid routines to take a small lead over Dominique Moceanu and Jaycie Phelps in the compulsories, which counted 60 percent of the total score. So far so good, and I was confident heading into the optional round. My first event was balance beam. This wasn't my favorite rotation, but I just had to deal with it. I saluted the judge and mounted the beam. I was ready; I was confident; I was . . . suddenly on the floor! I had fallen on my first tumbling series—a back handspring, layout step out, layout step out. *I go up on my first event and butcher it? Are you kidding me?* This was a huge, huge miss with so much on the line. TV commentators voiced their concern: "This doesn't bode well for her." I'm fortunate that the only voice I heard was Peggy's, and she was saying, "Get back up, minimize the deduction, and get on with it." So I did. There wasn't time to fret.

After landing a solid dismount, I came down from the podium and Peggy and Steve were waiting. Remaining positive, Steve said, "You hit the big stuff." He was talking about a couple of new skills in my routine that I hadn't tested in competition before. "Yes," I thought, "I performed all of my new skills, but I missed the one I've been doing since I was about eleven." I was just so disappointed and angry at myself. I wanted a do-over. Fearing I might be overwhelmed by discouragement, my coaches quickly stepped in and got me to focus on the three events ahead. Steve said, "All right, we've got some work to do. Let's go for it." Fortunately, he always had that attitude and told me after even the biggest mistakes, "Look forward. We have no time for you to look back."

What was I thinking? "I've been here before. I've fallen in the past, but I've pulled it out." I may have flashed back to age nine when I fell off the beam at the state competition but finished the routine and three error-free events after that to capture my first victory. Back then, I'd debunked the gymnastics adage that "you can't fall and win," and there was no reason I couldn't repeat that scenario ten years later. I could rely on my experience. After an unexpected setback, you need to have tunnel vision to move toward your goal. *Don't get sidetracked. Just put one foot in front of the next and keep moving forward.*

I was able to let go of my mistake. I couldn't control what had already happened, so my attitude was: *Control the things you can control and let God handle the rest.* This wasn't going to be easy, but nothing worthwhile ever is.

After spending at least a couple of additional years in gymnastics simply for the opportunity to represent my country on home soil in Atlanta, and enduring tremendous pain to get as far as I had, I was faced with a do-or-die situation. If I didn't nail the remaining three events, doing routines with new and difficult skills, my chances of being one of the seven girls on the Olympic team were miniscule. I'd then have no alternative but to compete at Trials, which would likely be the end of my career whether I made the team or not.

When my back was against the wall and the odds were against me, when reality said, "This is not possible," I felt my true character was revealed. I was a fighter. I accepted the challenge.

First up was floor exercise. There wasn't much time between beam and floor. I had to warm up, visualize my routine, and then salute the judges. Steve said, "Go out and give it all you've got. But remember this is fun!" I did a very challenging floor routine with four passes and a new double layout opening, a move I'd been working on for nearly seven years before I felt I could do it in competition. That night I performed the move well and competed one of the finest floor routines of my career. *Don't count me out just yet.*

Vault came next. I performed the best vault of my life on the first jump. I was getting excited but trying not to get ahead of myself, although a smile did creep through. On my second vault I pulled off a Yurchenko one-and-a-half twist. It was a new vault and had the highest level of difficulty. When I stuck the landing I received the highest vault score of the competition! I was clawing my way back. This . . . was . . . not . . . over.

The meet was flying by and all of a sudden I was facing my last event. I was hearing whispers as I walked toward the final apparatus: "Holy cow, she might win this thing!" Because of my wrist, my last event was also the most difficult: uneven bars. *I am not going to fail now.* After a painful, tear-inducing warm-up, I held my breath and hoped my wrist held up. I performed a solid routine. Afterward, Peggy hugged me and said, "Nice, comeback kid." Steve hugged me, saying, "That was fun, right? We train too hard to not have any fun." He was right.

I didn't look at the scoreboard, so I didn't realize that I had won until someone came over and told me. Jaycie Phelps finished second, ahead of Dominique Moceanu. After finishing behind Dominique Dawes in 1994 and Dominique Moceanu in 1995, I was again the U.S. Champion.

It was an amazing competition and for me, one of the greatest moments in not just my career but my life. When I face challenges, I always think of that night. At first all seemed lost. However, as I looked forward and broke down into small steps what I needed to do to accomplish my goal, the idea of success became realistic. In many ways that fall was a blessing. If I had completed four error-free routines, if it had been easy, in future years I wouldn't have been able to utilize what I accomplished at Nationals, which was to turn disaster into triumph, to get me through other seemingly hopeless moments in life.

This was a significant turning point in my life. Since then, every time I've come up against an obstacle—including when I went toe-to-toe with cancer—my comeback at Nationals and my decision to resume training despite a broken elbow and making the 1992 Olympic team have been my two main sources of inspiration. Maybe the Nationals holds a slight edge because I'd invested years of training and put my body through pain and discomfort for what I believed was my last chance to wear red, white, and blue and compete for my country at the Olympic Games.

I had pulled through. I had just won the National Championship. So you'd think I'd feel secure that my score would hold among the top seven at the Olympic Trials. But you just never know. I hoped it was enough, but there was nothing I could do at that point. Dominique Moceanu, who had a stress fracture in her right tibia, had also successfully petitioned to have her score from Nationals count as double and to skip the Trials. I have a snapshot in my head of the two of us sitting together in a suite at the FleetCenter in Boston as fourteen girls competed at the Trials, hoping our scores from Nationals were good enough.

They held up for both of us. I had made my second Olympic team!

After the competition, they took me and Dominique, or "Moch" as she would be known to her teammates, down to march out on the floor with the other five girls who had finished in the top seven after the Olympic Trials. Dominique Moceanu and I were introduced to the fans and media along with Amanda Borden, Amy Chow, Dominique Dawes, Jaycie Phelps, and Kerri Strug. The 1996 U.S. women's Olympic team was complete. We were all excited to have secured our spots on the team, but the Trials had been just the dress rehearsal. Now it was time for the show.

25

After a training camp in Greensboro, North Carolina, the women's Olympic gymnastics team traveled to Atlanta. We didn't stay in the Olympic Village this time but rather in a vacated fraternity house on the campus of Emory University. This was for security reasons and to keep us focused. Steve and Peggy were there, too. Our head coach was Márta Károlyi and our assistant coach was Mary Lee Tracy, who ran the Cincinnati Gymnastics Academy where Jaycie Phelps and Amanda Borden trained. My ranking wasn't as high as theirs because I'd missed months of competitions, so Steve wasn't given the assistant coach position at these Olympics and wouldn't be allowed down on the floor during team competition. That was something I hadn't experienced since the Junior Pan-American Games. Still, Steve and Peggy coached me through training and one of them would be on the arena floor with me during any individual competitions I might qualify for.

In 1992, everyone was happy our team won a bronze medal. In 1996, the expectation was of a different color. I believed we had a real shot to win the first women's team Olympic gold medal for the U.S. We were a very talented group, a perfect storm of the right girls peaking at the same time. Although I didn't know most of the girls very well, I knew them all as athletes and understood what they were capable of on the floor and how their hard work and talent could mesh with my own for history-making success on the world stage.

We had a terrific mix of veteran leaders who kept the young girls calm and younger athletes who kept us "old" girls enthusiastic and energized. We didn't socialize much more than exchanging brief comments around the chalk bowl. The grueling morning and afternoon sessions did not leave time or energy for much other than eating and sleeping. True friendships would form during the post-Olympic tour when we could enjoy time away from the unrelenting pressure of Olympic competition.

Dominique, Kerri, and I were returning Olympians. During the modern Olympic era, it was rare for any female gymnast to compete in more than one Games due to her physical changes and the tremendous toll years of high-level gymnastics take on her body. Yet, amazingly, there were three of us. Of the girls who would become known worldwide by the end of the team competition as "The Magnificent Seven," I knew them best.

Dawes, as she was known in order to differentiate her from Moceanu, had been my roommate at the 1992 Olympics and other international events. We were good friends who still approached gymnastics similarly. We were the first two of our era to push our way onto a scene ruled by Béla Károlyi. Although we never spoke about it directly, I think we both felt that we were pioneers in some ways and were showing the girls who followed us that you didn't have to train at a certain club and with a certain coach to be successful. *If you believe in yourself and work hard, then you can make the impossible, possible. You must dare to dream.*

Kerri and I knew each other well from when we trained together at Dynamo. She had been my travel companion and roommate at several competitions. After her departure from Dynamo in 1994, she headed home to Arizona to train and then returned to Béla after he came out of retirement. She seemed to have refocused because she was competing at a high level.

Amy Chow was as quiet as a mouse and a gentle soul. Anyone who confused that with weakness was in for a surprise because she was a tough competitor, a real fighter. She was highly intelligent and a concert pianist— and she had the heart of a lion.

Jaycie Phelps didn't wait until the tour to be a riot. If you needed a pick-me-up or just needed to laugh, you would call on Jaycie. She and Amanda

Borden trained together and were almost inseparable. Amanda was kind of like the mother of the team. At the competition and on tour, if you were having an issue with anything or needed someone to rally the troops, then she was the one. We selected her, unanimously, as team captain because she had a calm demeanor, smiled constantly, and had a positive outlook that was infectious. There was no need for an alternate on our team because Amanda and Amy shared a spot, with Amy competing vault and bars and Amanda performing on beam and floor. That gave Amanda time to be the cheerleader for the team, which was a perfect role for her. She was our glue.

Dominique Moceanu and I had battled at various competitions, but I didn't know her well at all. She was new to the scene and was coming on strong at the same time I was pulling back due to my injured wrist. The smallest and youngest girl on the team, she was cute and spunky and contributed plenty of energy. I'd get to know her better on the tour and though I was nineteen and she would be only fifteen that September, it didn't really matter because we were on a team together. Better than anyone, I understood that age has nothing to do with ability. Like Kim Zmeskal in 1992, Dominique was the media darling and under tremendous pressure to meet unrealistic expectations at the Games. She had tremendous talent but, like me with my wrist and Kerri with her ailing ankle, she was going into the competition with her fractured tibia.

I looked at myself as a veteran simply because I had been competing for so long and in so many competitions. I wasn't one to preach; I was much more comfortable leading by example. I certainly didn't need to explain to these girls how to compete, they were on this team for a reason, but I was always happy to help them better understand what to expect during their first Olympics. As much as a young gymnast will try to sustain the idea that "the Olympics is just another competition," the reality is that it's much bigger.

I believe my teammates appreciated my efforts and I was honored when they nominated me to be the U.S. flag bearer for the second straight Olympics. Each sport nominates one of its athletes for that position; then one Olympian is chosen from that group to carry the flag. Wrestler Bruce Baumgartner ultimately carried our country's flag at the Opening Ceremonies with great pride and respect.

The seven of us girls had such different personalities, but somehow we meshed. I doubt if we would have connected and bonded without gymnastics, but the sport gave us a commonality. We had the same drive to win the gold medal, but also we wanted so badly to perform and exhibit our pure love of the sport. I believe that's what made us such a good team.

Because so much was expected of us, we were a big story at the Games. Moceanu, who was on national magazine covers, was hounded by the media, but none of the girls were ignored. I'm not sure how the press approached Strug and Dawes, but I found it interesting that at the prescribed media sessions leading up to the Games, the questions I was most asked were: "How does it feel to be a veteran on this team?"; "Do you feel that you're too old to be on a second Olympic team?"; "Why do you want to chance sullying your Olympic record?"; and "Isn't it time to step aside and give deserving younger athletes an opportunity?" Members of the media also questioned whether I could duplicate my 1992 success now that I was five feet tall and weighed a scale-tipping ninety-five pounds. While Steve attempted to shelter me from the media prior to big competitions, it wasn't always possible. I was still soft-spoken, but I was older and much more comfortable doing interviews than in 1992. I patiently answered all the indelicate questions about my age and weight.

The issue of my staying around too long bounced around in my head. Gymnastics had been my life for as long as I could remember, and it was hard to even think about giving up what I'd been used to in order to venture into the unknown. Never mind that I was still capable of top-level gymnastics, the most important thing was that I loved the sport, enjoyed competing at major events, and was honored to don the red, white, and blue and represent my country in Olympic competition. Neither those second-place finishes in 1994 and 1995 nor my inactivity in 1996 was concrete proof that I was over the hill. It would not have occurred to me to state my thoughts on this topic out loud. I was a doer, not a talker. If I was truly capable and truly prepared, then it would come through in the competition, not in a press conference.

26

The day before the gymnastics competition began we had our podium training in the Georgia Dome, which we would share with the basketball competition during the Games. Podium training is basically a dress rehearsal. There had been an international draw to see when each country would compete and, for us, the podium training was essentially a mock competition. No one kept score, but we were told to perform full routines, as if we were competing. The TV crews used the day to figure out where the cameras needed to be placed for each gymnast. The judges used it to look at the teams and get an idea what types of routines they would be seeing. The coaches used to it help them decide on their lineups for the competition and to see if anyone was having trouble with a skill or piece of equipment.

We gymnasts used it as a showcase. To make a splash with the judges, we needed to do a good job during podium training. We also had to get used to unfamiliar equipment, including the different bounce to the bars, different spring to the floor, and even a different feel to the balance beam. When people watch gymnastics on television, they aren't aware of the little things that can cause athletes issues. Miniscule changes during a routine can add up to big problems. An inch here, a centimeter there, and you can be completely thrown off.

When we walked in, forty thousand fans rose to their feet and cheered. There were flashbulbs going off as if it were the Fourth of July! It was pure insanity and this was all for what was basically a workout! It anticipated what would take place in the arena each night of the actual competition. The biggest difference between Barcelona in 1992 and Atlanta in 1996 was the noise. The decibel level was so high in the Dome that I thought my eardrums were going to burst. It was fantastic to have such an enthusiastic audience. The chant "U-S-A, U-S-A!" was constant, and it lifted all of us to a higher level of performance. Looking into the stands, I saw a sea of red, white, and blue. All that positive energy was one of the reasons I had stayed the course to the Olympics. It was why the pain didn't matter. When you have that kind of support all negativity melts away. The opportunity to compete at home for my country made every hardship I'd experienced worth it.

Sometimes it was impossible to not let the pressure at a major competition get to me. In Atlanta, there was a new kind of pressure that I couldn't get past. It wasn't the pressure of the competition itself but that Americans were going to see everything I did firsthand. I needed to find a way to use that pressure to motivate me rather than overwhelm me because I had to stay focused.

I lay in bed the night before the Games began, feeling the enormity of the situation. I wanted to do well so I wouldn't let down my coaches, parents, fans, teammates, or country. I never wanted to disappoint them. I thought about why I had started gymnastics, what I still loved about it, and how much fun it was performing in front of a crowd. What I finally told myself was, "Whatever is going to happen is going to happen." I thought of how hard I'd trained for the Games and that I'd overcome so many injuries and worked through so much pain. And I knew I was as prepared as I was going to be. Steve's training really helped me at that trying moment, because he believed that it was important to shoot for perfection while focusing on trying my hardest. *Placements and medals didn't matter as long as I did my best.*

That night I closed my eyes and did exactly what I would do before every competition of my entire career. First, I said a prayer. I didn't pray to win. I prayed to do my best. I prayed that our team and every athlete competing would be safe. *Let us all hit our routines to the best of our abili-*

ties. Afterward, I went through each routine in my mind, seeing myself compete them all to perfection. I started on the event I would begin with the next day. I saw myself salute the judge. I focused on every skill and each correction. I did not allow myself to get sidetracked until I had seen myself stick the dismount on the final routine.

Muhammad Ali lit the Olympic torch to cap the Opening Ceremonies, and the next day the Atlanta Games began. As we marched into the Georgia Dome on July 21, wearing white leotards with stars on our right shoulders, the mostly American audience went wild. What a lift forty thousand cheering spectators can give you! I can't imagine the stress my parents were under up in the stands, hoping that we all did well, praying for good health and positive results. This was it—the time for our team to shine.

For the final time in Olympics annals, the team competition included compulsories. That was to my benefit. Scores for all gymnasts on compulsories would be combined with their scores on optionals. That would determine the final team standings and who qualified for the all-around and the four individual final events. While compulsories weren't the most exciting routines for the audience, they were critical to the team standings.

I was tested immediately. Uneven bars came first, so I would find out right away if my wrist would hold up during competition. I hadn't been able to pick up a cup that morning and was very concerned about bars. I knew the adrenaline would kick in and I'd pay no attention to the pain as I did my routine, but would I be able to grip the bar? Yes. I made it through without a hitch. What a tremendous relief!

I competed solid routines on the other apparatuses. At the end of the evening, Russia was in first place, but we were a close second and ahead of our other chief competitor, Romania. I finished the first night in second place among all competitors to Lilia Podkopayeva of Ukraine, which boded well for my making it into the all-around.

The optional competition took place two nights later. Bars had been a great first event in compulsories, so I thought it was a good omen that it was our initial apparatus during optionals. The four events always followed the "Olympic order," so bars would be followed by beam, then floor, and we would end the night on vault.

First in our lineup was Jaycie Phelps. Although I had always been careful not to watch other girls perform, for some reason I watched Jaycie that night, and that's why it stands out as a memory. She nailed it! We all watched her and were given a jolt of confidence. Amanda and I locked eyes and then all the girls looked at each other and we just had this sense that this was going to be *our* night. We just knew that we were not leaving that area without our gold medal!

We all did well on the uneven bars, particularly Dominique Dawes and Amy Chow, who would win a silver medal in the individual bar final. Beam was next and I had the highest score of the night, guaranteeing I'd be in the event final. Floor went well for the team and suddenly we were rotating to our final event. I was thinking how quickly everything was going.

America held a seemingly comfortable lead over Russia. As the result of several disappointing scores, Romania was out of the running for the team gold medal. It was down to the U.S. and Russia. Russia's last rotation was floor exercise; America's was vault. Jaycie and Amy both hit solid vaults. In third position, I did the same. Then Dawes nailed two incredible vaults. That left Dominique Moceanu and Kerri Strug, our two best on this event. Victory was in sight. I was now able to sit back and watch, although there was no way I could relax.

Moceanu unexpectedly missed her first vault. Then she missed again. We didn't see that coming, but we were still in first place and felt there was no problem with Kerri coming up.

Kerri went up, and she missed her first vault, too! *What?* The drama may have been great for television, but I could have done without it. My heart was pounding; my palms were sweating. You never want to see teammates fall because you know how hard they've trained and how much they want to do well.

What fans watching television may not have realized is that we held a secure 0.897 lead over Russia entering the final rotation, and that we'd already achieved enough to capture the gold, regardless of the falls by Dominique and Kerri. But there's always that worry in the back of your mind that the scoreboard has it wrong, or maybe an inquiry will change the scores. So you never let up, not until you've got the medal you want around your neck. I guarantee Kerri did not know her vault score wasn't necessary. And I'm not sure it would have prevented her from going all out on her second vault. She had hurt herself on her first vault and was limping, but you don't claw your way to the Olympic Games to give up on your last run. We had no way of knowing the severity of Kerri's injury. It wasn't unusual to sting your ankles on a bad landing. You shake it off, make sure things are working, and get back out there. The whole team was suffering from various injuries by the end of the team final and Kerri's shaking her left foot was not an unexpected sight. All we could do was support her by cheering for her as loud as possible, "Go, Kerri; you got it; you got it!" We knew she didn't want to end on a fall; no athlete would. "You can do it!" shouted Béla from the sidelines. She could do it.

When Kerri landed her second vault, her arms went up and she picked up her left foot. Her vault executed, she collapsed to the floor. That moment would be etched in the minds of millions of people around the world. It was a testament to Kerri's determination and will to succeed. It was a dramatic end to a hard-fought competition.

At that point, we still didn't know what had actually happened. From our poor vantage point, we had a hard time seeing the landings and we didn't get the benefit of TV replays. Instead, we were dealing with pure chaos down in the trenches. The rest of us were whisked backstage to line up for the award ceremony. One lady kept yelling at us to "March, march, march!" But we didn't know where Kerri was. She had been taken away so they could check on her ankle. This woman kept yelling as if it were life or death if we didn't march out immediately. Not typically one to speak sternly, I said, "We are waiting for Kerri; the team will march out together." One of my favorite memories of that amazing night was the moment the six of us planted our feet firmly on the floor mat and wouldn't budge. We were a team and we were not walking out without Kerri.

Finally, we saw Béla carrying her in his arms, an image that became iconic. He set her down beneath the podium. You could tell that Kerri was a reluctant hero, almost embarrassed by the attention.

Ever the pragmatist, I leaned over and made sure she knew I would come around and help her up onto the podium. I asked Moceanu to help on her other side. That night as "U-S-A! U-S-A!" bellowed from above, our amazing team of seven young women stood on the top podium as the first ever women's gymnastics team to win Olympic gold for the United States of America! We waved, we raised our flowers high, and we watched proudly as our flag was raised to the sounds of our national anthem. It was the end of a crazy night, and there were so many mixed emotions and thoughts racing through my head. I'm sure it was the same for the other girls. There was only one thing we knew for sure.

We were the Olympic champions!

It was stunning to be wearing an Olympic gold medal around my neck. I loved that it represented the effort of our entire team, a marvelous group of girls. Everyone on the team made unique contributions to the victory, and that is why that gold medal is such a treasured memory. Amanda, Amy, two Dominiques, Jaycie, Kerri, and Shannon. It was indeed a magnificent seven.

27

That night there was a whirlwind of activity that ended with a late-night party at Planet Hollywood. I even got to talk to "the" Hollywood supercouple of that time, Bruce Willis and Demi Moore, whose head was shaved because she was filming *G.I. Jane*. But in the back of my mind I heard Steve's words, "It's not over." Before leaving the Georgia Dome, I spent time with him and Peggy, who were proud and congratulatory but also squeezed a few corrections into our conversation. I had to complete the mandatory drug test along with many of the other gymnasts. After that, it was a whirlwind of media with many insatiable reporters and photographers. That night no one asked about my weight or my age. At nineteen, I had posted the highest score on Team USA. One of my favorite photographers, Dave Black, was there with tears in his eyes. He'd photographed me for the first time when I was nine, and as he took the Magnificent Seven's photo he told us that our winning the gold medal was the best thing he'd ever seen. It would be years before I truly understood the impact we had on the lives of others.

I also had the chance to see my parents in the USA Gymnastics suite, before they came to the party with my siblings. After my spot on the team was confirmed at the Olympic Trials, my parents had to scramble for accommodations in the Atlanta area. They were not going to jump the gun and buy tickets before I made the team. The only time they had purchased tickets in advance was for Mom for the Paris Worlds in 1992, and I ended up not competing. Fortunately, the trip to Atlanta was much easier to manage, although lodging was still tight. They were invited to stay with a family they met through our church, and had wrangled tickets to all of my performances. They were proud and happy for me.

Later that night my coaches took me aside to talk about our next steps. They had received the final standings overall and in each event during the team competition. The standings determined which athletes would compete in the all-around and event finals. By finishing in the top eight overall and on balance beam, I had qualified to compete in the all-around and the individual beam finals. I had also expected to compete in uneven bars after putting up a solid score. But I now learned that my bar score had been lowered by the judges, after the fact, and in an odd turn of events I had dropped into ninth place. Since only eight girls would be competing in the individual uneven bar finals, I was out. I was confused because no one could give me an explanation for what had happened. I was terribly disappointed, but there was nothing anyone could do at that point. *Control what you can control and let go of the rest.* I needed to focus on upcoming performances. At the time, I didn't know Kerri's injuries would force her to withdraw from the individual events for which she had qualified, and I'd be asked to take her place on vault. (Dominique Dawes would fill in for her on floor exercise and win a bronze medal.)

I was looking forward to the all-around that took place two days later, on July 25. I knew people expected a lot from me during this event, and after missing out on gold by a hair in 1992, I was extremely motivated. It helped knowing my family was in the stands watching. My parents had two tickets to the sold-out all-around competition through the United States Olympic Committee, but for them to get tickets for Tessa and Troy from an Olympic sponsor, I agreed to make an appearance following the Games. They were such a big part of my success and I couldn't imagine not having them in the arena. Also in the stands were Grandma and Grandpa Miller, who had made the trip from San Antonio and managed to find tickets to the all-around competition.

Ironically, it was on bars that I received my best score of the night.

After two rotations I trailed only Dominique Dawes in the all-around standings. However, hopes for a 1-2 American finish were dashed when the competition took a bad turn on floor exercise for both of us. On my first tumbling pass I stumbled after landing a little short on my double lay-out. Then on my last pass I overrotated slightly and touched my left heel out-of-bounds for a significant deduction. I was out of medal contention. I performed two solid vaults in my last event of the day and was able to finish eighth of the thirty-six competitors. Dominique finished seventeenth. Lilia Podkopayeva, or "Lily Pod," as we knew her, was having an exceptional Olympics and gave Ukraine the gold medal. Romanians Gina Gogean and Simona Amânar won the silver and bronze, respectively.

There wasn't much time to be sad or relive the mistakes I had made. I had two individual events to compete a few days later, vault on the twenty-eighth, and beam on the twenty-ninth.

On the night of the twenty-seventh, the Olympic Games that were being touted as "the World's Largest Peacetime Event" were jarred by a bomb detonation in Atlanta's Centennial Park. One person was killed by the explosion, another died from a heart attack, and more than a hundred people were injured. Naturally, it shook up the city and in the aftermath people were worried about security for the athletes and fans. In truth, it didn't have much impact on our team as competitors. It happened in the wee hours while we were fast asleep, and we only heard brief comments about it the next day. My coaches downplayed the issue and we didn't have access to a great deal of media. I wouldn't learn the full story until after my competitions were over, and I was out of the "bubble." My parents were a bit concerned about my well-being but took comfort that I wasn't staying in the vicinity. Security for the athletes might have been heightened, but our schedule didn't change, our procedures didn't change, our naptime didn't change.

I was sore and both mentally and physically fatigued from the team and all-around finals. I was on thin ice with my wrist, and wondering if it might finally give out. In addition, I was beginning to feel emotional. Usually I could set my emotions aside, which is why I came across as stoic at meets. While I wanted to compete the way I trained and think of this as just another competition, it wasn't. It *wasn't* just any competition—it might just be my last.

We had not even considered scratching vault. Wrist pain or not, I felt I owed it to Kerri to follow through. A healthy Kerri would have had a much better chance to medal, but I was going to give it everything I had. We could never have guessed that Moceanu would miss both vaults or Kerri would hurt her ankle, so when Steve and I discussed areas where we could cut back training in order to ease stress on my wrist we immediately looked at vault. The second vault would likely never be used, so we didn't practice it much leading up to the competition. It made no sense to pound my wrist working on a skill that I was unlikely to ever compete.

Yet here I was competing at the Olympic vault final. For my first vault we had chosen to go with my low-value Yurchenko with a half twist. I was typically able to perform it with much less deduction than my more diffi-cult one-and-a-half twist, so I played the odds. I performed it fairly well but had a large hop on the landing. So I needed to be perfect on the next vault to have any chance of stealing a medal. Unfortunately, my second vault was in trouble from the start. I always marked a spot with a large chalk line halfway down the runway so I'd know if my steps were correct, but this time my steps were off and I hit the line with the wrong foot. In hindsight, I should have veered to the right or left of the springboard and tried a second time, which was allowed by the rules. But I wasn't used to balking; I was used to going 100 percent. *Maybe I can salvage it.* I went for it. My rhythm was way off and my hand slipped over the top of the horse and the fans gasped as I landed on my rear end. It was a complete miss, a fall on vault during the event finals at the Olympic Games. Not my shin-ing moment. I was devastated and embarrassed. This was certainly not how I imagined my Olympics going. It was my first and only fall over two Olympic Games.

It still drives me nuts.

In the two years I had been training and competing that vault, I rarely missed it. Since I was nine I had never hit my mark halfway down the runway with the wrong foot. I may not have been in the running for a medal, but I should certainly have landed on my feet. Yet there I was, "splat," on my backside in front of the world. This was one of those hideous moments I would try not to relive unless I was using it to light a fire, to motivate, to drive me to do more, to work harder, to keep going. *From some-thing negative, create something positive.*

After I'd won team gold I was on cloud nine, but I'd gone from high to low in a matter of days. Everything seemed to be falling apart, unraveling at the seams. I stumbled on floor and then missed on vault. *What is happening?* The ups and downs were taking an emotional toll on me as I headed toward what would be the last Olympic event of my career. I needed to take back control, or I'd blow my final chance to bring home an individual gold medal.

28

I wanted so much to end my Olympic career on high note. Since I had qualified to be in the balance beam final, my goal was simply to go out and hit the best routine of my life. But after my back-to-back disappointments on floor in the all-around and vault in the event final, I struggled to regroup and not formulate a doomsday scenario for my final women's gymnastics event of the 1996 Olympics. That was so unlike me. My greatest strength as a gymnast was my ability to put a mistake on one event behind me and kill it on the events that followed, but I was having trouble doing that. All of the other competitions were a stepping-stone, but this was it. This was the end of the road, so I had to leave it all on the mat. I did not want to fail again. I had to shake the woe-is-me attitude and fight back.

I thought back to when I was nine years old and my new coach, Steve Nunno, would call me Chicken Little because when even minor things went wrong, I cried as if my life was over. It took me years to be kinder to myself and that made all the difference. When I brought my naturally optimistic attitude into gymnastics, it allowed me to reach the light at the end of a dark tunnel of brutal setbacks, serious injuries, and, now, skepticism by many experts that I could still perform at the highest level.

When things were darkest, I had always found the silver lining. Indeed, at times I seemed almost pleased that there was a negative situation so I could search for a positive to counterbalance it. In the midst of a crisis was when I often performed my best. Before Atlanta, it had been my nature to see failures as exciting challenges for me to fix what was wrong and do better, and I eagerly rose to my feet rather than staying down for the count. *You minimize your mistake and keep going no matter what.* I made many mistakes at competitions before the 1996 Olympics, including at the Nationals, my Olympic *qualifying* competition. If ever there was a time to rise like the phoenix from a funeral pyre, this was it!

As I approached what I believed to be the final event of my Olympic career and my final opportunity to bring home an individual medal in Atlanta, I was having little success finding my confidence.

My parents found me standing outside the USA Gymnastics suite after the vault final. My mother asked for a quiet spot for us to talk, and we were led to an empty suite overlooking the basketball court. There they made an effort to ease my distress and encourage me to believe in myself again. Mom reminded me how I went from being a skinny-legged little sprite to being a champion gymnast with an American-record six Olympic medals in my possession. She recalled my fractured elbow and pointed to my tender wrist and talked about all the obstacles I'd overcome. She reminded me that I had turned previous setbacks into golden opportunities. She told me that I needed to enjoy what I was doing because there were countless girls out there who would give anything to *fall* at the Olympic Games.

She asked what was really bothering me. I vented about my humiliating pratfall in the vault and confessed that I felt I had let down my family, coaches, and country and feared doing it again on balance beam.

My parents hugged me and told me how proud they were of me. Not for the flips and turns I had learned or the medals I had won. They were proud of the young woman I had become, gracious and humble, hardworking and determined. They encouraged me to look beyond all of the pressures that I felt I needed to handle. It wasn't about me and I wasn't alone. There were so many blessings already at work; I just had to see them. My mother explained that maybe I needed to stop thinking about how *I* was going to do this. "Let God carry the load." She wanted me to "climb up on that beam and express the talent, beauty, grace, and goodness God has given you." My tears dried and a smile appeared. I had suffered a blow, but I would not give up.

That final night as I entered the arena and walked to the beam area, I kept thinking about what my mother had said. *Remember why you're here. Remember what's important.*

Peggy was down on the floor with me and gave me last-minute instructions. Only one coach was credentialed, so Steve was behind the barricade. But he was within earshot and as always was shouting encouragement.

Once the score went up for the athlete ahead of me I stepped onto the podium. I made sure the equipment was set and the board was "square" to the beam. I looked down the beam to get a fix on my sight lines and took a couple of deep breaths.

My name was announced and there was loud applause.

I waited to see the head judge raise the green flag. This meant all the judges were ready for me to perform. I saluted. I now had thirty seconds to begin my routine. I never needed that much time. I did not look at either of my coaches or my parents in the crowd. I knew they were there and that was enough.

I approached the balance beam with my last chance to win an individual medal for my country. The 1996 Olympics had been significantly rockier than the 1992 Olympics, when nothing much was expected of me and everything went right, but now I was down to my last routine, the last ninety seconds of my entire Olympic career! *Was I ready?*

Before me was the beam, which at four inches wide and sixteen feet long was the most feared apparatus in gymnastics. But not by me. As I stepped on the springboard, I realized that I was lucky that my last competition, my thirtieth in the Olympics, was going to be on the balance beam, my favorite event. As I held my hands over the beam, my mother's comforting words played in my head: "All you can give is 100 percent. That's all anyone can ask of you and that's all you can ask of yourself. Go out there and *enjoy* this experience." Suddenly, after two days of tension, I felt completely calm.

I paused and took another deep breath along with everyone else in the arena. *God, I'm in Your hands.* Then I did my press to handstand mount. It was solid. I was on the beam at the Olympics, in front of the whole world, and feeling totally at ease. I enjoyed the heart-racing feeling that told me: *Hey, it's okay; I don't have to be scared of this.* I loved the feeling of conquering my fears.

There were forty thousand people present whose eyes were on me, but it was so silent in the Georgia Dome that I could hear the shuffling of papers and the occasional nervous cough. Then, just after I had finished my press mount, a gentleman on the left side of the arena yelled, "Hey, buddy, shut your flash off!" He was shouting at someone who was taking pictures while the flash on his camera was on, a big no-no. The funny thing is, the arena was filled with flashes. Silver fireworks were exploding everywhere. It was magical.

I'd never heard an individual yell anything during one of my performances in all those years. I was taught early on not to listen to the crowd or anything else while I performed. I couldn't identify the music that was playing on the floor venue at any meet I competed in because I was concentrating so hard on the skill I was doing at the same time. Sometimes I heard the crowd *ooh*ing or gasping, but I didn't think about whether it was for me or another gymnast. I just tuned out the sound and kept focused. Applause was a little different. It sounded like a wave of noise to me. It notched up my energy level.

My mother, who somehow was both calm and holding her breath while watching me from the nosebleed section in the stands, was surprised when I told her later that I actually heard the man in the crowd. She knew that I always tuned out all distractions. My thought was, "Aw, he's sweet for being concerned that the flashes might be bothering me." Then it dawned on me that if I was aware of him, I was *too* relaxed. I made a concerted effort to refocus on the task at hand. I was able to do that, but the reason that this routine stands out in my memories was not just because of its outcome, or that it took place in the Olympics, but because for the first and only time in ten years I allowed the audience in to be part of my performance. Every previous time when I was up there, it had been just me and the beam and the whole world disappeared. Not so on this night. *Enjoy the experience.*

Once my hands had touched the beam, the ninety-second countdown began. The crowd was with me as I performed a switch leg leap into a back handspring quarter turn to a handstand. That was followed by a quarter turn into two back extension rolls, each ending in a handstand. This was one of my favorite combinations. It was also unique and helped my routine stand out.

It was essential to set myself apart. Yes, I had some impressive skills, but my greatest ability was knowing how to put those skills together in an interesting and elegant way. That was always Peggy's goal when working with me. Don't just *do* a skill; you have to *perform* it! I wanted to display the artistry of the sport, tell a story, and reveal my personality through my moves. There is no musical accompaniment on balance beam like you have on floor exercise, but in my head my routine had its own beat, its own rhythm. In my mind, I was dancing and it was fantastic to have a supportive audience.

Next up was a front somersault that was tricky because of its blind landing. I kept my rhythm and performed my next move. I nailed my layout step out series, the move I had recently missed at U.S. Nationals. At this moment any misses in the past were out of mind. I had trained this skill a thousand times since then. My focus was to push out strongly with my legs, use my arms to keep me straight on the beam, keep my eyes on the beam, and pull up into a strong lunge position to seal the landing. The audience cheered. I had completed it as planned.

Only a few minutes before, I was dreading doing my routine while battling my nerves. Now I was up on the beam and having *fun*. I was actually able to enjoy the Olympic final. These many years later I can recall exactly how I felt during skills, routines, and landings. Today I can close my eyes and completely relive how I felt at that moment. It felt amazing.

Next came the Miller. It was one of my favorite skills but also carried plenty of room for error because of its many twists and turns. This was a complicated move that was incredibly painful on my wrist. But not on this night; I felt no pain. I did the best Miller of my life!

I wasn't thinking that this was in all likelihood the last time I'd ever do a particular skill in international competition. I was thinking, "Okay, that skill's finished; what's next?"

Next was my last leap series, which included a jump in a piked position, with my left leg straight in front and my right leg bent beneath. Although this piked jump is intriguingly called a "wolf jump," it's neither terribly difficult nor especially pretty. It just happened to be a jump that was worth the proper amount of credit for the routine. In fact, this leap series as a whole was the easiest part of my routine and an opportunity to rest before my difficult dismount. Yes, "rest" *while* I was performing in front of the entire world. Again, I couldn't lose my focus because many times it's the small stuff, the easy skills, that comes back to bite you. I was taught to think only about the skill I was performing. *Don't think about the dismount when you're not there yet. That's when mistakes happen.* I executed my leap series cleanly.

I was no longer competing for a medal. I was expressing the pure joy of doing a sport I loved. The routine flew by and all of a sudden there I stood, at the end of the beam arms raised high. I now had only one skill remaining in my Olympic career. The dismount. The full twisting doubleback somersault off the beam just happened to be the most difficult dismount being performed at that time. Even today it is a rare sight.

It was time to finish what I had started so many years ago. I said a quick prayer: *Please-God-let-me-land-on-my-feet.* Then I charged down the four-inch beam from one end to the other, trying hard to focus on my takeoff so I would have plenty of height and rotation. I had been finishing with this dismount for years, but there was always a little luck involved when I hit it. There wasn't much room to adjust once I was in the air, and I wasn't one of those gymnasts who had an impeccable air sense. I had to rely on mechanics and hope I had set the stage for a good landing. I left the beam for the final time, somersaulting high into the air. I didn't see my gymnastics life flash by. Not yet.

For me, gymnastics was never about winning. It was about the feeling of floating through the air, the fulfillment of doing what others said couldn't be done, the excitement and sense of accomplishment when all the hard work pays off, and the thrill of hitting the perfect landing.

I felt my feet hit the floor and I realized that I was standing up. There was a deafening roar from the crowd. I saw Steve jumping up and down, going crazy. I knew that meant I had done well. *Perfect? Almost.* But I realized it didn't matter; that's the moment all my emotions came flooding through. That dismount was fifteen years in the making and I felt joy, excitement, relief. This was a powerful mix of emotions and a moment that I can, even today, close my eyes and recall at will. In that moment I had no idea if I would win a medal or what color it might be; I just wanted to savor the feeling. The feeling, not of perfection but of satisfaction in having given it my all.

Peggy gave me a hug and a couple corrections. Corrections? This was my final event at the Olympics and perhaps my final event in competition ever. Yet giving me corrections to ponder was Peggy's way, and I was so thankful for that.

My score came up and it was the highest of the competition with four girls to go. What was my exact score? I couldn't have told you five minutes after it flashed on the scoreboard. I had never focused on scores and I didn't want to start in my final competition. It didn't matter. It would hold or someone would beat it. Regardless of my score, I had done my job. (Soon after the Olympics a stranger thought he recognized me at an airport, but when I failed his test by not remembering my final beam score, he walked away convinced I was an impostor.) I would be reminded many times over the years that I won the gold medal that night with a 9.862. The girls who came after me couldn't match that.

As the finals standings came up on the leaderboard, there was a deafening roar from the audience as my name stood at the top. Peggy was there with me and gave me a huge hug. Steve found me, too, and we hugged as well. I wasn't the type to pump my fist in the air or jump up and down. These days I might have, but back then, I took everything in stride. It took a few seconds (or maybe a decade) to sink in. I soaked in the tremendous applause from the home crowd and people chanting, "U-S-A! U-S-A!" I remember feeling thankful that they stuck with me on this roller-coaster ride that was my Olympic Games.

Soon I was standing on the center podium, flanked by Lilia Podkopayeva and Gina Gogean, who had won the silver and bronze medals, respectively. I was the first American to earn Olympic gold on the balance beam. With a total of seven medals now, I had improved my status as the most decorated American gymnast in Olympic history, which I still find hard to believe.

Four years before, in Barcelona, I had won medals in five of the competitions, and I was delighted with silver and bronze. Through the ups and downs of the 1996 Olympics, I won medals in only two competitions— team and individual balance beam, the first and last ones in which I participated—but both were gold. In between, there had been disappointments I hadn't experienced in Barcelona. While it had been a wonderful and richly rewarding experience, it also made me shake my head.

I learned later that more than a hundred million viewers on NBC watched me win the beam competition, and I imagine most were still tuned in as "The Star-Spangled Banner" played.

As I stood on the podium, watching the American flag being raised, I thought about the people who had helped get me there, my team. You don't land a gold medal alone; success is always a team effort. I thought of my parents, whose support of me never wavered. I thought of my coaches, Steve and Peggy, who had stuck with me and were so patient with me—a young, determined, often frustrated control freak—for all of those years. Steve was often the one in the limelight, but Peggy was also crucial to my success as a gymnast and in life. I also thought about how I had not retired after the 1992 Olympics and continued gymnastics simply because I loved the sport and the part it played in my life. I thought of how I trained up to eight hours a day with the thought of competing in an Olympics in my own country. I thought of how the hand specialist advised that I quit gymnastics rather than try for another Olympics. I thought about my painful wrist, which wouldn't improve for years.

I also thought of how skeptical people were about my chances in Atlanta because I had grown six inches, gained thirty pounds, and aged four years. My mind was flooded with all the bad falls and disappointments and doubt. I thought of how important it was that I continued to get back up after each and every fall, and to move forward after every setback.

What was the story of that girl on the podium? Maybe it was that you cannot succeed if you don't dare to try. That you must keep trying even after you fall on your backside. And that you should never let others decide how much you can achieve. *Dream big, work hard, and don't set limits on what you could do or be.*

I had success because I didn't know that I wasn't supposed to. It didn't matter that I was a girl or that I was small or that I was reserved. It didn't matter that my parents didn't have infinite resources. It wasn't about perfect; it was about making the full effort. It was about setting goals and steadfastly refusing to be derailed. *Keep passion alive.* Many people don't realize how strong they truly are until they are challenged. My sport did that for me. Gymnastics allowed me to see what I was made of. And when I had doubts or faced obstacles, it always reminded me.

29

Not until I was standing on the podium did it hit me. That was the moment. Somewhere in the back of my mind I knew that I'd soon retire, and for the first time I worried about my future, when I was no longer an Elite gymnast but a young woman trying to make her way in the world. "What am I supposed to do now? What do I do with the rest of my life?" I was thrilled to be up on the podium, but I wondered what would happen after I climbed down.

The day after I won my gold medal on beam, I sat in a room with a man from the sports agency that was representing me at the time. Unfortunately, this was not a successful meeting for him. I knew I was retiring from the sport, and I suddenly felt the need to be a part of the decision-making process with regard to my future. For me that meant starting with a clean slate. I needed an agent who was willing to talk to *me*, not just to my coaches or parents. However, I wasn't just looking for a new agent; I was looking for a partner, one who could guide me but, like my parents and coaches always had, make difficult decisions with my best interests at heart. This was my first attempt to be assertive off the gymnastics floor.

An acquaintance of my coach and parents recommended Sheryl Shade, who ran a firm, Shade Global, in New York City. She didn't represent many athletes and had no gymnasts as clients, so I felt I wouldn't get lost in the shuffle, as I might have at a larger agency. As always, it was a leap of faith with me, and the day after the Olympics I signed with Sheryl. As a member of the Magnificent Seven and with seven Olympic medals in tow, I suddenly entered a whole new world of opportunities that included tours, TV appearances, and endorsements.

Following the 1996 Olympics, there was much more excitement about the women's gymnastics team than in 1992. That team had won bronze, which at that time was a remarkable achievement, but the Magnificent Seven had won gold and America was overjoyed that Team USA had come out on top. We filmed a Wheaties commercial and I landed on the front (and back) of the cereal box. There was a huge spread in *Sports Illustrated* and the entire team went to New York and appeared on *Late Show with David Letterman*. I went on Conan O'Brien's late-night show. I had never been up late enough to see the show, and wasn't sure what to expect. I headed to the studio wearing my jeans and sweatshirt, with no makeup, and my hair looking wild. Luckily, Sheryl had thought to get me something nice to wear that night, and they applied makeup at the studio. However, I still blanch when I think of my crazy poof of hair.

The media couldn't get enough of us. Neither could the fans. USA Gymnastics had the foresight to set up a national tour. Arenas sold out across the country, so more dates were added for the second leg of the tour, which was called the John Hancock Tour of Gymnastics Champions. To this day it remains the longest tour in U.S. Gymnastics history. Eventually, we took our show to ninety-nine cities, and performed several exhibitions and professional competitions on top of that. I was grateful that my entrance into adult life was delayed for almost a year due to the busy schedule. I could put off that nagging question, "What do I do with my life?" for just a little bit longer.

Early on, Kerri Strug had opted to perform on a separate tour from the rest of the team, but after her tour ended she joined ours and the Magnificent Seven was back together. I had a feeling that when Kerri joined the tour she worried that we might be upset with her because she had gone a separate way. She quickly realized that wasn't the case and was immediately part of the group. We were a team and nothing could change that.

Touring was a blast. We got to know each other as people and formed lasting friendships. Fans could see me smiling. Jaycie and Amanda always had us laughing, and even Amy opened up and joined us when we engaged in our hijinks. She was a modest girl, but we coaxed her into playing classical piano for us for the first time and she was incredible.

The members of the men's team had basically grown up with us. They were as protective as big brothers but didn't hold back with the pranks. We were between fifteen and twenty-seven years old, and when we had free time, one of the few things we could do en masse that we all enjoyed was go to the mall. We'd be passing through Iowa and we'd get off our buses at a mall, to go shopping or just to walk around. For me, it was always nice to just feel normal. The boys came with us as chaperones but were typically leading the shenanigans. There was a lot of laughter. We were a family and that included the international athletes who joined us on tour, including Lilia Podkopayeva and Alexei Nemov. We were enjoying the sport we loved on our own terms, playing to crowds instead of judges.

We tried to do something entertaining when we had downtime in a city. In San Francisco we went to a Rolling Stones concert, my second concert ever. (My first was Tom Petty, which two morning show DJs in Oklahoma had taken me to after my success at the 1996 Olympics.) It was crazy! We'd also go bowling, sightseeing, or even catch a movie. We made time for fun, but the tour was a great deal of work. We had rehearsals each day, with group and individual routines to learn, and long bus rides that would have us arrive at our hotel in the dead of night. In each city, I would do interviews, gym visits, and other public appearances. I enjoyed visiting various children's hospitals and joining my Olympic teammates for the chaotic signings of our book, *The Magnificent Seven: The Authorized Story of American Gold*, that brought out thousands of fans.

Each night I would collapse on the bus, hoping for eight hours of sleep.

Wherever we went, fans came out in droves and we were treated like rock stars. We'd want to do our best every night for them because *our* sixty-eighth sold-out show was likely *their* first and only show. Months after the Olympics, tickets were still so hard to come by that they'd have to put extra chairs on the floor. I enjoyed all the hoopla and appreciated how people responded to our Olympic success, but I didn't fully grasp what the team or I had done to deserve so much attention. Fame and celebrity resulting from performing a sport I loved just wasn't something I fully comprehended at such a young age.

As in 1992, we were allowed to high-five folks, shake their hands, and even give out hugs. We put on quite a show with American and international gymnasts, acrobats, and even a comic master of ceremonies. A highlight was the full-cast performance to Michael Jackson's "Thriller" that we did just before intermission. The whole cast danced together, and then we broke off and did tumbling runs. It was a spectacular number. Around Halloween, we came out wearing masks and were decked out in an array of "scary" costumes. Anything to surprise the fans and keep it fun for us!

My balance beam routine was the final individual performance each night, prior to the full-cast finale. So I had to finish my beam routine and then quickly run backstage and change into the costume I wore for the closing number. Then I'd rush back onto the floor in time for the spotlight to hit me. The rest of the cast would already be on the floor and I was the only one changing, so I had no time to spare. Which was why certain cast members thought it would be funny to hide my costume. Because I'm Type A, I'd always lay out my costume for the quick change. When it was missing, I'd have to go back out for the final number in my beam uniform, while the pranksters tried not to laugh. "Okay, guys, come on!" Of course I wasn't the only one pranked. At times, there would be milk in the chalk bowl or a sudden change of floor music. On the tour stops right before our holiday break and at the end of the tour, the announcer would actually give the audience a heads-up that we were a little giddy. He'd tell the fans to watch out for some extraspecial fun that night.

There were almost a hundred tour stops, so Steve couldn't be at all of them. The girls' personal coaches also ran businesses, so they couldn't be on the road with us the entire time. They traded off different legs of the tour. Unlike in 1992, I wasn't training for future competitions, so I didn't fly ahead to work out in a gym in the next city. Training for me was just about staying in shape for the tour itself and getting my individual and group routines down.

I didn't do any separate training, even prior to appearances in a couple of made-for-TV "competitions." They were almost extensions of the tour and very relaxed. In most, I competed with a partner or as part of a group. We had so much fun wearing colorful costumes, competing with music on each event, and, of course, taking advantage of the rules being a bit looser than for Olympic competition. I have special memories of me joining forces with Amy Chow to compete in a pairs all-around competition at the Reese's International Gymnastics Cup in Anaheim. We were ecstatic when we won.

It was necessary for everyone to have some personal time off, even if just for a few days. There wasn't enough time for the international gymnasts to fly back to Russia or Ukraine, but I was able to get back to Edmond at times. I needed to do laundry, refresh my bags, and enjoy a mental break. It was great to go home every now and then to see my parents and catch my breath. After being treated like a superstar and performing in front of thousands of cheering fans on a nightly basis, going home was a way to ground myself and try to do normal everyday things, which was a theme of my youth. I was still living at home, so it was back to my room and getting a little downtime before returning to show business!

Girls were often leaving the tour briefly for personal commitments. On January 1, I was in Pasadena to serve as the co-grand marshal of the Rose Parade with Carl Lewis. It was an incredible honor to be in the lead car, side by side with the famous gold medal Olympic sprinter and long jumper. It was an experience that stands out in my memories. One of the blown-up photos that still hangs in my parents' living room is of me and Carl waving from the car. Every time I visit, I think, "Wow, I really got to do that!"

I couldn't have left gymnastics cold turkey. Touring helped me gently roll out of the sport. I was blessed with the opportunity to continue performing in front of a huge audience and do all those skills that I loved. So it was helpful in weaning me out of the competitive mind-set. Nonetheless, when the tour was over I felt a bit lost. What helped me get my bearings was going back to school.

I moved to Norman and into a dorm on the University of Oklahoma campus. My mother recently confessed that she desperately wanted to go with me and help me move into my room. She still missed having Tessa at home, so to see her second daughter move out of the house was very hard for her. But she understood that it was important for me to go off by myself. She knew I needed to start finding out who I was outside of gymnastics and what I was capable of doing on my own.

I realized quickly that dorm life didn't suit me, and it wasn't just because I wasn't crazy about sharing a bathroom. It was because I was at a different place in my life than most of the students. I was basically running a business while attending school. In fact, that first day I was trying to hook up a fax machine in my dorm room so I could stay on top of contracts and work. I wanted to be "normal," but it wasn't as easy as I thought it would be. I was now outside my element, which caused me to revert to my introverted ways. I was sure that I was the only one going through an identity crisis, and I felt like I had alternating neon signs plastered on my forehead that blinked DOESN'T BELONG and DOESN'T KNOW WHO SHE IS!

When I was afraid of something in gymnastics I would simply will myself to do it. We called it "chucking a skill." As if we were auditioning for a Nike commercial, we would "just do it." Outside the gym, I had not learned to chuck anything. I held back. I didn't want to be outside my comfort zone and that zone seemed to shrink, particularly after I moved into an apartment of my own. I told myself that I needed to come and go from where I lived with convenience because I was constantly traveling for appearances, sponsor work, and gymnastics clinics, but my move off campus was actually a way for me to run and hide. It was quiet and I could withdraw from the world. It was certainly not the best idea for me socially because it allowed me to become a bit of a hermit, which I was prone to do. I'd go to class, return to my apartment, get my homework done, and watch television. Now that I was no longer seeing my gymnastics friends on a daily basis, television became my best friend—Jerry Seinfeld and Jennifer Aniston didn't realize they were my best buddies. At least I was out of my apartment when I worked, because the bills needed to be paid and I wanted to save for the future.

People did reach out to me and I made several friendships that continue to this day. But I was timid as I tried to find myself after losing much of the self-esteem and confidence I'd gained on the gymnastics floor. Real life was just not a place where I believed in myself. Living a very open, public life was difficult enough when I was sure about what I was doing, but now, when I felt I didn't have the answers to the questions about my life and dreaded the unknown, I wasn't comfortable being under a microscope.

That summer, Steve asked me if I'd like to compete in the 1997 World University Games in August. I'd never given a thought to collegiate gymnastics because I wasn't allowed to participate in NCAA competitions as a result of having given up my amateur status when I was thirteen. I assumed I had to be on OU's women's gymnastics team to qualify for the World University Games, but Steve explained that anyone, even professionals, could participate as long as they were enrolled in college. I thought it ironic that my being a professional prohibited me from competing for my college yet I could represent it at these World Games. It was a tempting offer because it would allow me to get back, even briefly, to the life I'd left behind. However, I was barely in tour shape, much less competition shape. My body had retired! And so had my mind. And, although I did full bar and beam routines on tour, I hadn't done vault or floor since the Olympics. I didn't think muscle memory could save me at this point.

I liked the idea of having this one opportunity to represent the University of Oklahoma, but it definitely took some convincing from Steve because I hadn't wrapped my head around the idea of returning to competition. When I qualified at the World University Games Trials in Cincinnati by winning every event but floor, he told the press, "We decided to come to this competition just two weeks ago. I actually talked her into it, because I thought it would be fun and give her an opportunity for a nice international competition without the pressure of the Olympics."

Steve coached the American women's team that competed at the World University Games in Italy. We returned to the venue, in Catania, where in 1990 I won my first international competition and declared I wanted to compete in the next Olympics. Eight years later, the Italian fans still treated me like royalty and called me affectionately "Queen Yankee," as they did that first time around.

Since I'd gone back into training, my body hadn't been cooperating. In Italy, I had some really awful workouts, and I was embarrassed because around me were all these American college girls who were in great shape and flying all over the gym, and I was an Olympic gold medalist having a tough time getting through a routine. It wasn't going to be easy, because my body was not prepared and some of the Europeans were tough competitors I'd gone up against in the past.

There were some bumpy days leading up to the competition, but when the lights went on my body felt great. Everything was under control and I was ready to perform once more. Our team won the silver medal, and I captured the gold medal in the all-around. It was a fun competition with a wonderful group of teammates, and I was thankful to get another chance to perform on the world stage, particularly at the venue that started my Olympic dream. The World University Games may have been a side note to my career, but to stand up on the podium again while my national anthem played and to exit gymnastics with an all-around gold medal around my neck was an immense delight.

Afterward, Steve, the other girls on our team, and I traveled around Italy before returning home. That was a wonderful conclusion to a memorable trip. I was very glad Steve had talked me into going.

30

In September I had fun playing myself on the TV sitcom *Saved by the Bell: The New Class*. I was so nervous backstage. I waited for what seemed like several hours (but was probably only a few minutes), pacing back and forth in my dressing room, practicing my lines again and again. I had more butterflies than on the first night of the Olympics! I grew up watching the show, so it was exciting to do even a walk-on.

The show's title was appropriate because that month I returned to school after summer break. I was back to having a difficult time making a smooth transition to the real world, so getting into a learning mode was very helpful. Although I didn't know where I was going in my life, at least I was taking small steps to somewhere.

School was enjoyable and fruitful, but otherwise I was still feeling the letdown after gymnastics and experiencing withdrawal pains. I wasn't sitting around depressed and weeping, but I was still struggling to figure out who I was outside of my sport. Since the age of five, I had described myself as a gymnast, though I was able to balance that part of my life with school. Now I needed to find a different balance. I had never come across anything that could come close to replacing gymnastics in my life, so how was I now going to fill more than forty hours a week? It was troublesome without having a specific goal to work toward. My "job" filled some of my free time, but it was never the same week to week. Almost all of my travel was solo. I missed those regular friends that I saw every day in the gym. I missed having face-to-face conversations with my coaches and parents. I was lonely.

Another issue soon cropped up. I began to put on weight. When you gain four dresses sizes in a matter of months on a five-foot frame, it's a big deal. I had never worried about my weight or what I was eating. Burgers and pizza had always been among my favorite foods. It was hard enough just keeping up with the number of calories I was burning on a daily basis. But now that I kept eating the same amount of food I had as a gymnast yet was doing virtually no physical activity, it began to show. I was on my own, but I was not taking care of myself.

Around that time, I agreed to do an autograph signing at an office supply store. I sat at a long table in the furniture section, just me and the lady who was helping coordinate the event. There was a long line out the door, and the sponsor had provided a stack of 8 × 10 photos of me on beam at the 1996 Olympic Games for me to sign. In this setting, when it had to do with gymnastics, I had no problem talking to perfect strangers and always enjoyed meeting folks.

As I was signing, an older gentleman in a cowboy hat came up to the table and stood in front of me. I can still see him picking up a picture of me and staring at it. Then he looked at me. Then he looked at the woman sitting with me. In that moment, I realized he was looking for that girl in the picture, the fit, confident athlete standing triumphantly on the balance beam, the Olympic champion. He wanted to get *her* autograph. He was staring right at me, but he didn't recognize me because of the weight I'd put on. I no longer looked like a champion. And I didn't feel like one.

As I drove home, I felt a heaviness in my chest. I wanted to cry but was too angry with myself to do so. *How had I let this happen?* Even then I knew it wasn't really about the weight. It was, "What am I doing with my life?" I knew I couldn't spend the rest of my days signing autographs. I loved doing that and making people happy, but I needed to be part of society and I needed to give back to society. I had to figure it all out soon or be in danger of becoming a recluse. I could already picture myself with eighteen cats and rarely seeing the light of day. This was a dark period for me that would lead me down a road toward an ill-advised early marriage, grasping for that life I thought I was supposed to lead. But it was also when I really began to think about health and fitness. There was no way of knowing it at the time, but the seeds were planted for my wanting to run a company promoting women's health. Most people assume my mission to help women focus on their health and my foundation to combat child obesity grew out of my Olympic background, but it actually stemmed from what was going on in my life after retirement.

Like every other woman with weight issues, real or imagined, I tried every fad diet and quick fix; because I didn't want to wait. *I want to lose weight NOW!* None of these worked and I put on more weight. One day, I realized that if I was going to get back into shape, I had to do it the right way. I began learning more about nutrition. I started a food journal. I began to formulate the idea of an everything-in-moderation approach that became my credo. Of course, that came after I decided I would never eat chocolate again. I got rid of it all, threw out every morsel. I then proceeded to eat every piece of food in my apartment and then . . . went out and bought chocolate. I came to the realization that it was okay for me to have a little bit of chocolate or some other deliciously fattening treat if it would keep me from devouring everything else in the refrigerator. I focused on *portion size,* which is critical to maintaining a healthy weight.

I signed up for a gym membership, fearing what I would be subjecting myself to. Almost everyone knew me in Oklahoma, so walking into a gym as a very out-of-shape Olympic gold medalist was embarrassing. But I did it. I had never even been on a treadmill before, so I started slowly. I stuck with it by keeping an exercise log.

But I wasn't going to be able to just sweat off weight in a gym. I looked for activities I'd enjoy. I started Rollerblading, took up racquetball and squash, and learned to play golf with the clubs I'd received as a gift when I graduated from high school. I took lessons and got certified for scuba diving. (I admit I haven't been back in scuba gear since a trip to Hawaii when I found myself face-to-face with a ten-foot shark! That was definitely enough of an adrenaline rush for me.)

When a group of friends said they were going to Cushing to skydive, I went with them. Why? Because it had become very important for me to face my fears. I had confidence as a gymnast, but how could I get that to bleed over into regular life? When I was nervous to do a skill on uneven bars my coach would tell me I was safe and good to go, and I'd suck it up, count to three, and go. So I kind of looked at my new life of adventure that way. I was really scared to jump out of an airplane, so I counted— one, two, three—and jumped. It was an amazing experience. I was grasping at straws and looking for something to feel passionate about again.

Figure skating was the big one for me. After retirement sets in, almost every Olympian wonders if there is another sport they can do at an elite level. "Ice skating? That's kind of similar to gymnastics. It's so graceful yet powerful and I love the presentation and the costumes. I can even apply physics to the movements. It'll be a piece of cake!" They had opened a new ice-skating rink in Edmond, so at around five thirty in the morning I'd drive from Norman and take private lessons from a former National team member. I had fleeting thoughts of being an Olympian someday, but I was surprised that it wasn't as easy as it looked on television. I learned all the single jumps, but I had a lot of trouble with my footwork and understanding my blades. I found out the hard way that landings on ice weren't as soft as on the crash pads we'd used in the gym. And it was freezing! It turned out I wasn't Olympic-bound, but it was a fun activity and I gained a new appreciation for the athletes I watched take to the ice every four years in the Winter Games.

It didn't happen overnight, but eventually my weight evened out. I also discovered that I was stronger and had more stamina. I felt a sliver of that confidence I had as a gymnast.

Now that I was more energized, I began to be more efficient with time, and that helped strike a balance between college and work, including public and media appearances, clinics, and camps.

Life was better, but I still hadn't escaped entirely from that dark place. As one of many athletes whose career ends while they are still young, I continued wondering, "What am I supposed to do with my life?" I was not an overnight success at solving the identity question. Finding out who I was would take years, and a marriage, a divorce, and a comeback attempt would be part of the process.

31

In the last two years of the twentieth century, there were big changes in my life academically, athletically, and personally. I switched majors, I attempted a comeback, and I got married.

When it came time to declare a major at school, I picked psychology. I was a very curious person and fascinated by how people think and why they do the things they do. I enjoyed my psych classes, but soon determined that business administration and marketing would serve me better in regard to what I was already experiencing in my professional life. When people shoved documents under my nose I needed to understand them. I'd heard all the horror stories of athletes who worked hard but ten years down the road had nothing to show for it because they didn't know how to take care of their own finances. I wanted to try to be an adult and look toward the future, and I thought taking business classes would help me long term. I didn't know what kind of work I wanted to do in the future, but I figured I couldn't go wrong getting a business degree. It was a way of keeping my options open and not getting pigeonholed into one specific area.

The gymnastics-related activities and jobs I was doing helped me remain self-sufficient. I was able to pay for my undergraduate studies, my apartment, and other expenses. I was still reluctant to give speeches, but I accepted enough other requests to keep me busy when I wasn't in class.

In October 1999, I was asked by USA Gymnastics to go to Tianjin, China, as the athlete representative for our women's team at the World Championship. If the girls needed anything I was there for them as their go-between. The experience was rewarding, although the women's team placed fifth, not as high as we would have liked. As I sat there watching our gymnasts and gymnasts from around the world, I started thinking to myself, "Ahhh, man, I can do that! Ohhh, I can do that, too!" The die was cast. I was most definitely retired physically, but mentally I felt I could still do gymnastics at the highest level. When I returned to the States, I started to think seriously about trying to make my third U.S. Olympic team and compete at the Sydney Summer Games in mid-September 2000.

People inevitably question athletes' motives when they come back for another try after great success the first go-around. *What if you don't do as well? Why would you want to sully your record?* The most overlooked reason is their love for their sport. I loved gymnastics. I missed challenging myself to learn new skills; I missed performing; I missed competing on the world stage.

When Michael Jordan ended his retirement it was simply because he loved basketball, as there was nothing left for him to prove. My whole life I'd felt I had to prove myself, but there are times when it's not about proving anything to anyone. When I decided to make a comeback for the 2000 Olympics, it was about enjoying the sport. If I failed, I would have at least tried and that was good enough for me. Maybe it was illogical. Who takes off three years from training and tries to make the Olympic team in seven months? I believed I could do it simply because when I made up my mind to do something, I did it. However, I needed my coach on board. And I needed to discuss it with my husband.

I was someone who believed everything happens for a reason, so I never had regrets that so much of my youth was spent doing gymnastics. Nobody had a better childhood and I wouldn't have changed a thing. In fact, at twenty I handled a lot of adult issues that other young women may not have been able to, including parts of my business. However, socially I was much younger and more naïve than other women my age. Because I had been very sheltered in many ways, I wasn't fully prepared for adulthood.

I married the second man I dated. Chris was a medical student at the University of Oklahoma who was preparing for his residency in ophthalmology. We were engaged a few months later and married eight months after that. It's clear that I longed for the security and structure that gymnastics had brought to my life. I believe I married so quickly someone I didn't really know because I felt this union was going to be my security blanket. It seemed as if it was meant to be. I would get married, have kids, and live happily ever after. It turned out that this was not my fairy tale.

32

I waited for the new century before approaching Steve. I still considered him my coach and wouldn't attempt a comeback if he wasn't on board. I needed his honest opinion about my chances. Steve and I had seen each other on and off since the 1997 World University Games, but not that often of late. He was at a different stage in his life, too, as the father of young children. He wasn't necessarily eating, sleeping, and breathing gymnastics anymore, either. I hadn't been to Dynamo in a while when I walked into his office. I had no presentation ready, no PowerPoint to show how we could accomplish this task. I just said first thing, "Do you want to train me for the 2000 Olympics?"

He said without much enthusiasm, "All right." It was hard for me to hear him say, "Well, let's get you into good physical shape and we'll take it from there."

I would be twenty-three in Sydney, eight years older than I'd been in Barcelona. Steve had trained collegiate athletes, so he understood what it took to train someone my age. But he had never had an Olympic-caliber athlete take off three years and then try to make a comeback for another Olympic team. I'm not sure there was any coach who had done that. And he'd have to do it without Peggy Liddick, who was now living abroad as

Australia's national women's team coordinator. I was happy for her, but I had always relied on her and missed her greatly.

Steve had me do a stress test to make sure I was healthy enough for the vigorous training that lay ahead. Though I was only in okay everyday shape, and not nearly in competitive gymnastics shape, Steve and I agreed that there was no reason not to go ahead with our training.

That meant I wouldn't attend OU in the second semester of the 1999–2000 year. Although I had thought he would remain in Oklahoma, Chris received his residency in Houston. So when he left for Texas, I moved back in with my parents in Edmond and commuted each day to the gym, just like old times.

For the first couple of months of working with Steve, I hardly did any true gymnastics. I got up early and drove to a fitness center at Gaillardia, where Steve was living at the time. A personal trainer worked with me to get my endurance up and strength back. Those sessions were tough but felt good. In the gym I worked primarily on flexibility and very easy skills like cartwheels and back walkovers that I did when I was six. It was like starting from zero. I tried to work my way back by doing skills that I had performed for fifteen years and I couldn't do them! I had little air sense and I hurt everywhere. I was feeling a strain on tiny muscles that I forgot I had. But once I laid that groundwork and my body was back in gymnastics shape, the muscle memory kicked in and the skills came back. I was on my way!

The Mississauga Gymnastics Challenge in Ontario, Canada, was the meet Steve chose to be my first real competition in my comeback bid. He wanted me to use it as a trial run before I competed at the 2000 Women's National Gymnastics Festival in Tulsa, Oklahoma. I got a first-place finish for the first time since 1997, and surprisingly it came in the vault, the event that would play a big role for me at the 2000 Olympic Trials. I loved competing again, but Peggy was not there and I missed our old team.

Steve and I next went to Tulsa, where a good showing at the Women's National Gymnastics Festival would allow me to move on to the U.S. Championship in St. Louis. I wasn't worried because I had shown I was prepared at the newly instituted Olympic training camps. These camps had been added after I had retired. Gone were the days of simply training quietly in your home gym and proving yourself during competitions. Now you had to prove yourself each month at a rigorous training camp.

Also new in 2000 was the process for selection of the U.S. Olympic team. No longer would the seven girls having the highest scores from the Nationals and Olympic Trials combined be chosen automatically. Instead, a selection committee that included team Coordinator Béla Károlyi would evaluate the performances at both competitions and also take into consideration past performances and training camps, and choose girls based on the team's needs and not necessarily whether they excelled on all four apparatuses. That the compulsories, which favored girls like me who were fundamentally proficient, had been eliminated also was a factor. Putting together a team was now like doing a jigsaw puzzle and involved a great deal of strategy.

The era of the event specialist had not completely arrived, but it was fast approaching. I had mixed feelings about this change and its effect on our sport. I lamented that we would see fewer fundamentally sound all-around gymnasts. But I liked that we would be able to witness extraordinary routines and skills performed by athletes who had extreme talent on one or two events, but not on all four. This new system was controversial, but overall I thought it made sense for our sport. I could see how the new selection procedure would benefit Team USA at the Olympics.

My hope was that I would be chosen for the Olympic team because I was still doing both beam and uneven bars exceptionally well. I was content to be a specialist now, and I thought I could throw high-scoring routines on both apparatuses and help the U.S. medal. And in a pinch I could do a solid floor routine. For my comeback, my dear friend Kelly Garrison choreographed my Hungarian-folk-dance-influenced floor routine, during which violins played "Czardas." Conceptually, vault, because my start value was low, was the only event where I wouldn't be an asset. Beam, bars, consistency, and leadership—I felt I had a lot to offer. As much as I loved the sport, I wasn't there to waste anyone's time. I truly felt I could be in the mix.

The night before the competition in Tulsa, I had a good workout. Vault was my last event before heading for bed. I trained my Yurchenko half twist with no problem. Steve then had me do one more vaulting run so I could try my Yurchenko one-and-a-half twist, a difficult vault for me even in my prime. I was a little tired and landed short and stiff-legged on the hard surface that was in place for the competition. I hyperextended both knees and felt excruciating pain. It turned out I injured my right knee worse than my left, fracturing the bone.

In hindsight, which is always a dangerous because you are looking back instead of forging ahead, I should not have been doing such a difficult vault so early in my comeback. There was no need for us to worry about start value at that point, when I still had three weeks to train before Nationals and eight weeks before Olympic Trials. In making a comeback, you don't want to train or compete skills that you're not ready for because that's how injuries like mine happen. While you gradually get into better shape for competition, you train on softer landing mats. I was still in the "skill-and-routine" phase of my comeback. I was working on numbers and becoming more consistent. I'd had good showings at the training camps. Once I had full strength and stamina, the skills part would come easily, particularly because I'd done many of them for fifteen years. Only *then* should I have attempted that vault. Even then it might have been foolish because it was unlikely they'd even want me to compete vault at the Olympics when they'd have many more powerful vaulters to choose from.

This was the first time I'd ever injured a knee. I was fortunate that my leg muscles held and I did not tear my ACL or have major ligament damage. Doctors told me that my knee did not require surgery, and I just had to wait for the bone to heal. Meanwhile, I could begin rehab to strengthen the surrounding ligaments. I was instructed by my doctor to do pool therapy, which would allow me to work the rest of my body and keep myself in shape. There was no ground pool in my parents' backyard, so our neighbors allowed me to use their swimming pool to regain strength in my legs. I wore a life jacket and "ran" in the pool, going from forty minutes to an hour to ninety minutes at a time. How dedicated was I? I was training ten or eleven hours a day between my time in the pool and the gym. I was driven by a significant goal. I wanted to compete at least on a limited basis in late July at the 2000 U.S. Gymnastics Championship in St. Louis.

33

As an Olympian I had automatic entry to the U.S. Championship. Steve was in constant contact with USA Gymnastics updating them and Béla on my progress leading up to the meet. Although I'd trained all four events without too many hard landings, my knee was only at 80 percent. So everyone agreed that I should compete only on uneven bars to give my knee more time to heal.

Although I competed only one event at Nationals, it proved to be a big step in the right direction. That I tied Amy Chow and Alyssa Beckerman for second on bars behind Elise Ray confirmed that I could help the U.S. in that event. It was only the second time I had landed my dismount on my healing knee. I was able to show it was recovering fast and should be at 90 percent at Olympic Trials and 100 percent at the Olympics. Meanwhile, it was back to the gym for more rehab and training to compete all four events at the Olympic Trials that August in Boston.

Since I missed the meet in Tulsa entirely and competed in only one event at Nationals, Steve petitioned for me to be able to compete at the Olympic Trials. There hadn't been one year when I was able to compete fully in both the Nationals and the Olympic Trials. I went to Boston early and was able to "show readiness" to the women's selection committee for competition on all apparatuses. Basically this meant I went through a full competition just days before the real one began. The committee was comprised of Béla Károlyi, longtime judge Marilyn Cross, 1984 Olympian Tracee Talavera, and athlete representative Chari Knight-Hunter. My knee held up and the Monday before the two-night Olympic Trials, I was "verified" as a competitor.

On Friday at the FleetCenter, the Trials began and I got off to a promising start. I competed the two most important events without a major glitch. I kept in mind that scores in the all-around didn't matter as much as showing the selection committee that I was strong on beam and bars and that my knee was not holding me back. Uneven bars went well as I combined new skills like my inverted giants with old favorites like the "Miller 1," a hop full twist. I finished strong with a stuck landing. Beam had a solid beginning with my familiar front flip mount. My only error was a slight wobble on my layout step out. So I had impressive performances on the two events that I needed to do well before the selection committee. How I did on floor was of minimal importance and vault mattered even less, because I'd no doubt be a backup in Sydney, but the rules stipulated that I had to complete all four events, regardless. No problem. Although I wasn't the most skilled, strongest, or most flexible girl on the floor, I knew how to compete. That advantage hadn't gone away. I also wasn't terribly worried about my knee because I had trained full routines and it was only getting stronger. I capped off the night with a solid vault.

I had done exactly what I needed to do, which was to show my readiness for the second time that week.

On the final night, I started on vault. And ended on it, with the commentators who had stated the previous night that I was Sydney-bound now saying that my Olympic dream was over.

I was going for the stick and landed short and stiff-legged, like in Tulsa when I injured it. I didn't reinjure the knee, just tweaked it. From a sitting position, I lay down completely on my back. Steve and some others circled me as I winced in pain. Steve's familiar voice was all I heard though several people were talking at me. When someone suggested carrying me to the training room, I said no and got to my feet on my own. I was angry with myself. It was absurd that I would do this for a second time.

I was trying to shake the pain out of my legs while Steve was trying to keep me focused so I could quickly assess my condition and decide whether to chance doing my second vault. There was a sense of urgency and we had no time to think through what we needed to do and determine what my knee would allow, so I was trying to calm both Steve and myself. He instructed me to run a little before I took off on my second vault. My knee was sore, but these were the Olympic Trials. I go. The question was, *Will the knee work?* I thought it would, so I got ready to do my second vault.

Steve told me that if I didn't feel comfortable on the runway and couldn't do it 100 percent I should veer off. I went all out. This time I landed on my feet but took a few big steps backward. My knee seemed to be in shock, because it wouldn't do what I was asking it to do. I couldn't put weight on it. With the uneven bar rotation coming up soon, I was taken to the training room, where I had a big decision to make.

As I sat there on the training table while medics assessed the condition of my knee, people were asking me questions and determining my future, but all that noise seemed to float off in a bubble and fade away and I heard only what my parents always told me. Their comforting words reminded me that gymnastics was not life. It was a sport, one that I would always love with all my being, but wasn't worth doing if it could cause a permanent injury. I knew my body. As fearless as I was, it would have been reckless for me to attempt a full twisting doubleback off the beam in twenty minutes and risk landing on my head. Steve came to the same conclusion. He made the call, taking the decision out of my hands. It broke my heart, but I agreed.

There was a point when I wanted to shout over to the selection committee, "You're not going use me for vault anyway!" Maybe they could block out what happened on vault and just think about bars and beam? During a TV interview a short time later, I stated that I still hoped to be picked for the Olympic team. I sincerely believed that my knee would be fine again in a couple of days to the same extent it was before vault. I knew what I did to my knee was not serious and only temporary. I was like an experienced opera singer with laryngitis who doesn't mind sounding like a truck driver for three days because she knows she will be able to sing an aria beautifully at her concert on the fourth day. I'd trained with the bad knee, so though I looked finished, I knew that if they wanted me on that team, I would be ready in Sydney.

Steve told me that he would petition for me to be put on the team based on what I did leading up to the Trials and on the first night of Trials. I never expected the petition to go through. I just hoped, as you do when you buy a lottery ticket with the understanding that the odds are stacked against you. I understood the reality of the situation. If I had performed well then it wouldn't be an issue. It wasn't fair for me to think that the selection committee would put me on the team now. But I sat in that little locker room for twelve minutes prior to the announcement of the team, waiting and hoping. The delay offered me a little ray of hope that they were giving me serious consideration and understood that I'd be fit in a few days. I'd even be happy if they were considering me as an alternate. No such luck. My Olympic career was over.

I was not surprised that my name wasn't called when the 2000 women's Olympic team marched out to be introduced. It was a disappointment that I hadn't made my third Olympic team. However, it was better that I tried and failed than to not have tried at all. I dislike dwelling on what-ifs, but naturally three days later my knee was fine.

My competitive career really was over. I was fortunate to have had two peaks. One peak was when I won five medals at the 1992 Olympics and carried that momentum to have success at the next two World Championships. The other peak was at the 1996 Olympics, when I won gold medals as part of the team and on balance beam. The two peaks corresponded to the two separate parts of my competitive career, based on my having two distinct body types and there being two different Codes of Points. I wasn't worrying about it, but I knew my legacy was, essentially, that I was America's most decorated gymnast, male or female, having won seven Olympic medals and nine World Championship medals and fifty-nine international and forty-nine national medals. Although it would be years before I understood what I'd accomplished in terms of medals and awards, at the time the sun set on my gymnastics career, I felt extraordinary pride. I was respected for my hard work, drive, perseverance, and competitive spirit, and that was enough.

34

After coming home, I resumed training because I had been invited to be part of the 2000 post-Olympic tour. I soon received a call from Sheryl telling me that MSNBC wanted me to be an analyst for the network at the Sydney Games. So once again a negative, not making the team, transformed into a positive. Here was an opportunity that I never would have been offered if I hadn't been injured, and it let me add a major new component to my résumé.

In Sydney, I spent a week viewing both women and men's artistic gymnastics and providing my analysis on different MSNBC broadcasts. I was at the Olympics for the first time as something other than a competitor, and I found it gratifying to still be a part of the Games even if I wasn't wearing a leotard. Oddly, this was the first time in my life that I took the time to actually watch an Olympics. I had never been interested in sitting and watching any gymnastics on television, especially when I was doing it. Now, for the first time, I could look at it from the perspective of a fan.

After Sydney, I flew to New York and worked in the studio. Each day for another week, I sat with Brian Williams while he shared the news and then joined him for a segment in which we spoke about the most exciting highlights of the Games.

That was my initiation into the world of an "expert analyst." I had never planned to do commentary; it was never a job I wanted to pursue or even considered. But I realized that it was a wonderful way to remain part of the Olympic movement and gymnastics. It was a way to critique and inform. It was a rewarding way to help promote the sport I loved. It still is.

Soon after I returned home, the post-Olympic tour began. Although I wasn't a member of the 2000 women's Olympic team, I loved being asked to perform with Dominique Dawes, Amy Chow, and the younger girls who rounded out the 2000 team. The tour wasn't nearly as long as the one in 1996—but it was a really nice way to utilize all that effort I made while attempting a comeback. I assumed it would be my swan song, my last opportunity to perform for big audiences. (Little did I know I'd also be invited to take part in the 2004 and 2008 tours!)

While I was disappointed that Chris and I couldn't reside in Oklahoma, I was excited about a program offered at the University of Houston. This was an additional two-year program that offered an entrepreneurship degree. I was able to transfer many of my OU credits to UH, so as I neared my BBA in marketing, I applied for one of the thirty spots available for this program. I had kept up my grades, so I was hopeful when I applied. I was ecstatic to be accepted!

I try to live my life by continuously looking forward and not get bogged down in what could have been or should have been. So it is very hard to allow myself now to look back and relive the bumpy parts of my life that I, in fact, have tried to forget. I want to learn from my mistakes and move on. I wouldn't characterize my quick marriage as a reckless decision. It was more about my clinging to an image of what I thought I was expected to do at my age, an image of who I was supposed to be—the perfect wife. The marriage was short-lived, but I didn't want to admit that to myself or anyone else. That would make it a failure and I wanted perfection. Those years were a defining time for me, when I withdrew from life rather than participating in it, and then realized it was time to stand up for myself. I would soon find my voice and with the help of friends and family begin to rebuild my life and really discover who I was as a person. *Keep moving forward.*

I continued to work for my entrepreneurship degree. What I liked most about the program was that we were supposed to come up with an idea for a business and take it from scratch all the way through to fruition (conceptually at least). There wouldn't be a true launch, but we would factor in marketing and determine how it would work financially. That process was very interesting to me because of my expectation to one day start my own company. What I created in my mind was a health-and-fitness magazine called *Balance*.

One class that was offered toward the end of the program was business law. It really clicked with me. Taking that class was pivotal to my life. For the first time, I thought about going to law school. Finally, I began to think about what I wanted to do with my life in a real way.

My mother had gone to one year of law school, but I'd never thought about it for myself. I'd never even considered taking prelaw classes. Suddenly, I had a new train of thought about how it would be advantageous for me to go to law school. It would be to my benefit once I launched a business or a foundation. I'd be able to understand the language in the contracts I signed. And if my plans went awry, I'd have a law degree to fall back on. I was able to elevate these ideas from wishful thinking to long-term goals. So I took the plunge. I started to study for the LSAT, thinking, "If I score well, maybe I'll get into some law school. And if I don't, it's not meant to be."

When I got my degrees in entrepreneurship and marketing I was proud, but I didn't dwell on it. I didn't consider walking across the stage in a cap and gown at graduation ceremonies. I had a new goal and was already thinking ahead, studying and applying to law schools. It was like that when I was on a podium. Instead of truly appreciating my accomplishment, I was already focusing on training for my next competition.

It was one of the great moments in my life when I was accepted to Boston College Law School. The campus in Newton was absolutely gorgeous, and I could picture losing myself in enormous law books for days. During my time in law school, I would find a renewed sense of self-worth, regain my confidence, and find courage within myself.

Law school was the bravest thing I had ever done.

I didn't go thinking that I would become a lawyer. Instead, I was seeking an incredible education that I could use when laying the foundation for my own company. I found out right off the bat that I wasn't the only one there who had no plans to practice. And I wasn't the only one who hadn't arrived directly after earning an undergraduate degree in four years. There were other older students there. I enjoyed meeting classmates from all over the country and making some friends in a new environment.

Though I still had a thirst for knowledge and was a bookworm, I was terrified by the Socratic method employed by law professors. The horror stories about law school were true in that they called on students for answers whether they had their hands up or not. I had to always be prepared, even though I wasn't always sure what I had to be prepared for because they could ask us anything. Lectures in both giant halls and small classrooms were intense. A big lecture hall just meant more people would be looking at Shannon Miller to see if the gymnast was stumped by a question. I dreaded being called on in class. I didn't want to risk the embarrassment of giving a wrong answer, but it was unavoidable. There was no "free pass" in law school, no hiding. In gymnastics, I never considered myself the best even after winning numerous competitions and medals, so I was always trying to prove myself. It was the same at law school. I was glad that I had the grades and the LSAT score and had to remind myself that I deserved to be there.

That first year was tough, but it was new and exciting. There were probably a good six months when I actually thought I might practice law someday. I enjoyed intellectual property and estate law. Intellectual property was what I found the most interesting because it dealt with things relevant to my work, including marketing, trademark, copyright, and use of name and image. I was an absolute sponge when it came to those subjects I enjoyed. Of course, there were others like tax law that could put me to sleep in a heartbeat.

Taking difficult, thought-provoking classes and having conversations with other students helped me find my footing. Doing well at law school was empowering. Being forced to face my fear of failing in public head-on ultimately gave me strength. I came to realize that it was okay that I didn't always have the answers my professors were looking for. If I got something wrong, life went on. At law school, they scare you silly the first year, but if you make it through you will find yourself in an incredibly nurturing environment. My second and third years were much easier to navigate. I was finding out who Shannon Miller was without gymnastics. She was smart and self-reliant. She was worthy, not just as a gymnast, but as a person.

35

I lived a good forty-five minutes away from school, in Grafton, so I tried to bunch my classes on two or three days each week, and arrange my schedule so I could get away weekends for work. I was happy to accept a variety of opportunities, but I realized they were not going to last forever and I needed to find something that would be fulfilling long term.

I was finally at a point where I could consider accepting speaking engagements. Although I was still terrified, I knew it was time to face that fear and began talking to various groups, companies, and organizations. I wrote my own speeches and tailored them for specific audiences, but typically focused on my Olympic experiences, setting goals, finding motivation, assuming leadership, teamwork, and the gold medal mind-set. I was shocked that after resisting it for years, I enjoyed public speaking! It didn't matter if it was to thirty people in a small space or eight hundred in a banquet room, I loved connecting with my audience. I was able to share funny stories about the Olympics and also relate how the life lessons I learned through my sport apply to our everyday issues. It turned out that my nerves could handle it, and it opened my eyes to what was possible if I could set aside my fears.

About that time, I was asked to host a TV show with CN8 Sports-Comcast. It was called *Gymnastics 360° with Shannon Miller*, and from 2004 to 2007, I hosted this hour-long show with sportscaster Lou Tilley. I was very nervous when I started but felt much more comfortable as I became more experienced. Typically, I'd fly to Philadelphia, tape the show, and fly back to Boston. If we covered an event live, I'd host, provide commentary, conduct interviews, and do stand-ups to let viewers know what they just saw or what was coming up. Usually my interviews of gymnasts and coaches were accomplished prior to the events and they'd be slipped seamlessly into the live content.

Many times Lou and I would do live commentary of an event and they'd tape and edit it for the one-hour slots. On occasion, Lou would be off covering something else and not be available for a live event, so at times I had the pleasure of cohosting with Bart Conner, my good friend from Oklahoma. I doubt he realized he was such an incredible role model for me over the years.

From the start, I knew it was going to be a great deal of work for me because each event was different and required new research on my part. We covered NCAA gymnastics, international Elite, and the level just below Elite, which was now called Level 10. Elite and collegiate had completely different rules, so I had to become an expert on both. I needed to know the names and biographies of each of the girls. I also covered men's gymnastics, so I had to learn that entire sport and the names of the skills. This was an opportunity for Comcast viewers to actually see an entire men's competition, not just the highlights. It was a good way to showcase gymnastics, and I was excited to be a part of it. It was all on-the-job training and I learned as much as I could about being in front of the camera and what went on behind the camera. During those years, I had twenty or more different hairstyles because I could never figure out what to do with my hair.

I had been given a brief taste of broadcasting during the 2003 World Championship in Anaheim. I was asked to be part of a trial run of in-house radio broadcasting for gymnastics. For me, it was another way that I could remain involved with the sport. I had been an analyst during the 2000 Olympic Games, but color commentary was much more extensive. In addition, this radio show was quite different from TV commentary in that it was very relaxed, even a bit haphazard at times. Whereas TV commentary allows you to focus on one event at a time, doing in-house radio means you're trying to preside over a four-ring circus for women and a six-ring circus for men. So I found myself saying things like, "Don't miss this next floor routine by our leader . . . but, wait, the current Olympic champion is taking to uneven bars . . . but don't forget to watch this next vault closely because it lasts only two seconds . . . but wait . . ." Fortunately, I was game to try something new.

Standing in line at a Starbucks in Anaheim, I ran into David Michaels, a producer with NBC. We were both grabbing a quick coffee before the next round of competitions. He asked what I was up to and I mentioned the radio show among other things. He asked me to send him tapes of my broadcasts when I got back home. Honestly, I figured these would get lost or sit gathering dust. Several months later, I got a call asking if I'd be interested in doing commentary for NBC-HD's coverage of the 2004 Olympic Games. Yes, yes, and yes!

I had turned into an Olympic junkie and jumped at a chance to talk to millions of viewers about the sport I loved. So that August, I traveled to Athens, Greece, for the first Olympics held there since 1896, and provided network commentary for NBC-HD. It was the first time there was a high-definition telecast for the most popular Olympic sports, including gymnastics. That year, NBC Primetime and NBC-HD were separate and each had their own commentators. It was an exciting gymnastics competition to broadcast as both America's women's and men's teams won silver medals, and Carly Patterson and Paul Hamm won gold medals in the all-around for the U.S.

I had researched and prepared to the best of my ability. At first, I was very focused on each element in the gymnasts' routines. I'd state what each one was called and inform viewers about the deductions gymnasts could expect when they made mistakes. I quickly began to realize that it was not really about my going into such detail about the particular elements, but about having a conversation with viewers as if they were sitting next to me in their living rooms. The person on my left might be an avid fan who knows everything about the sport and the person on my right might watch gymnastics only every four years and know little other than it looks impossible. *How can I please them both?*

I hoped that what came through my commentary was: "Hey, I've been there, and I know that these athletes have spent most of their lives getting to this point. Hit or miss, they each deserve our attention, our applause, and our respect." It became my style to both inform viewers about what was going on in the competition with the gymnast on the screen and also share with them interesting personal facts about her or him. I had to be a critic, but I also invited people deeper into the sport so they could better appreciate what it had to offer. I enjoyed doing commentary at those Olympics and continue to relish the many opportunities I've had since then to be an analyst and commentator for this incredible sport.

Out of the blue, I was asked to participate in the 2004 post-Olympic tour. So when I wasn't doing commentary at the Games, I was stretching and working out in my small hotel room. I'd be doing handstands and back walkovers in this tiny space, trying not to kick a wall or stumble over the bed. I had to start from scratch because I had done no gymnastics since the 2000 tour. I was glad I didn't try a comeback that year! And I bet Steve was relieved I didn't ask him to train me. Over the years we would stay in touch and continue to be linked by our incredible partnership.

Back in the States, I resumed a law school experience that was different from most since I was working during the summers and touring on weekends in the fall. I wasn't under as much pressure as most of the law students at BC because I wasn't vying for a legal internship each summer. I had my hands full with sponsor work, speeches, my TV show, and other assignments that came along.

Because I wasn't a typical student, my mom was a little nervous that I would drop out of law school as she had done when she married and had Tessa. She told me again and again, "I just hope you finish; I just hope you finish." I felt like I needed to stay busy with work, but there was no doubt in my mind that I would finish school.

I was still living in Grafton, with my two big dogs, Sam and Gracie. I had always been a dog lover and I'd rescued Sam from a pound while in Houston. I was told that since he was five, if he didn't get adopted soon he'd have to be put down. He went home with me that day. I remember trying to teach him to swim. What retriever doesn't know how to swim? He fell in the pool the first time I let him into the backyard and couldn't get out, so I jumped in fully clothed and wrestled this eighty-pound dog out of the deep end. (They should make that an Olympic event!) I was hoping to get a companion for Sam (and for me, too) and went to look at a German shepherd that had been rescued. She was a bit too high-strung for me to handle, so I was relieved to be told there would be no problem placing her with another family. The woman there mentioned another dog I might want to meet. When she said it was a Rottweiler I was wary. I sat down on the curb and waited. Suddenly, this huge black and brown Rotty walked straight over to me carrying a red ball in her mouth and sat in my lap as if she were a poodle! I took Gracie home with me.

On Sunday mornings, Sam and Gracie and I would sit on the deck watching hot air balloons soar above the trees, and it made me appreciate what a wonderful place Grafton was. However, it was so quiet and peaceful and far away from school that I was beginning to feel isolated. I had a tendency to withdraw, so I knew I had to make a change. I decided to make a big change and try my hand living in New York City. I could still commute to BC from there and be closer to my agent.

The energy in the Big Apple was exhilarating and just what I needed. It was a fantastic change of pace. I continued to study hard, going from one coffee shop to the next. I was traveling back and forth between New York and Boston on the Acela, but the travel was worth it because I was doing a lot more practical thinking about my future, as well as dreaming.

I think it fell more into the "dare" than "dream" category, but I decided to run in the New York City Marathon. A friend of mine said we should run a marathon before we turned thirty. We still had a little time, but I decided I wanted to do it right away and check it off my must-do list. Despite some less-than-ideal training, I went for it and ran with Team for Kids, a group that raises funds on behalf of New York Road Runners youth services. My goal was to finish, period. I thought I could do it in five hours so when I found out my time was 4:06:05, that was almost enough for me to think I should train more and attempt to break the four-hour barrier. Almost.

As my final year of school approached, I realized that there were a few classes I was interested in taking that BC didn't offer. My amazing dean gave me permission to accept "visiting student" status at the Sturm College of Law at the University of Denver for 2007. I thought living in Denver would be ideal because it was only a short flight to Oklahoma and my best friend, Marianna, was planning to move there soon. We both grew up training at Dynamo and had a bit of a kinship because she was from my birth state, Missouri. She was the girl who kept everyone in stitches, even when Steve and Peggy were on the warpath, so I thought she'd be the perfect friend to have with me when moving to a new city. So, as I looked toward my future, everything seemed to be coming together.

Then I met the man who would turn my world upside down.

36

My parents raised me to "give back." So from the time I had my first gymnastics success as a young teenager, I happily lent my time and name to numerous charities. I enjoyed attending events for both local and national charities. I was even willing to embarrass myself by participating in charity golf tournaments. One summer I accepted invitations to fourteen tournaments. I was just about golfed out when a tournament from Jacksonville, Florida, called. The event helped raise funds for a foundation that had been started by Chicago Cubs catcher and Jacksonville-native Rick Wilkins to help adults with disabilities. It was a good cause and it was November, so sunny Florida seemed enticing.

John Falconetti, a friend of Rick's from Jacksonville, was present because the company he owned, The Drummond Press, was sponsoring the event. The story I've heard at numerous dinners and parties over the years, mostly from his friends, is that John noticed me at the pairings party and asked Rick who I was. Rick began to explain that I was an Olympian and John said, "Save the bio; is she here *alone?*" At these events, they typically seat a "celebrity" at a sponsor table during the dinner banquet. I was oblivious to this at the time, but John shrewdly upped his sponsorship donation to make sure that I sat at the table with his group. I'm not sure that he got his money's worth because we didn't actually sit together. In fact, I sat next to one of his best friends, Paul Van Wie, who would later become our son's godfather. So I spoke to John only briefly that night and didn't even catch his full name. I was ready to get back to the solitude of my books, and I left for New York thinking nothing more of it.

I hadn't given John any of my contact information, but he tracked me down through my publicist, writing a carefully crafted e-mail that he knew would be forwarded to me. Once I replied, the door opened. He e-mailed me and said, "I'm going to be in New York on business, do you want to grab a cup of coffee?" I was beginning to be more comfortable socially and was making a concerted effort to put myself out there—hence all the golf tournaments, speeches, and dinners—so I said, "Yes."

Was he asking me on a date? I didn't imagine that was the case. But was I wrong? I still had faith that there was someone out there for me who would be my true partner and whom I could love with all my heart. I still wanted a family. I still wanted the fairy tale.

John arrived in the city and we were supposed to meet that evening for coffee, prior to my leaving for Chicago the next morning to be inducted into the U.S. Olympic Hall of Fame. But that morning I woke up so sick I had to get to the nearest doctor. I knew I had more than just a cold. Yep. I was told I had bronchitis. I was thinking, "This is ridiculous. I feel horrible; I can't talk; I'm leaving early in the morning; I really have no idea who this person I'm meeting is. I need to cancel." But I had no phone number for him and wasn't sure if he would get an e-mail if he was traveling. So I sat in the lobby of my building half asleep, waiting. I must have looked like death warmed over and maybe that was a good thing. There was no glamour, just me, sick as a dog. Maybe he would run the other way and I could go back to bed. When he arrived, I said in a very hoarse voice, "I'm so sorry that I'm sick, so if you want to cancel that's fine."

He had no inclination to cancel and we ended up going to dinner. He did most of the talking while my head was foggy and pounding, and I was coming to the conclusion that he considered this a date. I didn't run away. As bad as I felt, I enjoyed our conversation. He was very much the south-ern gentleman, very intelligent, funny, and self-deprecating. John walked me back to my apartment, stopping at a nearby Starbucks so he could buy me a hot tea for my throat. There was no kiss good night, just an awkward handshake.

That was the last I saw of him until the spring, but we e-mailed constantly and had many phone conversations. The long-distance relationship was a good thing. We were able to really learn about each other and figure each other out. It forced me to think it through. I was much more cautious the second time around and wanted to make sure I was following my head as well as my heart. Of course, with my rose-colored glasses I still pictured myself living happily ever after as a wife and mother. The difference was that this time I had a better idea who *I* was as a person and what I wanted out of life. This time I felt more secure in myself. This time I'd make sure I stayed true to who I was and my identity wouldn't vanish.

We were talking on the phone late one night after I attended an event in Pittsburgh. He knew my upcoming plans for school and never once questioned it, but I had come to dread the move to Denver. I didn't want to scare him off by voicing my concern of what would happen to our relationship if we were that far away for another year. I was getting up the courage to broach the subject when he said, "Darling"—yes, he actually talks like that—"how are we going to fix this Denver issue? Am I going to need to move out there?" All my worries disappeared. I knew at that moment that I had found the one.

We had a very honest conversation and concluded that for us to have a real chance to be a couple, we needed to be closer geographically. As we were talking I started looking up law schools in Florida. It turned out that the University of Florida had a fantastic law school and offered the courses I planned on taking in Colorado. We took that as a good sign. So at 2:00 A.M., I e-mailed my dean to see if switching law schools for my final semester was an option under "visiting student" status. The next morning she sent me an e-mail approving the move. I was headed to Gainesville!

I took a few classes and by the spring of 2007 I had my law degree from Boston College Law School. I couldn't have been happier. Of course, my mother was elated.

When I made up my mind to do something, I would dive in with both feet, sometimes to my detriment. My parents understood this and could see the red flags before my first marriage. Of course, I didn't want to see any so I didn't, much to their chagrin. So now, when I decided to move to Gainesville to be closer to this man I'd spent only a few hours with in person, I sought their opinion. John understood how close I was with my parents and suggested we fly together to Oklahoma and spend some time with them. We still laugh about that trip. With all the kids out of the house, my parents had begun golfing. So the four of us looked for common ground by playing a round of golf. John's first shock was that the Millers don't use golf carts. My mother views golf as exercise. While it may not have been the leisurely afternoon he imagined, John won my parents over by simply being himself.

I'm not sure what John saw in me. Maybe he liked the challenge. I saw a lot in John. I liked that he was stable and smart and that faith was first and foremost in his life. We seemed to want the same things out of life. Like me, he was very close to his family. In fact, one of our first dates was going to his brother's wedding. John was salt of the earth and someone who loved his parents and was loyal to his friends. We spent time with his friends, many of which he had known for years, and every one of them adored him. It was apparent that he'd walk over hot coals to help someone close to him. When I looked in his steel-blue eyes, I saw a kind and caring soul.

One of John's best qualities was that he treated me and all women with respect. I shared with him my hope to run a business someday, and he assured me I was a strong woman and it was healthy and positive for me to step up and take control of my dreams. He always found a way to put others at ease, including me.

John had no need for the spotlight; his star shone bright enough. He ran a successful multicity commercial printing company that he had been working in since he was a six-year-old moving boxes in the warehouse. John knew I'd gone through a difficult divorce, and he said something that really struck home: "Don't ever let others steal your joy. You own that. You get to choose how happy you are." I often come back to those words. With these words and his knack for finding the humor in most any situation, I realized that being with him was the first time in a very long time that I found myself smiling and laughing, that no-holds-barred, gut-splitting kind of laughing. That was so healthy for me.

I was happy.

I accepted John's proposal in early 2007 atop a cliff in Kauai. We had a beautiful wedding on August 25, 2007, at St. John's Cathedral in Jacksonville. The reception was at the Cummer Museum of Art and Gardens, which is a marvelous building with a permanent collection of five thousand pieces of art and lovely, historic gardens along the riverfront. As a chocoholic, I remember we had the most delicious chocolate cake I've ever had. That was John's cake, although our true wedding cake was incredible, too. (One year later we ordered a mini-cake from the same bakery—we chose the chocolate.)

Marianna was my maid of honor and my bridesmaids were my Olympic teammate Jaycie Phelps and three-time U.S. rhythmic gymnastics champion Jessica Howard, whom I got to know on tour in 2000. While not all my gymnastics friends were able to make the trek, it meant so much that Dominique Dawes was there on my special night.

For our honeymoon, John and I spent two weeks in Italy. We flew in and out of Rome but otherwise went to places I'd never been when I was there for gymnastics. We mixed sightseeing with hiking, fabulous dining, and a bit of shopping. It was a wonderful, romantic honeymoon, but admittedly neither of us is really great at long vacations. We're workaholics. Two weeks was about as much vacation as we could possibly get away with before going nuts.

We started out agreeing, "We're not going to answer our cellphones." Four or five days into it, we agreed, "We'll only look at them in the morning to make sure everything is okay at home." Eight or nine days in, we were comfortable glancing at them throughout the day. That was the longest vacation I'd ever been on. We had an amazing time in Italy and still look forward to going back. But we were eager to get home and begin our new life together.

37

John helped me to learn to say no. I had a difficult time turning down any requests for my time, especially when it came to charities. Consequently, I was doing every charity dinner or event and visiting every school. I thought that was the best way to spend my free time, but by doing *everything* I was running myself into the ground.

One weekend, John accompanied me to an Alzheimer's event in New York. On the plane we started talking about how much we both enjoyed helping such a worthy cause. However, I admitted I was feeling a bit scattered because while I was committing myself to attend so many functions, I was also trying to think about our future together, which included having children. John said, "Shannon, if you commit to helping *every* good cause, you'll be booked at an event every single day of the year. That's not fair to you or the groups you're supporting." He convinced me that it really was okay to cut down and say, "Thank you for asking, but unfortunately, I'm not able to be there this time." He asked pointedly, "What is important to *you?*"

"I love kids," I said, "and I've been reading about the childhood obesity rate in this country and it's alarming." I started spouting statistics about how childhood obesity was gaining momentum in the U.S. I explained that an estimated one-third of all children were overweight and that could lead to their having life-threatening diseases over time. I pointed out that Jacksonville had one of the worst rates of obesity in the country. I'd seen firsthand that it was a huge issue in Florida because I had already gone into schools to talk about the importance of health and fitness. I had done a number of visits as cochair of the Governor's Council on Physical Fitness with Tampa Bay Buccaneers linebacker Derrick Brooks. (Tim Tebow, the University of Florida's Heisman Trophy–winning quarterback, would become an additional cochair in 2009.) The job of the twenty council members was to devise a plan of regular exercise and sound nutrition to reduce the number of Floridians who suffer from chronic diseases resulting from obesity within the next ten years.

John said, "Shannon, you're obviously passionate about this. This is what you need to focus on." So we talked seriously about starting a foundation together to combat childhood obesity. That didn't mean I couldn't continue to lend support to other charities, but I would set aside a significant amount of time and energy to work on this cause I was so passionate about. *You can't be everything to everyone.*

Neither John nor I tend to wait around for the grass to grow. By the time the plane landed in New York, we had formulated a plan for our foundation. The first thing we talked about was a signature event. We toyed with having a golf tournament or a gala, but ultimately decided that we wanted an event that was family friendly and got kids active. We mulled over several possibilities before deciding on a "fun run," an annual one-mile run for girls and boys fourteen and under. What would separate it from other runs was that it would be absolutely free to every child in that age bracket. We wanted to lessen the number of barriers that might keep people from attending, from getting active.

We started filing papers when we returned to Jacksonville. Mountains of paperwork later, the Shannon Miller Foundation became an official 501(c)(3) in 2007. Now we were off and running, literally. I won the naming rights, but it was John's foundation, too, and from the start we worked tirelessly to make it a success.

Our foundation was not about reinventing the wheel. There were already many fantastic programs emerging that worked to combat childhood obesity. However, it was a complex issue that could be approached from many different directions and we believed there was a place for us. Our focus would be primarily on the activity component. I traveled the country giving talks to raise awareness of the childhood obesity epidemic. I also partnered with other groups to sound the alarm about what was harming our children. Meanwhile, we made an effort to establish the foundation in the community and form partnerships.

During that first year we began planning our inaugural event while continuing to research the issue. We knew it would take an extraordinary amount of hard work before we could launch our first public event, but we were undeterred. We sold sponsorships to raise money for the foundation and worked with a number of companies and community resources to get it off the ground. In that crazy year, Starbucks served as our unofficial office.

In January 2008, I went touring yet again. However, this was quite different from anything I'd done in gymnastics. Four other Olympians from various sports and I had the incredible opportunity to visit our troops in Afghanistan. What a privilege! For two weeks we visited some of the outermost bases, those that rarely saw visitors. It was cold and desolate, but the mountains of Afghanistan were beautiful as we hovered over them in one Black Hawk after the next.

While we didn't arrive ready to perform our Olympic feats, the troops did coax me into a handstand contest or two. This tour wasn't about people cheering for us; it was about shaking the hands of these men and women and thanking them for putting their lives on the line for us every day. It was about letting them know we appreciated their effort and that they continued to be in our thoughts and prayers. They were eager to tell us about their daily routines and show us around the bases. For this girl from the heartland, the visit was a fascinating and inspiring experience.

Back home, also in 2008, I was honored to be voted into the U.S. Olympic Hall of Fame along with the other girls of the Magnificent Seven in the team category. As an individual, I had become the second female gymnast inducted into the USOC Hall of Fame, in 2006, so I now became the first female athlete in any sport to be inducted into the USOC Hall of Fame twice. That year, I also was inducted into the International Women's Sports Hall of Fame. It was overwhelming.

Everything seemed to be moving along so well. I was always a planner, so John and I began talking about when we'd want to start a family. But our happy time was interrupted by something you just can't plan for.

My mother called one night with tearful news: "Shannon, I have cancer."

Her words took my breath away. I felt like I'd been punched in the gut. I managed to hold it together as she explained she had been diagnosed with advanced-stage cervical cancer. Of course, I told her to be positive, as she had told me so many hard times over the years. I knew nothing about cervical cancer or many of the various types of cancer at the time, but I knew God was with her and so was I. She also had my father, my sister, and my brother to lean on.

That summer, I developed a more thorough understanding of what someone goes through during the various stages of cancer treatment. My mother underwent surgery, radiation, and chemotherapy. During treatment her weight plummeted to eighty-seven pounds and much of the time she was too weak to even talk to me on the phone. I needed to believe that it was all going to be okay. *She's my mom, she's going to get through this, and she's always going to be here. She has to be.* Mom's doctors were doing everything they could and she was doing everything in her power. The rest was up to God, in Whom Mom had ultimate trust. *Please, God, give her strength.*

Dad was able to take off work and be there for her 24/7 during treatment and recovery. He kept her medications straight and found foods or liquids that had the best chance of staying down. As any caregiver knows, it's stressful and often terrifying to see someone you love go through the few ups and many downs of treatment. I had never really seen my father in crisis mode, but he proved to be a calming influence who focused on the goal at hand. My mother, the woman I admire most, the one who has shown me what it means to be a fighter, made it through this dreaded disease. It was a long journey back to health and there are still issues that remain. My mother is a survivor in every sense of the word and proved it again in 2013 when, at age sixty-five, she ran her first *marathon!*

The Olympics were held in Beijing in 2008, but for the first time since 1992, I was not there as a competitor or broadcaster. I couldn't be half a world away while my mother was going through her ordeal. So for the first time in my life, I watched the Games on television, and it was pretty awesome. The U.S. women excelled. The team captured a silver medal behind China, and Nastia Liukin and Shawn Johnson won nine medals between them.

I got to know the current gymnastics stars better after the Games, during the 2008 Tour of Gymnastics Superstars. It was my fifth post-Olympic tour, which must be some kind of record. Again, I was surprised to be asked and had not done any gymnastics since the previous Olympic tour, which I believed would be my last. USA Gymnastics politely explained they wanted me to do balance beam and floor exercise because they were going for a "history of gymnastics" feel. So as we traveled to perform in more than thirty cities, I was a thirty-one-year-old on a bus with a lively group of teenagers. The front of the bus was unofficially designated for us "older" performers and the coaches. There was even a door that separated us from all-nighters of Guitar Hero. No matter that I was expected to be a den mother to the younger girls, I was excited to have the opportunity to push my body to the limits and perform once again.

I did balance beam to open the show, and in the second half I performed a floor routine while Disney recording artist Jordan Pruitt sang "One Love." As she moved from the stage onto the floor, I danced and tumbled. I can still feel my jitters before I went out to perform. Still, I relished those quiet moments standing in the dark before stepping into the spotlight. The other girls were amazing and the audiences were so enthusiastic. I was having a blast pretending to be a gymnast once again. In my mind I had never left, but my body disagreed. Eventually, the workload and intensity began to take its toll. After performing in Boston, I had a few days off and wanted to fly back to Florida to spend time with John. In the car on the way to the airport I experienced a moment of terror. My legs were done. They had completely given out. I was worn out and my body wasn't bouncing back nearly as quickly as it once did.

I was in better shape than I had been in some time, but pushing my body to the max, giving it my all night after night, was adding up. It took everything I had to get through my routines. I loved performing, but the tour was hectic and unrelenting, and by the end I was ready to hang up my leotard.

I was ready to move on to the next phase of my life. I could truly retire with the knowledge that I was now likely the longest-touring gymnast who ever lived! It was, however, difficult to come to terms with the idea that I'd never again do a giant swing on bars or a flip-flop layout on balance beam. I would miss performing.

I would miss being a gymnast.

38

The trip to Afghanistan in January 2008 was so rewarding that I immediately accepted an invitation to be part of a group going to Iraq in January 2009. Once again, I met awe-inspiring American soldiers who were stationed in one of the world's trouble spots. Again I was inspired by the men and women who wear our uniform.

Not long after I returned from Iraq, I spoke at and then participated in the Climb Jax race, a fund-raiser for the American Lung Association that would be renamed the Fight for Air Climb. So I ran up the forty-two flights of the tallest building in Jacksonville. I wasn't feeling well afterward, but figured I was just out of shape. I had no idea what the real reason was.

I soon traveled to Oklahoma for a company I was working with. I visited my parents but didn't tell them that John and I were trying to start a family because we didn't want to get their hopes up. We knew it could take a year or longer. After the short trip, I arrived back in Florida the first week of February. I unpacked and took a pregnancy test, which I'd been doing once a day, just in case. . . .

It was positive! I could not believe it. I poured a glass of wine *for John* and met him at the door when he got home from work. When he walked in the door of our condo, I announced, "I have some news!" We were both over the moon and couldn't wait to be parents.

I immediately went into planning mode. When you have a Type A personality, that's what you do. *What's the baby's room going to look like? Where are we going to put the crib? How do I change a diaper? What classes do I sign up for?* I had never babysat when growing up and didn't know much about babies. Now I wanted to know everything! While nesting and rearranging rooms, I came across some research stuffed away that I had been saving for a series of fitness books I'd once thought about writing. I suddenly had an urge to tie up loose ends. I had to finish those books before the baby arrived!

I'd been searching for a new direction in my life. Of course, I was now busy with the foundation, gymnastics analysis, and motivational speaking, but as far as I was concerned, I still had free time. I wasn't good at not being ridiculously busy. I looked over my notes on the fitness books. My inspiration for writing these small and portable books was that when I'd get to a fitness gym I'd forget all the fun, interesting abdominal exercises, stretches, and yoga moves I'd read about in magazines or seen online. I actually started tearing instructions out of magazines and stapling them together so I'd have them with me at the gym. I thought, "Why don't I create a small lightweight book that has fifty of these great exercises? I can have different routines in the back, so that if you're in the gym and want to do an abdominal workout you can simply choose the one you want and get to it."

My original title to the first book was *Gold Medal Abs*. I was already six weeks pregnant and didn't know how long my abs would be in shape! I needed a photographer quick.

John asked, "How about Nick Furris?" Nick was a longtime friend of John's who owned a multifaceted production company called Spectrum Films. In fact, the year before we had worked well together on an educational video with a goal-setting theme. At eight weeks, I went to Nick with the list of photos and we got them shot. Everything was happening so fast.

In addition to my working on the books, the foundation's first children's fun run was also quickly approaching. I found ways to promote the excitement and benefits of children getting active within the community; I spoke to school officials, nonprofit organizations, and individuals to alert them about the one-mile fun run. We received a strong response to our suggestion that schools and nonprofits encourage their kids to run twenty-five miles in the fourteen weeks leading up to the fun run and the last 1.2 miles on race day to reach 26.2 miles, a marathon.

The Shannon Miller Foundation's first fun run took place downtown at the Jacksonville Landing on May 30, 2009. We called it the Shannon Miller Kids Marathon. Our initial family-friendly, health-and-fitness event was a huge success. We had hundreds of children participate, including those who had been running for fourteen weeks prior to race day. Many parents ran alongside of them. After our first event, we immediately began making plans for a bigger splash in 2010, with more runners, more vendors, and more sponsors. It was a great start!

In the meantime, my agent and I were trying to find someone to produce prenatal and postnatal fitness videos, another idea that I came up with while experiencing pregnancy. I thought it odd that I knew how to be fit as a normal person and as an athlete, but I had no idea how to stay in shape now that I was expecting. Now was a time I really needed to be fit and healthy, but I wasn't sure what was safe and what was risky.

For instance, I had signed up to participate in the Gate River Run, the largest 15k in the nation. Although I still wasn't much of a runner, a friend had talked me into giving it a try. It turned out that the run fell on the week after my nausea had seriously set in, but I didn't want to withdraw and let her down. On the day of the race she brought a bag full of ginger and lollipops to help get me through. So I spent the day before my thirty-second birthday running my first 15k and stopping every ten minutes or so to heave. It was after that event that my fear began to set in. Was what I'd done dangerous for my baby? I had learned to push through all kinds of physical issues as a gymnast, but was doing that now unhealthy for my child?

I began to educate myself and realized there was a need for the type of information I found. The pregnancy fitness videos on the market were few and far between. There was a need for both prenatal and postnatal videos that were up to date and featured routines that were easy for women to do in the comfort of their homes. I also wanted to go beyond the fitness and provide information on such important topics as gestational diabetes. I knew from personal experience how unnerving this diagnosis could be. I craved information and knew other women did, too.

A few production companies expressed interest in doing the *postnatal* fitness video. But they weren't interested in the prenatal portion. In fact, one producer declared, "Women don't care about being fit *during* pregnancy. They only care about what they look like afterward." I thought, "Whoa, wait a second! That's not true." I utilized this inaccurate, insulting comment to reenergize my efforts. I was determined to prove that expecting women *do* care about being fit, because we want to be healthy for ourselves and for our children. I asked Nick if he'd be interested in filming both videos. He didn't hesitate and we got to work.

Our time frame was tight. My baby wasn't waiting for books or videos. The prenatal fitness video had to be shot quickly because I was getting really close to my second trimester. Of course, we had more time with the postnatal video. As we prepared for the shoots, Nick and I initiated even bigger plans. He is a very intelligent, boisterous Greek man and I was a bit intimidated when he sat me down at his conference table and asked, "What are you going to do with all this *stuff*? What do you really want to accomplish?"

I said, "I want to create something that makes women's lives better."

I told Nick I had spoken to Sheryl Shade in New York about my dream of branching out into areas beyond sport. It was a difficult call because she'd been with me for so long and we'd been through so much together. She understood that there were big changes in my life, with marriage, our baby, and my foundation. She knew me and understood I was ready to strike out on my own.

Nick felt that the best way for me to achieve my goal of helping women was to form my own company. That had been my dream all along. He realized that anything to which my name was attached had to be something I was passionate about and in line with my core values. So we talked about becoming partners in business. His creative business mind and my logical outlook were in fifth gears, and we came up with a number of names before settling on Shannon Miller Fitness. We had some logos drawn up using that name. But Nick continued to listen to me talk about my vision, until one day he firmly stated, "No. You're *not* describing Shannon Miller Fitness; you're describing Shannon Miller Lifestyle." He explained, "You're talking about fitness, but you're also talking about nutrition and about seeing your doctor and about preventive care for diabetes, heart disease, and other illnesses. You're reaching out to women about time management and balancing the everyday details of life. This is not just about going to the gym. This is a *lifestyle*."

After hearing his explanation, I suddenly had a clearer picture of what the company would be, how much more it would encompass. Shannon Miller Lifestyle made perfect sense. Our plan was to work hard putting the pieces together and molding our new business along the way, until we were ready to launch in the summer of 2010.

I hired a woman named Jackie Culver as my fitness trainer for the videos. I had initially learned about Jackie through a friend of John's. His kids went to a local school where Jackie was a volunteer mother who was very involved with children and running as well as a certified fitness instructor. I had met Jackie during one of my school visits prior to the race. She became a volunteer at our first fun run. Intelligent, active, and outgoing, she was perfect for our videos—and I kept her in mind with regard to my foundation.

I wrote the books and the outline for the videos; Nick provided photographic support and graphic design. We hadn't stopped to formalize the company just yet, but we were on the same page and working hard to create a solid foundation. We shot the videos in my second and third trimesters. Fortunately, I finished shooting the prenatal DVD, *Fit Pregnancy*, before our son arrived.

During that time, I enjoyed the everyday activities of preparing for our baby. I built his crib, using the skills my dad taught me when I was a girl. Once I set my mind to do something, I needed to do it immediately. So by the time John got home to help, the crib was finished.

I was sick 24/7 for a solid seven months and during that time John took care of emergency eating situations. I had many more food aversions than I had cravings. I recall one particularly difficult day early in the pregnancy when I hit that "if I don't eat in sixty seconds I'm going to die" kind of hunger. John asked what he could get me. The two things I wanted most were a vanilla milk shake and mashed potatoes. "And, I need them now." John went immediately into action mode and found a KFC and a McDonald's on the same block, and I lived.

John and I were both so anxious for the baby to arrive and for us to meet our son. We had heard from so many of our friends that a baby changes your life. We had no idea.

Rocco was born on October 28, 2009. His arrival changed everything.

39

John and I were prepared for how the logistics of our daily life would change once the baby was born. We certainly knew we'd have to balance our lives in a different way. However, we hadn't believed those who said parenthood would change us. We weren't thinking about the true, fundamental change. The depth of love we had for this little person shocked the both of us.

We had friends who were always talking about their kids, and John and I would laugh, "Let's not be those people." But we were *so* those people. We could have spent five hours telling absolute strangers about the cute faces Rocco made that day. We'd have to force ourselves to talk about something else so we wouldn't drive our friends away.

With the first child, we were worried about everything. We were terrified we were going to make a mistake and scar our baby for life. My concerns were evident in my preparation: finishing the nursery months in advance and having my "go bag" ready by the front door a full six weeks prior to my delivery date. I even had the bathing instructions for an infant laminated and posted by his bath area so I'd know exactly what to do. Once Rocco arrived, John and I were put to the test. He would lie in his crib and cry and cry, and we'd be outside his door strategizing as if we were on some top-level military mission, saying, "Let's try to last two more minutes, and if he's still crying, we go in." He'd fall asleep after one minute and fifty-nine seconds, and then John and I would breathe a sigh of relief. Five minutes of silence later, we'd be wondering, "What's he doing in there?" We would look on the monitor. "Can you see him breathing?" I would stare at the monitor while John tapped on the door to make him move. Being a new parent can be a harrowing experience!

Rocco was very easygoing from the start, and a good sleeper and eater. He was the perfect baby to ease us into parenthood. As a new mother I came out of my shell even more. There was no time to be shy. Whatever it took to make sure he was safe, happy, and healthy I'd do. I was mama bear. Of course, I had a fear of the unknown, those things I couldn't control that would drive me crazy. *There is no perfection in motherhood.*

For seven weeks I was almost exclusively a mother. During that time I started getting active, and I especially enjoyed taking long walks in the park with Rocco. He was certainly *my* child, because he spent quite a bit of time hanging upside down in my arms. (To this day he yells out, "Mommy, hold me upside down and spin me around!") As much as I loved spending entire days playing with him, I eased back into work.

Before our company could launch, I worked furiously with Nick to devise a strong and inviting content-based Web site with informative articles by me and other writers that were devoted to fitness, pregnancy, motherhood, health, wellness, and nutrition.

We offered our two pregnancy videos (which also landed in Target, Best Buy, and other stores across the country) along with my series of fitness books and journals and the *Shannon Miller Healthy & Balanced Pregnancy Cookbook*. Our goal was to reach women through multiple vehicles including social media, articles, programs, radio, television, events, products, and partnerships.

On Sunday, July 4, 2010, we launched Shannon Miller Lifestyle: Health and Fitness for Women. My dream of owning a company had come true.

I had plenty of book knowledge, but I hadn't had any hands-on experience running a company. Nick was a wonderful mentor, as was my husband and a man named Paul Caine, the chief revenue officer at Time, Inc. I'd met Paul at a race car driving event! It was in 2006 that the two of us were among the celebrities who took part in the Toyota Long Beach Grand Prix. (I was terrified and had never driven stick before, but it was the opportunity of a lifetime for a girl who grew up watching NASCAR and Indy races with her dad.) As my company began to grow, I felt I was being tugged in all directions. One day Paul shared some words of wisdom: "In gymnastics you had a very specific goal every day when you got up. Business is no different. Yes, you're going to be pulled in many different directions at any given point, but you must ask yourself, 'What is, at the core, my single most important mission each day?'"

Since then, every morning I've woken up thinking, "How am I going to help one woman make her health a priority today?" Maybe it's giving her a gentle nudge to get to a doctor's appointment . . . sharing with her the importance of an extra hour of sleep at night, to take time and recharge . . . offering a new fitness tip or exercise or even a tasty, yet healthy, recipe . . . conveying the importance of using baby steps to get through a trying time . . . or expressing to her that with most health challenges, an everything-in-moderation approach is vital.

Obviously, at SML, we wanted to help *many* women make their health a priority. When we'd get phone calls from companies and people who wanted to partner with us or wanted me to endorse their products, there was a filter. I'd ask myself, "Will this help a woman make her health a priority?" It could be a great cause or great product, but if it fell outside of our focus, I was obliged to say, "No, thank you." We had an important mission and stuck to it.

We focused on everything pertaining to women's health, including heart disease, diabetes, and other life-threatening illnesses. We didn't have a specific cancer area on our Web site, but it wasn't ignored as a topic because it was a health concern for all women. In the fall, I would do a great deal of speaking, about women's health and fitness, and cancer awareness was part of that topic.

Recognizing that I was now excited about venturing outside my comfort zone, Nick often pushed me to leave my logical $2+2=4$ side and find my creative side. So in early 2010, he asked me if I'd entertain hosting a health-based radio show to coincide with the launching of the business. I use the word "asked" loosely. He was so confident that I could do it that it was more of a statement about what I'd soon be doing. I did my best to hide my panic. In all the years I'd talked only about gymnastics on air, so it was with some trepidation that I agreed to do the show. I took the reins of *Shannon Miller Lifestyle* in partnership with St. Vincent's HealthCare, and each Sunday morning for an hour I tackled a different health topic with an expert guest.

I was nervous at first, but I eased into the role and it became fun and interesting. I was proud that these shows caused people to give more thought to their health, which was a goal of SML. I loved that people could call in and ask questions directly to our experts and physicians. Some callers found it too embarrassing to ask their own doctors about certain topics and needed assurance that making the trip to their physician was worthwhile. Countless callers were prompted to have similar discussions with their own physicians. Maybe they could now speak to their doctor by approaching a problem or concern from a different angle. Many times our topic was cancer, because there are so many types of cancer that people confront.

Radio was part of my company's multipronged approach to helping people think about their health. I also began to use social media in a big way. I found it amazing to have real-time feedback and conversations. It was exciting that there were so many ways for me to reach women and fans and for them to reach me.

As Shannon Miller Lifestyle grew, it took a large role in sponsoring my foundation's annual race and bolstering our health fair addition to the race as a way to give back to the community. We added a 5k race and the event became the Shannon Miller Lifestyle 5k and Children's Fun Run.

The foundation also made enormous strides, and in the fall of 2010, I appointed Jackie Culver as its executive director. We immediately began to formulate an in-school running program for elementary and middle school students.

Physical education classes in the Jacksonville area, like most places in the nation, had been eliminated or scaled back due to the lack of funding. Beginning in January 2011, by word of mouth alone, we initiated a Shannon Miller Foundation Running Club, our in-school program to replace or supplement PE for over 2,800 children. Kids could run, skip, jump, hop, or even dance as long as it was forward moving. Fast or slow, loud or quiet, we didn't care as long as they were active.

Every child should have the opportunity to associate joy and confidence with physical activity.

I was a skilled multitasker and didn't mind that life was a bit overwhelming. I was reveling in parenthood with John, trying to grow my company and foundation. So much was going on that I wasn't paying enough attention to my own body when it was trying to tell me something. At times in October and November I had stomachaches that were aggravating enough for me to mention them to John. When they'd disappear, I just shrugged them off. When they didn't, I cut back on treats, downed a few Tums, and kept busy. Not for a minute did I think they were a symptom of a bigger issue. I couldn't baby myself when I had a real baby, could I? I was still a new mother and had only recently finished nursing, so at the time I assumed my body was out of whack to a normal degree. I didn't even bother saying anything to John or my doctor about my sudden weight loss. I just chalked up my losing six pounds in less than a month to more after-baby body changes.

Anyone can become gravely ill despite having superb body awareness, but I wholeheartedly believe we have a better chance of detecting when something is amiss if we listen to our bodies. In hindsight, it's disappointing that my body awareness wasn't where it should have been. I hadn't been focusing on myself as I did when I was a gymnast. I wasn't hearing my own talks to women or applying my company's mission to myself. I wasn't making my own health a priority.

40

Although I was overextending myself, I felt everything was working for me, everything was moving in the right direction, and everything was clicking. My marriage was blissful and I loved being a mom. Also, I felt I had found my calling as a passionate advocate for women's health based on my own experiences on and off the competition floor. My foundation was making major strides into the community with the advent of the running club, and Shannon Miller Lifestyle was going rapid fire and about to launch its new Walk-Fit Program. It was the first time since I was a gymnast that life truly made sense.

Getting a frightening diagnosis from my doctor wasn't part of my plan. Not then, not ever.

I was rarely sick as a child, and as an adult my good luck had continued into my early thirties. My philosophy was "everything in moderation," and, in that sense, I practiced what I preached by eating healthily for the most part and exercising thirty to forty-five minutes most days, with an effective mix of cardio, light weights, and flexibility work. Becoming critically ill didn't even cross my mind. So I wasn't surprised when my gynecologist, Dr. Long, found nothing wrong with me during my post-baby wellness check in early November. When he asked me how I had been feeling, I said, "Great!" He believed what I said because I believed it my-self. When interviewed in the weeks after my diagnosis, I would say flat out that I had no symptoms. But the truth was that I'd been experiencing discomfort without really taking notice. I hadn't realized these minor incon-veniences were *symptoms*.

In fact, in early December, John and I decided the time was right to take that next step and try for a second child. I thought it would be smart to make an appointment with my gynecologist as I had before Rocco to confirm all systems were go. I'd go in and make sure I stocked up on prenatal vitamins, and get a refresher course in case anything had changed since the last pregnancy.

As my appointment neared, life became even more hectic than usual. In addition to work, it was the holidays and there were a million extra things to do. I planned to do a little more on Christmas because Rocco would be one year old and could begin to experience the festivities. When I found out I would need to be out of town on the day of my scheduled exam, I felt no urgency to cram a doctor's visit into my overpacked sched-ule. I could simply put it off. I could certainly go buy prenatal vitamins. I didn't think I really needed to pay Dr. Long another visit until the *next* November or a positive pregnancy test.

I called my doctor's office, but before I could cancel my appointment, I was put on hold. As I waited for the receptionist something kept nagging at me. Maybe it was the countless physicians, nurses, and cancer survivors I had just interviewed on my radio show during breast cancer awareness month—the ones that said repeatedly: *Do not delay your doctor's visit.* Could it have been that whisper from God or His angel trying to steer me in the right direction? Or could it have been flat-out guilt for being an advocate for women's health who was considering skipping her own exam? Most likely, it was all three.

I reminded myself what I'd been telling other women: "You're always going to have something else to do on the day of your exam; you'll always say that you can't miss work or you simply don't have time." So when the receptionist came back on the line, I followed my gut and asked for the first appointment available.

Dr. Long was my regular gynecologist at North Florida OB/GYN in Jack-sonville. However, the facility encouraged women to rotate through all its doctors during pregnancy to make sure they would be comfortable with whoever was on call at the time of delivery. Dr. Long wasn't available that morning, so I had no hesitation going to a satellite office and seeing Dr. Virtue instead. He had a cancelation that morning, so I drove right over. If I hadn't gone then, I'm not sure when I would have rescheduled.

I entered Dr. Virtue's office positive I'd fly through his checklist and get back to my to-do list. I didn't think twice about whether or not I was healthy. Cancer? Not on my radar. But after my pelvic exam, I wasn't given the green light, the all clear, the good news I had been expecting. Instead, he told me he had come across a cyst on my left ovary "that is about seven centimeters."

I was absolutely stunned. In a matter of seconds my foundation of a healthy life cracked and crumbled beneath me. That was the last thing I'd expected to hear.

Is it cancerous?

I was trying to remain calm on the outside even while the questions and confusion spun in my head. As a former athlete and relatively young woman with a healthy lifestyle, I had felt invincible.

It was unfathomable that something had been growing inside of me that was now the size of a baseball. Sure, I had had some stomach discomfort, but at the time I didn't even remember that. It was possible that I had the cyst at the time of my annual exam with Dr. Long, but Dr. Virtue explained that cysts sometimes hide and detection is often incredibly difficult. Sometimes it's pure luck if they are sitting in a detectable place at the time of the exam.

I had just received the shock of my life, but I felt some relief when he said, "Cysts come and go in women all the time; many just disappear on their own. So there's no need to worry yet. I think we should just wait and observe it for the next four to six weeks."

Still in a daze, I called John. He's even-keeled and very good when I'm in crisis mode. He said assuredly, "There's no need to panic. We're just going to do what the doctor says and observe it. It's going to be okay." I called my mom and she called Tessa in Rochester, Minnesota. Mom, a cancer survivor, and Tessa, who worked in research at the Mayo Clinic, both told me, "Don't worry; it's probably nothing. You will be fine."

But I was numb. There were conflicting thoughts going on in my head.

There was part of me that wanted so badly to agree with everyone else that I had nothing to worry about. But there was another part of me saying, "What if it *is* cancer?"

When I got home, John and I talked about what the doctor had told me and all the possible future scenarios. We concluded it was best to consider but *not* assume the worst and hope for the best. We didn't make light of it or try to convince ourselves that there was no need to do follow-up tests and exams. We also were willing to follow Dr. Virtue's edict to hold off trying to have a baby. I was so terrified of rupturing the cyst before they could find out what it was that I didn't just cut down on my exercise as my doctor advised; I completely cut it out. Looking back, I must laugh a little at how I was walking around like a zombie, afraid to move and risk twisting this alien mass inside me.

The idea of observing for four to six weeks was not something that appealed to me. Waiting around? It wasn't in my makeup. If there was an option to get moving on a test or a strategic conversation, I wanted to do that instead.

Fortunately, my attentive doctors, Virtue and Long, beat me to it and were being proactive. There wasn't a whole lot of sitting around. I went in for blood tests and ultrasounds. I was pleased to learn that my doctors, who were growing in number, had consulted with a nearby gynecologic oncologist, Dr. Stephen Buckley. Dr. Buckley, who was one of the most respected doctors in his field, wanted to see me January 4, after all the test results had come back.

Waiting for that appointment after the holidays was excruciating. It felt that my life was on hold. Every time I looked at Rocco, I wanted to cry. I feel as if I held him in my arms nonstop during those trying weeks. The more insistent poor John and my family were that I was fine, the more I wanted to scream, "Easy for you to say! This is my body, this is my life, and I'm terrified!" But, not wanting to make them as anxious as I was, I smiled and agreed. For a distraction, I decided not to cancel a short trip John and I had planned with some friends right after the New Year. It helped that John and I didn't talk to our friends about what was going on with me. We hadn't told anyone outside of the immediate family because we really had nothing to tell, having zero information ourselves.

John and I entered 2011 with a mix of wariness and optimism. On

January 4, we met with Dr. Buckley at Southeast Gynecologic Oncology Associates. He looked at the latest ultrasound and he, too, said, "Well, it looks like this might be a simple cyst. Let's plan to watch it for the next four to six weeks. Hopefully it will go away on its own." *Another four to six weeks? Was the clock starting over?* John seemed relieved to hear Dr. Buckley's proposal. I didn't share that feeling. John looked at me and smiled, but I was incredibly disappointed. He may have felt we had dodged a bullet, but I felt I had a ticking time bomb in me.

I thought this was the day I was going to have a definitive answer. Good or bad, I could move forward in a specific direction. I couldn't imagine remaining in limbo for another month and a half! Whatever was inside me, I wanted it gone.

Despite my anxiety, I wasn't quite ready to voice my strong opinion. I didn't need to because in about ten minutes the issue had been resolved. Dr. Buckley said, "I'm going to take you into the next room because it's easier to see things when I do an ultrasound here." Fortunately, he wasn't satisfied looking at the several-days-old, static ultrasound that had been sent to him. He was being very cautious, making sure he had all the information he needed before sending me home. So I went into the next room to get a new ultrasound, while John remained in the hall.

Within minutes, my life changed forever. During that time Dr. Buckley looked at the ultrasound and saw that it was not a simple cyst but a solid mass on my left ovary.

I'd heard people say their world stopped the moment they learned they had a tumor that might be cancerous. Now I knew that to be true. For a few seconds I was stuck in time, as things spun around me. I'm not sure I even took a breath. Everything that I thought was so important now seemed trivial.

From John's perspective I had gone off to do the ultrasound to confirm what was already known, not discover a completely new course of action was needed. Suddenly, we were sitting together holding hands, a bit dazed, hearing words like "mass," "malignancy," and "cancer." Dr. Buckley was forthcoming and matter-of-fact. He calmly told us, "I don't know if the mass is benign or malignant, or if it has spread. We can't know until after surgery." *Surgery?* He continued, "I now know that this will not go away on its own. When are you available for surgery?" he asked. *Surgery.* The option to wait and observe was now off the table. He wanted to get me on the operating table as quickly as possible. The urgency was confirmed when he declared, "This is not something we can put off."

In an odd way, I was relieved. Not that surgery was at all appealing, and Dr. Buckley made it clear that it would be an invasive surgery with a long recovery period, but I was so grateful that he was going to remove the mass. I wanted answers. I wanted forward motion. I needed to get on with my life.

Minutes later we settled on January 13 as the date for the surgery to remove the tumor along with my left fallopian tube and ovary—and, we hoped, nothing more. Dr. Buckley would perform the operation himself.

The nine days until surgery went by quickly. We had a couple of more appointments with Dr. Buckley and made preparations for my hospital stay. I spent most of the time before surgery being a doting mom. Rocco must have noticed that I was smothering him with more kisses and hugs than ever. I was troubled when I was informed that I wouldn't be able to lift him for two months while recovering from surgery, so I was surely over-doing it, carrying my little boy everywhere. (Maybe that's why it took him fifteen months before he started walking!)

I broke the news to Nick. I probably played it down in the beginning. On some level, I expected I'd have surgery and move on as if nothing had happened. A positive attitude or wishful thinking? No matter, that's how I had to think for me to cope. I couldn't allow my mind to go to a darker place.

We still didn't share the news with many other people because we had nothing concrete to tell them. We didn't want to upset anyone or spend time answering questions that we didn't know the answers to. *Let's first figure out what we're dealing with, get our arms around it, and then move on from there.*

Since I am in many ways a control freak, the loss of control was ex-cruciating. There was nothing I could do except prepare, trust my doctor, and do a lot of praying. I was nervous, but held on to this thought: "They're going to get it out, and that's a good thing." After surgery, we would un-derstand what we were dealing with.

I tried not to dwell on worst-case scenarios. My brain can only handle so much and then it shuts down. So I allowed just so much in, and then

I had to draw the line. My mother always told me that *worry* was not trusting in God. I had to get to a point where I could truly put myself in His hands and let Him show me the way.

As surgery approached, John and I sat down one more time with Dr. Buckley in his office. He told us, "I have a plan during surgery, but I have to ask, are you planning on having more children?" His question pretty much sucked the wind out of the room. "I asked for a reason," he said. "My hope is that we complete the surgery as planned and the right ovary will kick in and take up the slack for the ovary that will be removed. But if it is cancer, if it has spread, if there is any kind of an issue, we need to have an alternative game plan. I need to have an understanding of how aggressive you want me to be. Is a hysterectomy something you would consider if it's warranted or would you rather me try to salvage what I can? Now is the time to make these decisions."

I truly appreciated Dr. Buckley's concern and frankness, but it was an immense dose of reality for both me and John. I guess I always just assumed I'd have the ability to have more children. Denial? Maybe. Or possibly it was just me trying to take one punch at a time and steady myself before the next swing. I had already been on such an emotional roller coaster and I was coming to the realization that it might not be over anytime soon. I was incredibly sad and upset in that moment. I thought of Rocco and the unbelievable joy he brought me each day. Now, the opportunity for more children might be taken away.

But as quick as those thoughts came, the faster I had to push them away. I didn't want them to take hold, to bring me down.

I turned to Dr. Buckley and said, "Yes, we would love to have more kids; we were even planning for a second baby before the cyst was discovered. *However*, right now, we have an adorable little boy who needs his mommy. So I need you to do everything you can do to make sure that I am here for him. If this turns out to be cancer, we need to do everything possible to get rid of it and make sure it doesn't come back. If it's in God's plan for us to have more children then *He* will figure it out."

During the time before surgery, so much was unknown. I needed my husband to be there and assure me that what we were doing was the right thing. He was my rock. His faith and contagious optimism helped us get through. While John and I were very engaged in my ordeal, we were also focused on my father-in-law. John's father had been diagnosed, around the same time, with stage 4 colon cancer and his surgery took place the day before mine in another hospital. I wasn't able to see him because I was dealing with the all-day preparation for my surgery, but John and his mother were with him. So my husband had a wife and father going through surgeries over two days with unpredictable outcomes. He had to hold it together for his mom and me, take care of our son, and run his business. John was the guy you wanted on your team in a crisis, but this was more than anyone should have to handle.

The night before my surgery was difficult. As part of the preparation for surgery I had to do a lovely "cleanse" because it was essential to flush everything out of my system so there was less chance of bacterial infection. It was a difficult process that I did at home, and in about twenty-four hours I lost ten pounds. I woke up in the middle of the night to use the restroom and was so weak I fainted in the hallway. I was fortunate to have banged into a wall or two before blacking out, because John woke up and caught me before I hit the floor.

Yes, it was a rough night. The morning of January 13, 2011, was no picnic, either. As I said good-bye to our little boy, Rocco, I was trying so hard not to break down. He had no idea what his mommy was going to do that day.

Soon I was checked into St. Vincent's Medical Center in Jacksonville. I was glad this was where the surgery would be performed because it was the hospital where both John and Rocco were born. And everyone there would take fabulous care of me.

The wait was finally over. One of the roughest parts of my journey was being wheeled into surgery not knowing what I would wake up to. If the tumor was benign, then my biggest concern was not being able to pick up my fifteen-month-old son during recovery. But what if it was malignant? Would Dr. Buckley need to perform an entire hysterectomy? Would I lose the opportunity to have more children? What if it had spread? Heading into surgery, there were just too many unknowns. It was the loss of control that was eating away at me. It was terrifying.

When I opened my eyes afterward, it was all smiles from John and Dr. Buckley. My first question was, "John, what did they have to do?" Dr. Buckley spoke before the words could even pass my lips, explaining that the surgery went according to plan. My left fallopian tube and ovary and the tumor had been removed successfully. My logical next question was: "So what exactly are we dealing with?"

Cancer.

No word can evoke such a myriad of conflicting emotions.

Dr. Buckley explained that what he found was a malignant 1A mixed germ cell, a form of ovarian cancer that typically strikes females in their late teens or early twenties. Incredibly rare, germ cell tumors account for only 2 percent of ovarian cancer cases. That Dr. Virtue had found this elusive tumor was remarkable. One reason ovarian cancer is referred to as a silent killer is that it's terribly difficult to detect until the later stages. Early detection is crucial. I was very fortunate to have had that, and since all signs of cancer had been removed, the prognosis looked good. I could smile, too.

John and I breathed a sigh of relief and turned our sights to recovery and taking care of family.

41

Surgery had been no fun and left me with a six-inch scar as a constant reminder that I'm not as indestructible as I'd thought. Because it had been quite invasive, I remained in the hospital for several days before going home. I was very thin and weak from losing 10 percent of my body weight. I was also dealing with quite a bit of post-op pain. I had much more trouble controlling the pain at home than in the hospital because I was no longer hooked up to an IV drip, and my stomach couldn't tolerate anything much stronger than ibuprofen.

Being told not to lift my son was harder to bear than the pain. Considering all I'd been through, I imagine most people would regard this as a minor inconvenience. But not new mothers. I couldn't get him in or out of his crib. I was permitted to hold Rocco only if we were on the same level. We were used to playing airplane zooming around the house, but such games were on hold.

Once I was home, I wasn't supposed to lie in bed for recovery (as if I could with a young child), so I started walking and increased my movements every few days, adding gentle yoga to regain strength. I was regaining my appetite as well, and it was nice to indulge a bit more than usual. Things were looking up, and I was feeling grateful and looking forward to healthy days ahead with my husband and son.

I wanted to get back to a normal life as quickly as possible, and that meant going back to work. Toward the end of January we launched our SML Walk-Fit Program to help people in the community become active by counting their steps each day. I also resumed hosting my radio show. And the foundation launched the Shannon Miller Foundation Running Club.

I went to visit each of our participating schools, and at assemblies I spoke about goal-setting, leadership, and empowering our youth to take care of themselves by accepting ownership of a healthy and active lifestyle. The principals, teachers, and kids were as excited as I was. We helped their children see for themselves that getting active can be a lot of fun! That first year, 2,852 elementary and middle school children would participate.

A couple of weeks later, John and I were on our way to dinner with Rocco. While in the car, I checked a voicemail on my cellphone. It was Dr. Buckley asking if John and I could see him in his office the next morning.

Not good.

We couldn't wait until the next morning to find out what was going on. We called Dr. Buckley back that evening. John and I got on different phones, and as I paced back and forth Dr. Buckley gave us the news. He explained that after the surgery they sent my tumor to pathology and it turned out to be a higher-grade malignancy than they'd originally thought.

What did this mean?

Dr. Buckley had spoken to several of our country's few specialists in combating this rare tumor, including one at Harvard and another at MD Anderson Cancer Center in Houston. They concurred that we should take a "hit it hard, hit it fast approach" on this kind of malignant tumor. They believed that my best chance for nonrecurrence was an aggressive nine-week chemotherapy regimen.

Chemotherapy!

John and I hadn't seen this coming. We thought we would soon be announcing to our parents that another grandchild was on the way. Instead, I was calling to let them know I had cancer. Our baby plans had been put on hold when the original cyst was discovered, and we were now on hold indefinitely.

Finally it registered. It was at this moment that my denial vanished and the full weight and realization of what we were dealing with came through. It suddenly became very real to me. It didn't matter that I was an Olympic gymnastics champion. It didn't matter that I was fairly young. It didn't matter that I was a new mother with a child who needed to be taken care of. It didn't matter that it was the last thing I had time to deal with. I . . . had . . . cancer.

This was another powerful blow, but the shock to my system was less than after my original diagnosis of having a large, mysterious cyst on my ovary. Somehow this was different. When I was first told about the cyst, I had such a fear of the unknown that worst-case scenarios filled my head. By the time I was told about needing chemo, I had a different mind-set. I was weary and lacked strength and stamina, but mostly I was just tired from not being in control and being a passive victim. That phone call from Dr. Buckley changed everything because for me chemotherapy was a way that I could fight back against cancer.

I wanted to be active in regard to my own health, so I went into competitive mode. I reflected back on what I did in gymnastics when I was facing an obstacle or big challenge. I had broken down barriers, ignored any limits imposed on me, and exceeded expectations. All those years of reaching goals through dedication and hard work had prepared me for this moment. I was ready to fight!

Since Dr. Virtue first discovered there was something inside me, I had kept asking, "How did this happen? What caused this to occur?" The question I now added was: "What did I do wrong that caused this?" Emotionally that can be a very dangerous path to go down. It would be explained to me that what I had was a rare tumor and at this point in time it is unclear why it occurs. There was no genetic component, so even my mother's cancer had no bearing on my diagnosis. Quite frankly, that explanation frustrated and annoyed me. Many times it's easier to deal with a diagnosis when we can specifically identify the reason behind it. I wanted to place the blame somewhere, and I preferred thinking that I was responsible because I had been doing something wrong to my body, such as not eating the right foods or eating too many of the wrong foods. If I knew what I did wrong, I could change it. But now I was being told that I could have been doing everything right, and it happened anyway. It was hard to wrap my mind around the feeling that I had been sabotaged by my own body.

Did I think what was happening to me *unfair?* I never used that word. That's not me. We are all faced with challenges in life. It may take every last ounce of strength and fortitude we have to keep going when facing unexpected setbacks and seemingly insurmountable obstacles. But you can't win, you can't succeed, if you don't dare to try and keep on trying, even after you've been knocked on your backside. I was just one of the nearly 22,000 women who were diagnosed with ovarian cancer in 2011. I had no intention of being among the more than 15,000 women who die each year due to this merciless disease.

I am an optimistic, "glass half full" type of person, so I tried not to dwell on the negative of my situation, but kept moving forward and thinking positively. I was in a better place mentally because I now had a specific goal. I knew what I was dealing with and what I had to do to have the best possible outcome. Moving forward for me meant switching from a "poor me" mode to an "I've got to attack" mode. Up to this point I had felt so useless. The tests were going to detect whatever they detected, and Dr. Buckley was going to perform surgery without my giving him tips or holding a scalpel. However, chemotherapy was a process that allowed me to actively fight for my own health.

It helped that I saw cancer as my competitor. Not the type of competitor that you race to the finish line. This was the type of competitor that you need to out-train and outmaneuver. I learned in gymnastics that many times you win a competition before you even step on the floor. You prepare, dig in, and do the work. I would do that now. I always needed goals, and my goal was to prepare and compete to the best of my ability and as fully as I could.

Little did I know that my passions—my background in competitive gymnastics and my role as wife, mother, and health advocate—would ultimately save my life.

42

It was essential for me to recognize the distinction between cancer, my competitor, and chemotherapy, the tool I needed to help me defeat cancer. I was still a goal-setter, and chemo was my means to achieve my new long-term goal . . . *to live*. That meant everything to me now, and it defined all my actions and choices. A friend of mine pointed out that the word "che*mother*apy" contains the word "mother," and that made sense because it would help me continue to be a mother to my son. I also wanted to continue to be a wife to my husband and continue as an advocate for women. Chemotherapy would give me my best chance to do all those things.

Certainly chemotherapy isn't easy for anyone to embrace. But when you are trying to maintain a positive attitude and not feel like a victim, you have to dig deep and decide what can help you fight back and say, "No more!" Cancer wants to strike you unexpectedly and victimize you. It boasts, "Look, you have no control anymore and I'm going to do whatever I want. I will decide your fate." You can't let cancer dictate how you respond to the challenge. You don't have to roll over. You fight back! I came to embrace chemo as my means to regain control and cease being cancer's prey.

As I did with gymnastics, I went into planning mode. I needed a strategy, so my thinking going into chemo was, "Okay, I can prepare for this; I can be proactive. There are parts of this I can control and that will give me the best chance of getting through it."

The chemo regimen I was put on was BEP (bleomycin, etoposide, and cisplatin). That's what the doctors had referred to as the "hit 'em hard, hit 'em fast approach" and that's what I began calling it. I would undergo chemo for nine straight weeks, divided into three cycles. During the first week of each cycle I'd have chemo on five consecutive days for five or six hours each day. In the second and third weeks I'd have it only on Monday for approximately four hours. The process would start anew each cycle for a total of three rounds.

I would do whatever it took. I was a fighter. I had always been one. My gymnastics career was a struggle every day for years. But it was worth the blood, sweat, and tears. If going through this brutal treatment would give me a better chance to be here with my son . . . it was worth it. I felt I had the right attitude from the beginning because of my life experiences. I felt prepped and ready. *I can do this; I'm going to do this. No problem.* All of the Olympic training came rushing back. *This is the recipe for success, so I'm going to apply it here as well.*

I didn't even ask about losing my hair at first, because my mind was racing and trying to make sense of everything. It's easy to feel you're being petty worrying about hair when you are fighting for your life, but it is something you think about. My mother's hair had thinned because of chemo, but she hadn't lost it all and I remembered her relief. Dr. Buckley said I was definitely going to lose my hair; it would happen within the first two weeks. He didn't make any false promises because he knew I'd had enough surprises.

I was shaking my head, wondering what else they could spring on me. But I was in a good place mentally. Preparation was key, and I'd always been good with that. From having watched my mother, I knew that the chemo process would be a shock to my system. It would be a long and bumpy road, and I wanted to be in the best shape before I began that journey. I reasoned that the stronger I was mentally and physically going into chemo treatment the more likely I wouldn't miss any treatment days, and my recovery would be quicker.

I spoke to Dr. Buckley about diet and exercise leading up to and through treatment. In the weeks before chemotherapy began, I challenged myself to walk for thirty to forty-five minutes each day. I added swimming, yoga, and even a bit of strength training with my trusty two-pound weights. My diet was focused on consuming enough calories to regain some of the weight I'd lost. I was pretty excited about having the license to eat anything I wanted, including my Five Guys cheeseburgers! *There is always a silver lining. Discovering the positive in even the worst situations can help you find the will to go on.*

After our conversation with Dr. Buckley, John and I talked that night about what lay ahead. I suddenly understood something else I needed to do. I realized that instead of keeping private about what we had been going through, I had to be vocal about it.

If there was ever a time to share my story, it was now. I was about to have chemotherapy for ovarian cancer, and I had all these questions and concerns. There were so many others out there struggling with something similar. We will all touched by cancer at some point in our lives. It might be you, a friend, or a loved one. This was a unique opportunity to use my resources and voice to help others in a way I never imagined.

It wasn't going to be easy talking to thousands of people about my ovaries and difficult treatments, but I made a conscious decision to swallow my pride. If I had to go through this, I hoped to help others along the way. If my journey could help even one woman, then it was worth it. I saw my decision to be open and public as an extension of what I was already doing with regard to women's health and fitness. The most important thing for me was that women, as well as men, take a closer look at their own health.

When my diagnosis hit the news it was a shock to many. People who grew up watching this young gymnast couldn't believe that I was now battling cancer. I wanted to help spread the message that cancer does not discriminate. It doesn't care who you are, where you're from, or how many gold medals you have. That is why it is critical for every one of us to focus on our health each day.

I was inundated with letters, e-mails, and postings on social media. People shared their prayers, advice, and stories of their own cancer battles. I was deeply touched. Amazing people that I had never met were filling me with hope. There were so many stories of strength and courage. I realized very quickly that it was a two-way street. I may have initially set out to help others but found that I was receiving much-needed support as well. On those very difficult treatment days when I just didn't think I could carry on, I would read some of those notes.

I started a blog on my Web site, kind of a journal of my experience as I journeyed through chemo. My intention was for others to understand that they were not alone. It was a place where we could all feel safe sharing our own stories: the good, the bad, and the absolutely devastating.

On the eve of my starting chemo, an old friend, a gentleman whom I had not seen for quite some time and had never guessed was a cancer survivor, shared the words I needed to hear: "Shannon, it's going to be tough, but remember it's just like falling off the beam. You fall off . . . and you get back up. And you'll fall off again, but each time you just . . . get . . . back . . . up."

Through it all, those words would reverberate over and over again in my head. They made such sense to me because of my gymnastics experience. The saying in gymnastics was always "You can't fall and win," but I'd debunked that "truism" many times in my career. After falling at my Olympics qualifier, I got up and performed some of the best routines of my life. I was reminded once again that *when you fall, you must get back up* and *when you hit a seemingly insurmountable obstacle, you start climbing.* This is true in life, too. We're all going to hit a wall, stumble, and get knocked down. But then you move forward. I carried that lesson with me during my diagnosis and treatment and recovery. *No matter what, you keep going.*

43

On March 7, 2011, my chemotherapy began.

In the morning, my husband drove me to Southeast Gynecologic On-cology Associates, a women-only facility where I would receive my treat-ments for nine weeks. There were about a dozen chairs lined up with a few feet of space between them. I could bring my belongings and settle in. I had my favorite blanket, the one I had with me when my son was born, and my Kindle was filled with books I could escape into when needed. My bag also had snacks and other items for the long day ahead.

I had pictured in my mind a place that was going to be dark and sad. This facility was the opposite. Windows lined the entire wall and the space was filled with natural light. The chairs were incredibly comfortable and were conducive to working on your laptop, knitting, reading, or sleeping. I brought my laptop thinking I'd get tons of work done and then watch some movies. I managed to answer a few e-mails, but I soon became too tired and too sick to do much but read a little or sleep. Now and then, if we were feeling well enough, I'd have conversations with the women sit-ting next to me. Although we were all receiving chemo, we were each on our own path. With cancer, no two experiences are the same. We bring different backgrounds and diagnoses, we are all at different stages, during our journeys. All the women around me shared a sisterhood, something that connected us. We understood the fight. We learned what it means to find the strength within.

The nurses at SEGO took care of so many of us, yet they made each of us feel as if we were their only focus. In fact, I thought of them as *my* nurses. They were the ones with me every step of the way during these long hours of treatment. If one nausea medication wasn't working they'd try something else. They'd offer other options and try to make me as comfortable as possible. They made everything easier.

I was feeling so positive heading into my first day of chemo that I didn't think about not hosting my Sunday radio show after that first week of treatments. I had heard that it would take a little time for the treatments to take effect, so I taped several shows ahead of time for broadcast on future Sundays, but I just assumed I would be okay to do a live show that first weekend.

Sunday morning came and I expected to drive to the studio and host a live one-hour interview with a physician. But that morning I wasn't feeling well at all. I wasn't able to keep down anything, including water. It wasn't in my nature to back out, so I asked John to drive me to the studio. I had made a commitment and I was going to get through it, or so I thought. The program began and I could barely think straight. Who knows what questions I asked. I literally had to run out of the booth every two minutes to vomit.

John could stand by only for so long. After fifteen minutes he leaned into the booth and said, "I'm taking you to the hospital." I stayed in the hospital overnight as they tried desperately to get the nausea under control. I blew through nine or ten different nausea medications. The one thing that helped to some degree was getting fluids into me. They hooked me up to an IV and kept the fluids coming. The next morning I lay in bed thinking, "How can I do this for another eight weeks?" *Shannon, it's going to be tough, but remember it's just like falling off the beam. You fall off . . . and you get back up.*

The nausea was never fully under control. It was a vicious circle: I couldn't keep liquids down, which meant I would get sicker, which meant I definitely couldn't keep anything down. It was decided that I'd have to use an IV at home. Learning how to plug in and out of my own port was a new and empowering experience. I went through two bags of IV fluid every day. Yes, I was a lifelong fighter, but I had no idea what kind of competition I was up against. I thought I was going to battle through this, winning round after round. I came out swinging, but I got flattened in the first round. *Shannon, . . . you'll fall off again, but each time you just . . . get . . . back . . . up.*

The twice-a-day hydration helped me keep down a bit more food, although I lost my taste for just about everything after the first week of chemo. I ate solely to keep up my energy and get the nourishment I needed. There really was nothing I enjoyed and keeping anything down was a constant struggle. I drank water when I could. I sipped apple juice, decaf hot tea, and two or three protein shakes each day. I drank the chocolate shakes mostly, but ironically I lost my taste for chocolate itself, as my mother did during her chemo. What I ate most was chicken soup, fruit, vegetables—which I was careful to wash thoroughly because chemo weakens the immune system—and caprese salads, with tomato, mozzarella, basil, and olive oil. I don't know if my taste buds were changing or the nausea made most everything seem unappetizing, but I had no desire to eat many of my favorite foods.

On the few days I could manage it, I added to my cancer blog. I thought of it as a diary, a place where I could write down my thoughts and feelings as I went through treatment. Somehow writing made the days a little more tolerable. It gave me the opportunity to vent my worries and troubles, and as I did so, I gained insight into the bigger picture. I would feel discouraged, but through writing I found renewed strength. In all honesty, I'd be petrified to see what I wrote on those many days when my mind was a blur because of the bucketful of nausea medications I was taking. On most days I was unable to write anything, so I would read a few of the comments and messages I received. The decision to be very open about my issue was something I never second-guessed. Letters, texts, e-mails, tweets, and posts came pouring in, all offering support. Many felt comfortable to share their own stories of trial and triumph, knowing I was a kindred spirit. I knew full well I wasn't the only one going through a rough time. Sadly, there were many others with similar stories. Too many. Cancer is a new world with a new language and can be confusing and scary. It helps to know that you are not alone in the fight.

I received a letter in early March, days after my diagnosis went public. A woman from Austin, Texas, wrote: "I watched you growing up and cheered for you during the 1996 Olympics in Atlanta. I just learned of your battle and want you to know you are in my prayers . . . I'm writing because I am a wife and a mother of three. I have not been to the doctor in years. I simply can't find the time, or so I thought. After hearing your diagnosis I called my doctor. He is going to see me next week. You have given me great joy over the years and now you give me inspiration. . . . God Bless."

I can't explain the gratification and the joy her words brought me. But there were also tears rolling down my cheeks by the time I finished reading. All of the anger, fear, anxiety, and appreciation—every feeling I'd had in the last two and a half months—came flooding to the surface, one after another. *There's no shame in crying if it helps you move forward.*

It was certainly a blow to my ego to land back in the hospital the first week. I understood now that this was not a walk in the park. But I could do this. With my faith and tremendous support from family, friends, and perfect strangers, I would make it through.

On day thirteen, I was at an appointment with Dr. Buckley. I was busy explaining to him that I really thought I was one of the lucky ones who get by with no hair loss. How awesome is that? He smiled. But I detected skepticism in his eyes.

The next day my hair began falling out. This was not a few strands or a slow loss. I woke up to clumps of hair on my pillow. There is nothing that can prepare you for that. As survivors we joke and laugh about it to get past it, but losing your hair is tough no matter who you are. I didn't even like my crazy frizzy hair, so I didn't think it would be a big deal. But when it happens, the loss of your hair seems like a symbol of sickness. And you truly feel like you've lost your identity.

The previous October, I had interviewed a woman on my radio show named Jeri Millard, who ran a nonprofit called In the Pink that helped women cope with a cancer diagnosis. The store carried special bras, wigs, and other paraphernalia for women whose physical appearance was changed by their cancer fight. We stayed in touch and she reached out to me when she learned I was diagnosed with ovarian cancer. She was a shoulder to lean on and the person who really helped me deal with the loss of my hair.

Jeri told me, "As soon as your hair starts falling out, call me. The process can be very depressing and it can be a bit painful because your head is so sensitive. When the time comes, invite close friends and family and come out to my shop. We'll have a party and lift our glasses in celebration because losing your hair is *not* a sad thing. It can be empowering. Shannon, it's going to be okay."

I waited a little too long, but I did give her a call. My scalp was starting to look a little patchy and I couldn't put it off any longer. So we had a small "wig party" at her store. I was surrounded by a few close friends and John held my hand the entire time. (My parents could not get there from Oklahoma, but I talked to them almost daily.) Some friends shared heartfelt stories about people they knew who had experienced cancer. Some shared spiritual stories for me to remember during my journey. Of course there were tears shed, but there was also quite a bit of laughter. We were having so much fun laughing and trying on all kinds of wigs that it was easy to put off the inevitable. But finally I looked at John and we both knew it was time.

I sat in a salon-style chair. Jeri asked if I was ready. I nodded reluctantly. Then she began to shave. A minute later, I was 100 percent bald. It was shocking. I took a glimpse in the mirror but didn't linger because I wasn't ready. Other people could look at me, but I didn't feel the need to.

As the party came to a close, I chose a wig to take with me, after having tried on a dozen. My hair had been getting darker with each passing year and blond wigs didn't quite suit me. John voted for the "fiery redhead," but I picked one that was a simple bob in a shade darker than my normal hair. I liked it and it was comfortable, but I ended up wearing it more the year after chemo than I did during. Mostly I'd wear soft caps when going on walks or when I was chilly.

My biggest concern with the hair loss was in regard to my little boy. What would Rocco think of bald Mommy? Would he be scared? Would he not want to hug me? We had a wonderful friend named Trisha who helped with Rocco when I was too weak or sick. She had watched him while we were at my head-shaving party. When we returned home I sat with her for a few minutes. As a mother of two, she understood my fears. She said very sweetly and wisely, "Shannon, if you're not okay with it, he certainly won't be." That made a huge difference in my outlook.

Since the shaving, I could barely look in the mirror and hadn't even touched my head. I figured that if I couldn't see it or feel it, then it wasn't so. But for Rocco's sake I needed to get over my denial. I took a few days of looking in the mirror and feeling my scalp and then had the nerve to introduce Rocco to Mommy's new look. He didn't even flinch! Apparently, it was just another hairstyle. What an incredible relief.

Because Rocco didn't care, neither did I.

I became very content with my new look. Here I was, bald and proud. I had not had that level of self-esteem my entire life. It was like standing up tall in front of the judges at the most important competition of my life and showing no fear, only confidence. *If you pretend you are courageous over and over, you may eventually realize that you have become courageous.* Almost as startling as having no hair on my head was that my eyebrows and eyelashes fell out a week later—I handled that, too. I was showing cancer that it was not going to get the best of me.

When you lose all your hair, suddenly you're just not embarrassed by much. I took my look to the grocery store and to grab a cup of decaf once my stomach could tolerate it. Shyness was no longer an issue. Like Jeri predicted, I felt empowered. I blogged what she had told me: "Losing your hair is such a personal thing but you should embrace it as a symbol of health, as a symbol of *I am doing this so I can be here for my family.*"

I felt worse than awful all the time, but my husband maintained his compassionate sense of humor and we would laugh about the zaniness of some of the things going on. Although I wasn't terribly clearheaded, I have fond memories of weekends when I just lay in bed and he sat near me and we watched sports on television. I'd listen to what was on and drift in and out. Rocco would crawl across the bed to snuggle with me. He didn't mind the IV wires; he thought they were interesting. This was life for us.

It was not the time to give up. I stayed focused on my nine-week sprint. I kept thinking about a happy future, but I looked only far enough down the road to keep informed, not to a point where I'd become paralyzed by a fear of the unknown. *Have a goal, but stay focused on the baby steps you need to take each day to get there.*

I remembered an important lesson from my days training for the Olympic Games: *Don't try to do this alone.* My faith remained first and foremost. I knew that I was not walking alone. I also made sure to surround myself only with people who could give me positive reinforcement and to tune out anyone who wanted to dwell on the negative. I certainly didn't need anyone to pass along cynical, pessimistic thoughts to me while I was trying to move forward. *You can't fill your mind with negative thoughts and expect a positive outcome.* A positive attitude doesn't come with guarantees, particularly when your foe is cancer, but it certainly helps in any competition. I was grateful that everyone in my circle remained very calm and upbeat. That attitude was important, with the understanding that some days I needed to vent and or boot out even the most positive visitors and be by myself.

I don't think anyone fighting a life-threatening illness can be happy and positive twenty-four hours a day. I learned that it's okay to break down because you need to allow yourself those real, raw, emotions along the way. There will be days when you want to hide under the covers. You may want to scream and cry. Do it! You may want to give up. Don't do it! You don't give up. You pull those covers down. You plant your feet firmly on the floor and you keep going. *You fall off the beam . . . you get back up!*

It was okay for this mother to put herself at the top of her priority list. To be there for my son, I had to take care of myself first.

During the second cycle of chemo, the IV began to work a little better at controlling the nausea. However, on most days just getting out of bed and getting dressed was a chore. Of course, I didn't do well with limits, so I'd set goals, as I did in gymnastics, and exercise when I could. Perhaps I'd try to walk for five minutes around the house. If I got up, got dressed, and strolled to the park with my son, getting some fresh air, then it was a very successful day. I was so proud of myself the first time I took the stairs to my doctor's office for one of my treatments. Three floors, very slow, very winded, but I made it. A goal reached!

The blog grew as I went along. We added interviews with makeup artists who discussed skin care and with nurses and physicians who openly discussed cancer diagnoses, treatments, and recoveries. I was grateful to my SML team for helping me continue to educate and bring vital information to others, and making this blog, this diary of sorts, a resource for those who read it.

As a gymnast, I was always moving forward, whether it was to leave behind a mistake or just to prepare for the next challenge. It could be to my detriment, as it was the many times I refused to stop and enjoy my successes, or tell myself, "Hey, good job," or consider that what I did may have inspired young fans. But my ability to move forward with tunnel vision was instrumental to my improving what I was doing wrong so I'd have success at my next competition. With cancer, this idea of "keep going" was essential to my physical and mental well-being. I was always in the mode of "All right, what comes next?"—and that forced me to do the necessary work.

I also carried over from my gymnastics days as a girl and into my cancer battle as an adult the idea that *what you do each day matters.* You don't wake up one day and decide that you will go compete on the Olympic team. That might be your goal, but you have to work every day for years to make it happen. I was always the girl who did a few extra push-ups, an extra lap around the gym, and a few extra leg lifts. It added up! *What you do today matters.* This certainly applied to chemo. What work and effort I put into one day definitely led to my having more energy and strength to cope with chemo the next day and the next.

I was thankful for my close relationship with my mother. She was always just a phone call away. She would remind me that no matter how difficult the road seemed, God was with me. I pulled out those old stained and wrinkled cards she put in my travel bag prior to a competition. I kept them with me throughout the days of treatment and reread her special messages, such as Psalms 56:3: *What time I am afraid, I will trust in thee.* One from Isaiah, which I leaned on during those long training days when I thought my legs would give out, included the phrase: *They shall run and not be weary; and they shall walk and not faint.* In gymnastics and now during chemo treatments, I took those words literally.

When you go through a game-changer such as cancer, you look for people who have gone through similar things, with whom you can identify. When I reached out to my mom and other survivors for advice or support, it was for a different conversation. It was a conversation that, as supportive as he was, my husband could not give me. However, I found a kinship with his father through the unlikely topic of cancer. We shared war stories and gave our opinions on the best protein shakes, and discussed the neuropathy that was greatly affecting his feet and my hands. John was told that his father would not likely leave the hospital after surgery. Papa didn't get that message, or simply didn't care because he defied all expectations. A tough Italian from New York, he was going to go out on his own terms. That meant fighting strongly for two more years, during which time he played a few more rounds of golf. He would get to know his only grandson and Rocco would spend precious time with his grandfather. We would lose Papa on March 23, 2013, but continue to be inspired by his courageous attitude toward life.

ABC newscaster and sports commentator Robin Roberts, whom I had met years before at various award dinners, was a big inspiration to me. I identified with her as a fellow athlete and was impressed that she, too, made her fight with cancer public. At the time I did not know her cancer story well. I had only one image in my head: Robin Roberts, bald on national television. That image of her without a wig and looking gorgeous and strong was a terrific lift for me. I wanted to be strong like her in my own battle.

I was delighted when Robin flew down to Jacksonville to interview me for *Good Morning America* about my cancer battle and the importance of early detection. I'm not one to be starstruck, but if cancer survivors have a hero, I'm pretty sure it's Robin! On air, I talked with her about my mission to help women focus on their personal health and how critical it is for women to get appointments and screenings, even if they feel fine. I told her that I thought I was feeling okay, too, at the time I was diagnosed, and thought my stomachaches and weight loss were the symptoms of a busy woman, not a sick woman. At one point, Robin asked me, "Has there been a day yet when you have not thought about cancer?"

I shook my head and answered, "No." I couldn't even imagine it.

She looked me straight in the eye and with a confident voice declared, "You will."

44

On May 2, 2011, I walked out of my last treatment. My nine-week regimen of chemotherapy was over!

Dr. Buckley explained that I had an excellent chance of nonrecurrence. However, there would be some more follow-up visits and tests before he could give me a clean bill of health. My mother and everyone else who had experienced chemo had told me not to expect too much on the exact day treatment ended. *You likely won't feel good for six months to a year.* Did I listen? Of course not. If most people do it in six months, I'll do it in three! Ever the competitor. Somehow in my head I had built up this date, May 2, as my return to normal life. I imagined walking out of the doctor's office and the clouds would part, the sun would shine, the birds would sing, my hair would reappear, and all would be right in my world. But it wasn't any different from the day before.

I was still bald; I was still nauseous; I was still exhausted. A few days after that, still nothing had changed. I began to think I'd never feel good again. I needed to hear from someone who had gone through cancer to give me some reassurance. So, yes, I called my mother. She said, "You'll be fine, but it's going to take some time. Your gold medals didn't come overnight; they were the result of fifteen years of hard work. This will be similar; you just need to plug away every day. Give it two weeks and then let's talk about it again."

Two weeks to the day I called her and said, "You were right!" I was doing better with the nausea. It had not completely subsided, but there had been a significant shift. My energy was beginning to return, although that would also be a work in progress. Most important, I knew that I was headed in the right direction. I had renewed confidence that it was going to get better.

Today I often talk to survivors about how it is common to feel more at a loss after recovery than during treatment. During treatment you have a battery of doctors and nurses all focused on you and ready to answer every question that comes to mind. You have family and neighbors ready to jump in and help carry the load. However, when your treatment is finished, many times your support system sees this as a cue that you are now ready to return to "normal" and go back to daily life and pick up right where you left off. It doesn't work that way. Cancer changes you.

It would take close to a year before I felt more like me. Crossing the finish line with chemo was just one step, albeit a *big* step, in the process. The trouble with cancer is that there is no clear start and no clear finish. That's why it takes such a psychological toll in addition to the physical devastation it brings.

During my treatment, I'd struggled past obstacles, plugging away every day to stay on track. My recovery was the same way.

My short-term goal was to be well enough to travel to Oklahoma for my brother Troy's wedding in June. I wasn't a pretty sight, but I got there. It was a festive wedding and at the end of the day I realized I hadn't thought about the nausea or about not having hair. I tweeted Robin Roberts: "It was today!" That was the first day I didn't think about cancer.

Little by little I regained my strength and stamina. I made sure to get plenty of rest, arranging my schedule so I could take naps in the afternoon or lie in bed answering e-mails while my son napped. Each week, I added a little more to my fitness regimen. I did yoga, walked, and swam. I also worked at getting my appetite back. For the first six months after treatment, I ate the same foods as I had during, including those ever-present protein shakes in the morning and caprese salads for lunch and dinner.

Every morning, I'd walk a thirty-minute loop through a park to our neighborhood Starbucks and back. That was such a long way after my very short walks during chemo. I'd push Rocco in his stroller through the park, and once we arrived, I'd get my nonfat two-Splenda decaf latte and a milk for my son, and then we'd mosey back through the park. I'd usually be wearing sweats and either was bald to the public or had on my little soft cap, and I wore no makeup. My skin was still very pale and my eyelashes and eyebrows hadn't grown back, so I'm sure I was quite a sight. After what I'd been through, I didn't really care. For me it was a daily reminder that I didn't need to feel any embarrassment.

It seemed that Starbucks was the standard meeting place for everyone in Jacksonville. I often had meetings there because it was so convenient to downtown. So I might return later in the day to meet someone about the foundation or to purchase another latte before heading to SML to film something. Only this time, I'd have on my nicely styled wig, be dressed to the nines, and be wearing makeup and false lashes. Those poor baristas would be utterly confused!

It wasn't until my treatment was over and I began to work a little more outside the house that I began to wear my wig with any regularity. My work had for years included regular filming and public speaking, and a bald head was not conducive to every activity. Outside of work or certain functions, I was more comfortable without a wig. I continued to have hot flashes during my recovery period, a vexing side effect of having an ovary removed, and a Florida summer is incredibly hot and muggy, so wearing a wig wasn't always the best choice.

As the cooler weather approached I began to have a little more fun and ventured out with new hairstyles. I loved wearing wigs for events or work because they were so fast and easy! I admit that every so often I'd see a picture taken of me and my wig would be completely crooked. Oh, well. It wasn't as if it was a big secret that I was wearing one. At some point you just shrug and say, "If my wig's a little crooked or falls off today, it's okay because I'm here, I'm alive."

About nine months after chemo, I was asked to do a guest spot in a TV pilot that was being shot in L.A. I would need to do a handstand walk along an obstacle course! I was game, but there were a couple of issues. First, I hadn't done a handstand in years, much less walk on my hands up and down stairs and over speed bumps. So I had to practice pretty quickly to pull it off. Second, my hair was still only about an inch long and was patchy in places. I thought it would be so much easier to wear a wig, but how could we prevent it from falling off my head when I was upside down? The amazing stylists attached that wig to my head so securely that I wondered if it would ever come off.

In July 2011, my doctor gave me a clean bill of health. I was cancer-free!

That didn't mean I had nothing to worry about ever again or that I didn't have to be vigilant of a recurrence. But it did mean that for the foreseeable future I was cancer-free. *I'll take it!*

I moved on to the next step, which was getting used to the idea that I was going to be observed by doctors from then on. I was going to be having blood tests every three months and CT scans or MRIs every three or four months. I hadn't considered that before because I had been so busy getting through treatment and recovery. At first, I was extremely depressed that I had to keep going back to the doctor. I wanted to hear the word "cancer-free" and never have to think about it again. I didn't want a constant reminder; I wanted to be finished. However, after thinking about it the next couple of weeks and trying to peel away the emotional portion of it, I realized it was actually very comforting to know I would be checked up on more often. We all must deal with our feelings about treatment and diagnosis in our own way and in our own time. I just needed a little separation before I could come around.

As I regained my full strength and settled in as a mom, business owner, foundation president, and health advocate in the new year, I continued to make it a priority to be very open about my treatment and recovery, at the computer and when speaking at events. I was increasingly being invited by cancer organizations to talk about my cancer experience. I was eager to do so and that quickly became another major part of my life and work.

I felt passionate about helping women focus, not only on their health, but also on their inner strength and courage. Facing the difficult diagnosis of ovarian cancer had forced me—*freed* me—to find the silver lining in my situation. I rediscovered a strength inside of me that I thought I'd lost long ago when I left the competition floor, and it pushed me to continue the fight. That inner strength was my silver lining and every cancer survivor I have ever spoken to also discovered they had it. I have heard from so many that they didn't realize that they could be that strong until cancer forced them to be. Crisis brings out untapped strength. There were times that gymnastics did that for me and cancer most certainly did. You find your inner strength because you have no other choice.

At SML, Lauren Fox knew that I had been reaching out to women through multiple partnerships, events, and speeches, but understood that I wanted to do more. I wanted to celebrate survivors. She devised a plan that would encourage cancer survivors to do something they had always wanted to do but hadn't the resources or courage to try. Going through cancer gives you a new perspective on life, so you are likely ready to make the leap.

As we moved forward with our project, Seize the Day!, everyone at SML was full of crazy ideas of things the women could do. But the amazing women we chose to participate had their own ideas. Our first adventure was swimming with dolphins. Elaine, a survivor who had been diagnosed with stage 3c ovarian cancer, was all smiles as we suited up and joined these beautiful creatures in the water. To hear her story and see what joy she had that day was incredible. Next, we revved it up with a turn at the Richard Petty Driving Experience. If anything could come close to scaring us as much as a cancer diagnosis, it was topping out at speeds over 150 miles per hour! We continued on with one survivor after the next getting up close and personal with the tigers at the Catty Shack Ranch, flying through the air at Trapeze High Florida, and even zip-lining over snapping alligators. It was wonderful to see proof that cancer doesn't have to break you. Cancer changes you, but not always in negative ways.

It was exhilarating for all of us. It reminded us that we need to live each day to the fullest. Sometimes we need to try something new. *We don't want to only survive; we must thrive!*

Many times it's the horrifying stories about cancer that we tend to recall, but the vast majority of stories are ones of perseverance, courage, and hope. The more I got out and spoke with people around the country, the more stories I heard of women who found their own lumps, those who were given no hope but didn't back down, and those who survived and then turned around and reached out to others. We all need to hear those positive stories, and it helps to know that we have more survivors today than we've ever had before. People are living longer with the disease, many have a better quality of life than was available in the past, and more cancers are cured than ever before. When I talk about health and fitness, I also talk about the importance of getting those exams and screenings. Early diagnosis saves lives. The earlier we are diagnosed, the more options we will have. *Do not delay.*

My battle with cancer has been my toughest battle thus far, a truly defining moment in my life. However, it was never only about me. Cancer never just affects the person being treated. Cancer attacks the entire family. I continued to rely on John's support. He was managing the household and my medications, and moving back and forth every day between our place and his parents', helping with his father. He also was running his business and likely trying to maintain his sanity. What an amazing and selfless role he accepted. Caregivers have to take time to focus on their own health and well-being. No, it's not easy, but it's important. *Who takes care of the caregiver?*

On New Year's Eve, John and I clinked champagne flutes and John said, "To a better, healthier 2012." That simple toast forced me to realize how difficult 2011 had been on *him*. In many ways, he'd had a much rougher year than I did.

45

I wanted to get back to life as it was before my diagnosis. But, as any survivor will tell you, it doesn't work like that. Life will never be the same. A year after completing treatment I was still dealing with fatigue and loss of appetite. I suffered from neuropathy due to the chemo and couldn't open a bottle of water without help. Chemo-brain is something I probably still battle. At first, I was terrified I would forget words when giving a speech or doing an interview. There were plenty of times I did. I would be in mid-sentence and not be able to find the simplest words. My two-year-old son would often fill in the blanks for me. (He now has a very broad vocabulary because he feels it is his duty to use every word.) Rocco also helped me remember the grocery list and what was on our daily schedule. There were many times I'd head out the door to a meeting and Rocco would give me a big hug and say, "Mommy, don't forget your hair." This was the *new* normal and I had to embrace it.

I was getting sleep, forcing down liquids, and working on expanding my diet. Protein shakes remained a staple, and I focused on six small meals each day. This was something I had been practicing since my late twenties and it worked well with recovery. During treatment I was unable to tolerate most foods and had high hopes that my aversion to chocolate and sweets might become permanent. I wasn't that lucky, and soon I began craving my sugary treats. I can't say that my appetite has recovered even now. Like many things, it's a work in progress.

In the late summer of 2011, just months after finishing treatment, I was asked to provide commentary during the 2012 Olympic Games in London. Assuming I would be completely recovered by then, I wasn't hesitant about accepting the assignment. For me it was a no-brainer. It was one of those times when you jump in with both feet. *I'll figure it out.* All of a sudden I found myself with multiple jobs at those Games. I commentated on both the men's and women's artistic gymnastics for networks around the globe, including the live feed for NBCOlympics.com. I helped promote the Games with the United States Olympic Committee, worked with various sponsors, and covered artistic gymnastics as an expert analyst with Yahoo! Sports. It was a horrendous schedule for anyone, much less someone squeaking along the recovery trail at what seemed like a snail's pace. I had stopped taking afternoon naps only two weeks before I left for London, and as the competition approached I worried about whether I had the energy to keep up. With long days ahead, I learned the importance of pacing. I focused on a balance of work and rest.

In my free time, I took the opportunity to attend a few Olympic events as a spectator for the first time! I cheered Serena Williams as she easily took the gold in tennis. Then I capped my 2012 Olympic experience watching the U.S. men's basketball team. I screamed and stomped as loudly as anyone else in the arena when Team USA made its move in the final seconds of the championship game to claim gold once again.

The Olympics had played such a big part in my life and in my competition with cancer that I felt privileged to be in London to cover the gymnastics competition. I enjoyed the view from press row while commentating on the women's artistic gymnastics competitions. Watching our girls, who were affectionately called "the Fab Five" and later "the Fierce Five," win our first team gold medal since 1996 brought all my Olympic memories back as if they were yesterday. I had tears of joy for the girls who did well and tears of sadness for those that missed the mark. I've been on both sides and knew this emotional roller coaster intimately.

I looked at the competition and thought, "I'm so glad I don't have to do that!" These girls were so powerful, so talented. It's amazing how far gymnastics has come since Nadia Comăneci's perfect tens in the Olympics. Everything about the sport seems to have changed—the skills, the equipment, even the scoring system. The skills athletes were now competing seemed absolutely impossible in Nadia's day and even in mine. But it's still the sport I have known and loved since I was a child.

The entire Olympic experience has changed as well. I feel antiquated when I think of 1996. We were given pagers to communicate with each other during the Games. We didn't have cellphones and there was barely an Internet. (I remember purchasing my first computer after the Olympics and using AOL instant messenger to practice my typing.) What struck me most this time was the power of social media and the influential role it played. In fact, the 2012 Games were promoted as the "world's first social media games." Everyone from athletes to fans to celebrities to news organizations was using Twitter, Facebook, Instagram, and other social media platforms.

I tweeted about my personal experiences at the Games. I also texted and called home often to check on Rocco. We tried to keep his TV time to a minimum, but we wanted him to enjoy the Olympics. He would pretend he was a swimmer one night and a gymnast the next. He had no idea I used to be a gymnast, but he now knew the names Gabby Douglas (the all-around gold medalist) and Jordyn Wieber. He would raise his arms, salute the judge, and then run as fast as he could down the hallway, do a forward roll, throw his arms up, and shout, "I'm on the Golden Team!" He still does it on occasion.

Soon Rocco began jumping for joy for another reason.

During surgery, they had taken my left ovary. John and I remained hopeful the right ovary would kick in and do its job. Then came the second blow . . . chemotherapy. Would treatment damage my remaining ovary to the point we would be unable to have more children? With each step the chances diminished. We spoke to Dr. Buckley about our options. We wanted to keep as many on the table as possible. He gave us one month to save eggs before starting chemo. We took the opportunity. *If you bring your umbrella, it won't rain. . . .*

Dr. Buckley asked that we wait for at least one year to try for our second baby. I thought it would be difficult to do any more waiting, but I soon realized my body needed that time to heal. I needed to be healthy enough to carry a child.

In late August 2012, Dr. Buckley said all my tests looked good and he gave us the green light, suggesting that we try to conceive naturally for a full year before moving to other options. Although we were anxious to expand our family, we weren't particularly stressed about the situation. Knowing we had other options allowed us to relax a bit. *God has a plan, so let's follow His lead.*

Of course, I did a pregnancy test almost every single day. Although we knew that it could take months or that we may even need to go to plan B or C, I couldn't help myself. I was invariably disappointed by the results.

September was a busy month and one day, for whatever reason, I forgot to check the results. It wasn't until late that afternoon that I saw the test still sitting on the counter. I went to throw it away, but immediately stopped when I gazed at the result. I could feel my heart pounding. It was positive! I was sure the test must have malfunctioned because I had taken it about seven hours before, so I took another one right away.

My world was once again changed with one word: "pregnant."

There was no need to go to plan B. I was having a baby.

I frantically dialed John at work and almost screamed the good news into the phone. We were both ecstatic. It had been only fifteen months since my chemotherapy treatments had ended.

During the initial weeks after the cyst was discovered I had been very upset about having to put our baby plans on hold. On one particularly difficult day John said something that stuck with me: "When our baby does arrive, he or she will be our *miracle*. Because it was the *thought* of this child that prompted you to go in for that exam." That I was now pregnant after all we'd been through gave us just one more reason to consider this child our "miracle baby."

John's wish for a better 2012 had come true.

I was more relaxed with this pregnancy than the first go-around and didn't feel the need to read *every* book on the subject, just most of them. We had planned for a boy because every indication seemed to point that way. So of course we found out we were expecting a girl! I admit I was shocked but excited for the explosion of pink in our lives. Rocco was thrilled to find out he would be getting a baby sister.

I was so excited to meet this baby and find out what personality she had. Sterling Diane was born on June 25, 2013, and we showered her with love. Rocco had been named after his great-great-grandfather on John's side and Sterling was named after her maternal great-great-grandfather. Rocco loved to hold and kiss his new little sister and even offered to share his toys with her!

It was certainly a different pace with our second child. As new parents with Rocco, we second-guessed every decision and worried endlessly. We still worry but have found that the juggling act sometimes keeps you too busy to worry as much as with the first one. With Rocco, I came home and slept most of the first week, waking up to feed him or eat myself. With Sterling, I came home from the hospital and did two loads of laundry, the dishes, and played with Rocco while baby girl slept in her Moses basket. It was a joyous time and Sterling proved to be a calm, happy baby. Like Rocco, she slept through a full twelve-hour night at around fourteen weeks. She had a set of lungs but mostly used them to make pterodactyl sounds in bed. I'm a planner and I'd lay out a daily schedule for both kids, including mealtimes, play times, nap times, and when they went to bed for the night. Sterling's was obviously a little more flexible, but I had to create some kind of a game plan.

I'm now figuring out my life as I go. I'll be commentating the Olympic Games one day, changing diapers and making fish faces the next. I'll drop Rocco off for school and head to Japan for a limbo contest and be back within forty-eight hours. Then it's on to the Congressional Women's Cancer Luncheon in Washington, D.C., while solidifying plans to get back to Oklahoma to be the keynote speaker for the Oklahoma Medical Association. Packing lists include everything from cocktail attire to baby food and plenty of wipes!

My closet is divided according to my jobs. For shooting fitness segments I have my "nice" fitness clothes, the ones I haven't worn completely ragged. After that I may need a business suit for a luncheon or meeting. John has about as many events as I do, so there's always a cocktail dress at the ready and hopefully the dog hasn't chewed on my favorite black strappy heels. Then I have my mommy clothes, not necessarily suitable for wearing out of the home. I'm still a sweats, jeans, and boots kind of gal. I'll put on a sundress or two because we do live in Florida, but I will always be that Oklahoma girl at heart.

I literally wear all kind of outfits and I figuratively wear all kinds of hats. After I left gymnastics I had trouble finding my identity. Now I have almost too many identities, including wife and mother. I have many balls in the air and I enjoy the challenge of juggling.

Shannon Miller Lifestyle has grown tremendously and we have been honored to partner with some amazing organizations along the way. Our mission is specific in its purpose but broad in action. We help women make their health a priority.

The Shannon Miller Foundation Running Club has also grown dramatically. Now, more than eight thousand children from over twenty schools and nonprofits are part of our in-school program, and we're looking to continue our expansion. We received a letter from a woman whose five-year-old was enrolled in the program the first year. She said she had been morbidly obese and could barely walk twenty feet, but because she was afraid to let her son practice running alone in their neighborhood, she forced herself to run with him, a little at a time. Two years later, she wrote gratefully, she ran her first marathon! When parents as well as children benefit from our efforts, we know we're doing something right.

At age thirty-three, my world changed. My journey is not over, but it has renewed my passion to help others focus on making their health a priority and encourage them to prepare and plan for the unexpected. My experience with cancer causes me to pause long enough to appreciate those big and small moments in life. I do believe my new appreciation of my gymnastics legacy of awards and medals has much to do with having children. Seeing the world through their eyes has helped me put my career into perspective. I have finally learned to stop and smell the roses.

ADDENDUM

I thank God every day for life.

I want to know myself and live life to the fullest. I continue to believe anything is possible and that we can achieve our dreams, live our passions, and, yes, turn lemons into delicious and nutritious lemonade. What I have enjoyed over the last few years—and maybe even back when I was a gymnast—is that I'm able to take my peculiar traits, particularly the drive, and make it about not just accomplishing something for myself but actually achieving my goal of helping others.

I believe that once you face down cancer, you can do anything. We can amaze ourselves with the strength we have when we rise to conquer new challenges. I was self-assured as an athlete, but rarely off the gymnastics floor. Now, the confidence I had in my sport shines through in my everyday life. I'm more confident as a person than I have ever been.

I am grateful for the opportunity to, in some small way, use my voice to help others through their own challenges in life and help them make their own health a priority. Looking back on my life now, maybe for the first time, I certainly recall the low moments, especially my cancer diagnosis and treatment, which was not so long ago. But there always seemed to be a silver lining, even if I had to search hard to find it. I was blessed to learn some very critical lessons at an early age and life has proved a ripe source of opportunities to utilize them. I've come to see the obstacles of life as opportunities to employ all those life lessons I learned as a girl and relearn every day as an adult.

There have been so many beautiful and important lessons. Among them was the importance of goal-setting, and bringing a positive attitude to a difficult challenge. I learned what it meant to be a part of a team and that teams come in all shapes and sizes, and sometimes from unlikely places. I learned that forward momentum can be a good thing, but it shouldn't prevent you from taking the time to enjoy each moment along the way. It's the bumps and bruises in life that reveal our true character. Each of these lessons allowed me to do the one thing that is critical to any success . . . *believe in myself.*

Those life lessons I learned through gymnastics are not specific to me. These are lessons that anyone can utilize. Many of these lessons were strengthened when I was forced to apply them to life outside the sport and to a diagnosis of cancer. We all face challenges; it's how we handle them that matters. We have to remain focused on our goal.

I am a perfectionist. I have always strived for perfection in every activity, every crevice of my life. However, what I have learned in gymnastics, my career, and my personal life is that while it may be admirable to *shoot* for perfection, *it's not about perfect.* It is about going out and giving it your best every single day. It's about getting back up after a fall with the understanding that a 9.862 can still win you the gold, in the Olympics and in life.